D1615348

BRITISH REGIMENTS
AT GALLIPOLI

By the same author:

Collecting Metal Shoulder Titles
(Leo Cooper, 1980)

British Battalions on the Somme, 1916
(Leo Cooper, 1994)

BRITISH REGIMENTS
AT GALLIPOLI

by

Ray Westlake

LEO COOPER
LONDON

First published in 1996 by
LEO COOPER
an imprint of
Pen & Sword Books Ltd
47 Church Street, Barnsley, South Yorkshire S70 2AS

A CIP catalogue record for this book is available
from the British Library

ISBN 0 85052 511 X

Typeset by Phoenix Typesetting
Ilkley, West Yorkshire

Printed by
Redwood Books Ltd,
Trowbridge, Wilts.

for Laura Westlake

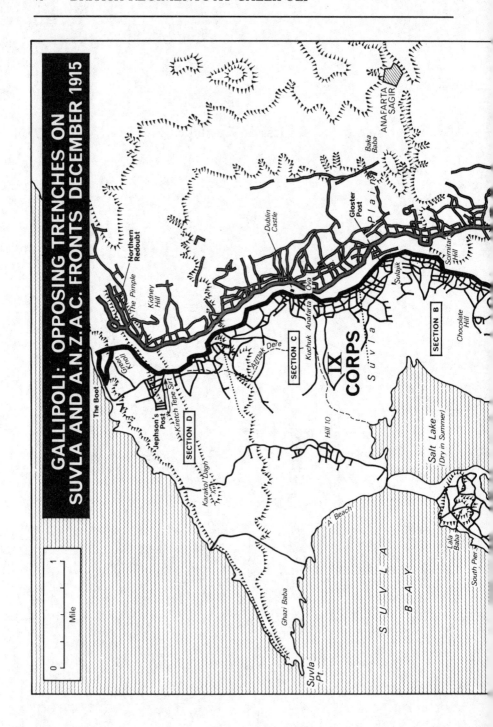

GALLIPOLI: OPPOSING TRENCHES ON SUVLA AND A.N.Z.A.C. FRONTS DECEMBER 1915

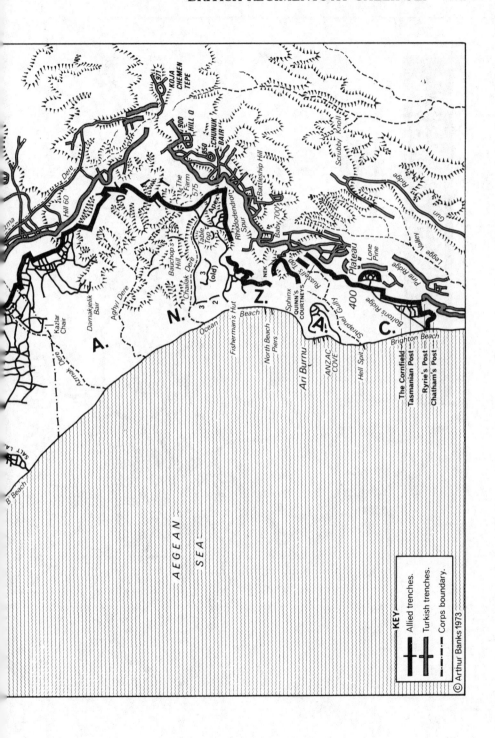

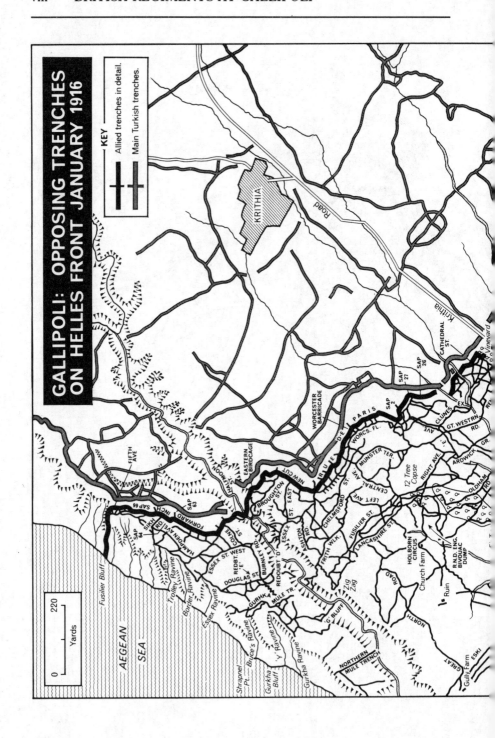

GALLIPOLI: OPPOSING TRENCHES ON HELLES FRONT JANUARY 1916

KEY

Allied trenches in detail.

Main Turkish trenches.

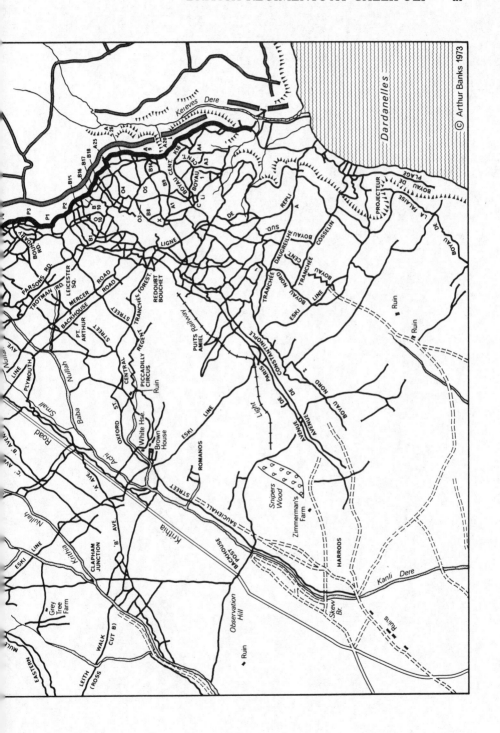

Introduction

With the huge success of *British Battalions on the Somme* (Pen and Sword, 1994) it seemed natural to follow on with something of a similar style covering some other important period of the Great War. The idea for the Somme book had came about as a result of many years of enquiries, not only from researchers keen to establish what part each regiment had played in the battle, but the family historian eager to know just where relatives had served. Now that the Gallipoli Peninsular is more accessible, more and more people are visiting the area and forming an interest in this often neglected campaign. As with the Somme book, it is hoped that the family historian can once again "follow in the footsteps" of their grandfathers, fathers, uncles, etc. While at the same time military historians can for the first time, in a convenient handy volume, access important information on a regimental and battalion scale.

British Regiments at Gallipoli is not intended to be a history of the campaign. Other and more knowledgeable authors having already covered this important period of British military history adequately. What has been provided, however, is an account of every infantry battalion and yeomanry regiment of the British Army during their service on the Gallipoli Peninsular. Battles and engagements, along with movements both in and out of the line, being dealt with at battalion level rather than on a larger and less detailed divisional scale. My start point has been the day in 1915 that each unit left the United Kingdom for overseas service. The Allied landing at Gallipoli commenced on 25th April, 1915. Evacuation of the Peninsular was completed during the night of 8th/9th January, 1916.

Normally locations given are those where the majority of the unit bivouacked or camped. Often small parties or single companies moved away for temporary attachment to other formations, or on work detail, and this has been mentioned where known. While in the forward areas trench names have been given according to war diaries. Normally a front (or firing) line wound be held by one or two companies, while the remainder of the battalion occupied support and reserve lines. Place names are as given in war diaries and the spelling used is as seen on contemporary maps. Casualty figures, where given, are generally those recorded in war diaries and are made up from killed, wounded and missing lists.

Infantry regiments appear in the book according to order of precedence. Battalions are then located by numerical seniority. Regular battalions of a regiment are listed by number only. Territorial Force units can be identified by the letters "T.F." while New Army formations (Kitchener's Army) include the word "Service." Yeomanry regiments are listed in *Army List* order. Titles used are those appearing in *The Army List* for 1915. Battle honours awarded for service on Gallipoli appear below each regimental heading.

Sources of Information

The main source of information for this book has been war diaries and unit histories. The latter amounts to some 250 volumes, making a list impractical. War diaries are held at the Public Records Office under W.O. 95 classification. References drawn from published memoirs, letters, diaries, etc, have been acknowledged in the text. My own records (RAY WEST-LAKE UNIT ARCHIVES) have also been put to good use – the 6,000-plus files formed over the last twenty-five years providing in many cases hitherto unpublished information. The following works have been essential:

History of The Great War – Order of Battle of Divisions. Major A.F. Becke. H.M.S.O. 1935, 1936, 1937, 1938, 1945.

History of The Great War – Military Operations Gallipoli. Brigadier-General C.F. Aspinall-Oglander. William Heineman Ltd. 1932, 1939.

British Regiments 1914-18. Brigadier E.A. James. Samson Books 1978.

The V.C. and D.S.O. Sir O'Moore Creagh, VC and Miss E.M. Humphris. Standard Art Book Co. Ltd. 1924.

Monthly Army Lists 1915. War Office.

To What End Did They Die? – Officers Died at Gallipoli. R.W. Walker. 1985.

Gallipoli A Battlefield Guide. Phil Taylor and Pam Cupper. Kangaroo Press 1989.

Ships of the Royal Navy. J.J. Colledge. David & Charles. 1969, 1970.

Officers Died in the Great War 1914-1919. J.B. Hayward & Son. 1988.

Acknowledgements

The help given by the following individuals, regimental museums and organizations has made this book possible – Argyll and Sutherland Highlanders Museum, Bedfordshire County Record Office, Major P.J. Ball, Major A. Cobbold, Major J. Carroll, Terry Carter, Cheshire Regiment Museum, Bill Cotton, C.B.E., Geoffrey Crump, Andrew Davies, Colonel C.D. Darroch DL, Military Museum of Devon and Dorset, Peter Donnelly, Duke of Wellington's Regiment Museum, Green Howards Museum, Tom Hawthorn, Lieutenant-Colonel C.G.O. Hogg, Jim Kellerher, King's Own Royal Regiment Museum, King's Own Scottish Borderers Museum, Museum of Lincolnshire Life, Nigel McCrery, Lieutenant-Colonel N.D. McIntosh MBE, Major R.P. Mason, Northamptonshire Regiment Museum, Ernie Platt, Prince of Wale's Own Regiment of Yorkshire Museum, Public Records Office, Queen's Royal Surrey Regiment Museum, Paul Reed, Royal Fusiliers Museum, Royal Gloucestershire, Berkshire & Wiltshire Regiment Museum, Royal Hampshire Regiment Museum, Royal Inniskilling Fusiliers Museum, Royal Scots Museum, Major G.E.M. Stephens MBE, Lieutenant-Colonel T.C.E. Vines, Royal Warwickshire Regiment Museum, Royal Welch Fusiliers Museum, Welch Regiment Museum, Lieutenant-Colonel A.W. Scott Elliot, South Wales Borderers Museum, Staffordshire Regiment Museum, Alan and Margaret Stansfield, Graham Stewart, Suffolk Regiment Museum, West Sussex Records Office, Tameside Local Studies Library, John Woodroff.

THE ROYAL SCOTS (LOTHIAN REGIMENT)

"Helles" "Landing at Helles" "Krithia" "Suvla" "Scimitar Hill" "Gallipoli, 1915-16"

1/4TH BATTALION (QUEEN'S EDINBURGH RIFLES) (T.F)

MAY

Larbert, Stirlingshire. Part of 156th Brigade, 52nd (Lowland) Division. Moved by train to Liverpool (22nd). Strength – 30 officers, 942 other ranks. Embarked *Empress of Britain* (23rd). War Diary records strength now 30 officers, 941 other ranks – 1 man having deserted from quay. Called Gibraltar (28th). Arrived Malta (31st).

JUNE

Sailed for Egypt (1st). Arrived Alexandria (3rd) and moved by train to camp at Abukir. To Alexandria (8th) and embarked *Empress of Britain*. Sailed for Lemnos 6.30 a.m. (9th), arriving Mudros Bay 9 a.m. (11th). "C" Company under Captain Rutherford sailed *Carron* for Helles 2 p.m. (12th). Headquarters, "A" and "B" Companies sailed *Reindeer* 10 p.m. War Diary records vessel colliding with the *Immingham* (sank) and forced to return to Mudros badly damaged. Men transferred to a French ship, the *Moulooya*, and later to *Empress of Britain*. Enemy aeroplane dropped bomb near ship during transfer. Headquarters with "A" and "B" Companies sailed *Basilisk* and "D" Company *Grasshopper* 9 a.m. (14th). Landed "W" Beach 2 p.m. and moved inland about 1 mile north of beach. Began to dig in under shell fire. Employed in digging communication trench (16th). Ordered to front line (18th) but returned to dug outs after marching about half mile. Relieved 1/5th Royal Scots in front line (19th). Relieved by 4th Worcestershire 6 a.m. (24th) and to rest camp. Message received (26th) from Major-General G.G.A. Egerton (G.O.C. 52nd Division) congratulating Company Quartermaster Sergeant Dewar for his good shooting. Sergeant Dewar was a winner of the "King's Prize" for marksmanship and was responsible on 21st June for killing a sniper operating in rear of firing line. The Commander also conveyed a message from Lieutenant-General A.G. Hunter-Weston (G.O.C. VIII Corps) – "Sergeant Dewar never made as good a 'bulls-eye' at Bisley as he did on this occasion." To front line east of Gully Ravine (27th). Attack on enemy trenches H12A and H12 at 11 a.m. (28th) – "C" and "D" Companies under Captains Rutherford and Ross charged and took H12A. "A" Company under Lieutenant Young followed. Major John

Ewing, M.C. in his war history of the Royal Scots records that the first few yards of the advance was thick with dead and wounded. Most of the officers were casualties, the men being gallantly led by N.C.Os. The bravery of Pipe-Major Buchan, who although twice wounded played the men over the top before being killed, is also mentioned. "B" Company (Captain MacCrae) moving forward changed direction half right and charged enemy then bringing enfilade fire on leading companies. Attack under C.S.M. Lowe then moved on to its second objective, the Turks being cleared from H12 at the point of the bayonet. Heavy enemy counter attacks 10.30p.m. and 11.30 p.m. repulsed. Machine guns under Lieutenant F.B. Mackenzie noted as doing excellent work. Casualties – Major J.N. Henderson, Captains R.W.Rutherford, G.A.S. Ross, G. McCrae, J.D. Pollock, J. Robertson, Lieutenant R.E. Mackie, Second-Lieutenant W.J. Johnstone killed; Lieutenant-Colonel S.R. Dunn (died of wounds), 7 other officers wounded. Major J. Gray, Lieutenants C.F. Allan, A. Young, Second-Lieutenants C. Paterson, T.D. Aitchison, R.J. Gibson missing – later ascertained as killed. Other ranks – 204 killed or missing, 141 wounded. Relieved 1.30 p.m. (29th) and withdrew to reserve trenches. Attached to 88th Brigade, 29th Division.

JULY
To rest camp (2nd). Employed on fatigue duties. Formed composite battalion with 1/7th Royal Scots – 1/4th Battalion providing "X" and "Y" Companies. Relieved Indian troops at Gurkha Bluff during evening. Relieved by 1/7th Scottish Rifles (9th) and to reserve trench in Bruce's Ravine. To rest camp (10th), Divisional Reserve at Backhouse Post (12th). Moved forward in support of 1/4th Royal Scots Fusiliers 12 noon. In action at trench E11. Gains held. Casualties – 17 other ranks killed, 45 wounded, 8 missing. Relieved 5.15 p.m. (14th) and to reserve trenches at Brown House. Employed in clearing communication trench to Regent Street. To rest camp (15th). Employed on fatigue duties at "W" Beach (16th-31st).

AUGUST
Continued fatigues at "W" Beach. Draft of 14 officers arrived (10th). Battalion reorganised as separate unit under command of Colonel A. Young (11th). Moved forward to reserve positions – Eski Line (13th). Moved forward to Redoubt Line in support (16th). One company to Wigan Road (17th). Relieved 1/7th Royal Scots in firing line west side of The Vineyard (21st). Took up new positions in firing line – Argyle Street and Queen Street (23rd). Relieved by 1/4th Royal Scots Fusiliers and to Eski Line (26th). To

firing line (29th) – position west of Krithia Nullah running to Royal Naval Division line.

SEPTEMBER
Moved to support lines – Redoubt Line and redoubt west of Krithia Nullah (2nd). To firing line (6th), rest camp (10th). Began fatigue duties at "W" Beach (11th). Relieved 1/5th Royal Scots Fusiliers in firing line (14th). Relieved (19th) and to Divisional Reserve at Oblique Trench. To firing line (26th). War Diary records celebration of successes on Western Front – "our troops cheered, pipers played."

OCTOBER
Relieved by 1/7th Highland Light Infantry and to rest camp (10th). To firing line (17th), relieving 1/5th King's Own Scottish Borderers in centre of right sector. Position extending for 142 yards west of Sap 6 in Argyle Street. War Diary records "this part of the firing line is a very safe part with well made trenches, the enemy's trenches being on an average 100 to 120 yards distant." Moved position 50 yards along Argyle Street to the east (18th). Men from 1/1st Lanarkshire Yeomanry attached for instruction (19th). Part of 1/1st Ayrshire Yeomanry attached for instruction (24th). Occupied new firing line in Main Street (27th). Argyle Street now support line. Relieved by 1/5th H.L.I. (31st) and to rest camp. War Diary records spirits of Battalion excellent during month. General health bad, however, 6 officers and 62 other ranks sent to hospital suffering from jaundice and dysentery. Battalion strength at end of October recorded as 12 officers, 330 other ranks. Effective strength just 181.

NOVEMBER
Formed composite battalion with 1/7th Royal Scots (4th). To firing line (7th) – Russel's Loop sector. Provided supporting fire during attack on enemy line opposite Russel's Loop (15th). Relieved and to rest camp (21st). To firing line (28th) – positions from F12 Bomb Station to junction of Nelson Avenue and Main Street. War Diary (29th) records hard frost rendering many rifles and machine guns unserviceable. Second-Lieutenant F.J. Cook killed (30th). Strength at end of November – 12 officers, 306 other ranks. Effective strength – 163.

DECEMBER
Relieved and to Eski Line (5th). Battalion's right on Krithia Nullah. To rest camp (10th). Relieved 1/6th H.L.I. in firing line – Rosebery Street to Rue de Paris (14th). War Diary records "this portion of firing line is rather

difficult and dangerous, as the hostile trenches approach to within 30 feet in some places." Relieved and to Eski Line (21st). Positions held between "C" Avenue and Small Nullah also Oblique Trench. Moved to Redoubt Line and new trench in front of Eski Line between Mule Trench and Oxford Street (22nd). Relieved and to rest camp (26th). To firing line – Achi Baba Nullah sector (29th). Strength at end of December – 18 officers, 283 other ranks. Effective strength – 16 officers, 189 other ranks.

JANUARY, 1916
Relieved and to support positions (2nd) – Parsons Road, Redoubt Line to east of Plymouth Avenue. Machine guns remained in firing line. War Diary records much aeroplane activity (3rd-7th) – "Turkish planes occasionally showing great bravery and flying very low over firing line." Began evacuation (8th). Embarked *Prince George* which was struck by torpedo (failed to explode) soon after leaving Helles. Arrived Mudros (9th). War Diary records that of the original battalion that landed on Gallipoli only Captain A. P. Watson (Medical Officer) and 148 other ranks remained.

1/5TH BATTALION (QUEEN'S EDINBURGH RIFLES) (T.F.)

MARCH

Leamington, Warwickshire. Part of 88th Brigade, 29th Division. Moved by train to Avonmouth during night (20th/21st). Sailed *Caledonia,* strength – 28 officers, 916 other ranks. Transport (2 officers, 100 other ranks) sailed *Melville.*

APRIL
Arrived Alexandria, Egypt (2nd) and to camp at Mustapha Pasha Barracks. Transport arrived (6th). Embarked *Dongola, Haverford, Marquette, Melville* and *Kingstonian* (6th). Officers: Lieutenant-Colonel J.T.R. Wilson (Commanding), Major A. McDonald, Captains J.D. MacIntosh, D.C. McLagan, D.A. Lindsay, A.H. Mure, A.W.H. Macrae, J.W.S. Wilson, W. Russell, F.W. Robertson, Lieutenants J.M. Smith, T. Darling, A. Kerr, W.H. Steel (Quartermaster), W.E. Turnbull, D. Sillars, R. Maule, W.S. Kerr, A.H.S. Paterson; Second-Lieutenants C.J. Kemp, G. Gibson, J.L. Gunn, W.B. Hislop, J.B. Aitchison, G.O. Sutherland, T. Nelson, J.L. Geddes, B. Murdoch. Captain W.D. Hepburn (Seaforth Highlanders, Adjutant), Major J. Scott (R.A.M.C., Medical Officer). While at sea, War Diary records men practicing climbing rope ladders in marching order and

disembarkation with all stores both by day and night. Arrived Lemnos (13th). Practiced descending rope ladders into boats and landing under fire. Two companies sailed for Gallipoli 3.30 p.m. (25th). Landed "V" Beach, Helles 12.30 p.m. without casualties. Moved forward to support trenches. Two remaining companies landed and provided working parties on beach. Captain A.H. Mure was with the beach companies and noted in his book *With the Incomparable 29th* how his men waded back and forth from beach to the boats unloading food, water and ammunition while under constant fire – "it was one rain of death." He also mentions that it was necessary to walk over the dead and dying. One company to firing line (26th). Commenced general advance 4 p.m. (27th). War Diary records 8. a.m. (28th) – "heavy casualties, had to retire from advanced position." Casualties – Captain W.D. Hepburn killed, Lieutenant A. Kerr died of wounds, Lieutenant-Colonel J.T.R. Wilson, Major A. McDonald, Lieutenants D.Sillars, J.L. Gunn, G.O. Sutherland wounded; Lieutenant W.E. Turnbull, Second-Lieutenant W.B. Hislop missing. Moved to left flank and built redoubt (29th). Here Lieutenant-Colonel Wilson recalled to Captain Mure how he was wounded and eventually found his way back to his battalion. A Turkish sniper had appeared from a bush about 12 yards away. His first bullet hit the bolt of the Colonel's rifle and a second Sergeant Allsop. A third passed through the Colonel's arm. Captain Mure reminds his readers that it was not unusual for a commanding officer to be carrying a rifle. All officers in the early days carried rifles and wore the same uniform as the men. Having made an escape, the Colonel came across a party of Turks from whom he asked directions. They were not, he says, interested in taking him prisoner, but would not help him in any way. Moving on, Colonel Wilson then encountered another sniper who fired 3 shots. The C.O. lay on his back pretending to be dead and hoped that the stories whereas Turkish snipers never came to view their kill were true. They were. Later to reserve positions astride Achi Baba Nullah and Krithia Road.

MAY
Came under heavy bombardment (1st). Enemy attacked during night, War diary records – "the Turks broke through first line of trenches and came rushing down gully, but were met by the Battalion with fixed bayonets." Major John Ewing, M.C. in his war history of the Royal Scots records the enemy charging with desperation and breaking the line in front of the 1/5th . . . "but Captain McLagan restored the situation by a brilliant counter-attack." Captains D.A. Lindsay, W. Russell and Lieutenant J.M. Smith killed during the charge. Remainder of battalion arrived (3rd). Relieved and to rest trenches (4th). Moved forward to firing line between Krithia Road

and Achi Baba Nullah 8 p.m. (6th). Captain J.D. MacIntosh killed by sniper. Attack on Fir Tree Wood (7th) – advanced 10 a.m. and entered wood. William Ewing served as a chaplain with the 29th Division and in his book *From Gallipoli to Baghdad* he recalls how the 1/5th Royal Scots well supported by artillery rushed the wood. There they found many snipers situated on small wooden platforms in the branches. These, he notes, "were promptly dealt with." Driven back after 3 hours fighting. Second Lieutenant J.B. Aitchison killed, 4 other officers wounded. Battalion reduced to strength of 2 companies. Withdrew to reserve trenches (9th), rest trenches (10th). To reserve line (11th). Moved forward to support and firing line during night (16th). Lieutenant C.J. Kemp killed (25th). Relieved and to rest trenches at Pink Farm (26th). Draft of 3 officers and 98 other ranks arrived (27th). Came under heavy shell fire (28th-29th) – Lieutenant R. Maule killed. Began work digging mule track forward from Clapham Junction.

JUNE
To firing line near Fir Tree Wood (3rd) and ordered to "hold this line at all costs" during planned attack next day. War Diary records few casualties (4th) due to counter attack. Relieved by 1/5th Royal Scots Fusiliers and withdrew via Gully Ravine to rest camp at "X" Beach during night (9th). Relieved 1/5th Royal Scots Fusiliers in firing line during night (13th). Enemy attacked during night (18th) and occupied part of line held by troops on right of Battalion. Some casualties among "Y" Company who counter attacked 4 p.m. (19th) and regained position. Lieutenant J.S. Merriles killed by bomb, Captain W.Russell killed whilst leading the charge, Second-Lieutenant C.N. Rundle killed on parapet of enemy's trench. Total casualties – 20 killed, 40 wounded. Lieutenant-Colonel Wilson awarded D.S.O. Relieved by 1/4th Royal Scots and to rest camp at "X" Beach. To support trenches (23rd), reserve line (27th). Attack on trench H12 (28th) – moved forward to support lines 11 a.m. then firing line 2 p.m. Lieutenant W.H. Steel led platoon of "Y" Company into Turkish communication trench 4 p.m. Charged forward 4.30 p.m. and was soon killed. Lieutenant O'Sullivan also killed at second attempt. Remainder of Battalion advanced 7.30 p.m. and were also unsuccessful. Captain T.A. Tresidder killed. War Diary records the charges being made with great bravery. Losses from shrapnel and machine gun fire very heavy. Casualties – 3 officers killed, 7 wounded. Total other ranks casualties estimated as 34 killed, 156 wounded, 80 missing.

JULY

Withdrew to "X" Beach (3rd). Major John Ewing notes that Battalion had been reduced to less than the strength of one company. None of the original officers except Lieutenant-Colonel Wilson remained. Relieved 1st King's Own Scottish Borderers in firing line (7th) – top of Gully Ravine to right. Relieved and to "X" Beach 4.p.m. (11th). Captain P.S. Picot (14th Notts and Derby, attached) killed by sniper while showing reliving battalion around trenches. To "V" Beach 10 p.m. and embarked for Mudros. Sailed for Gallipoli (28th). Landed "V" Beach, Helles during evening and to "X" Beach. Moved forward to Eski Line in reserve (30th).

AUGUST

To "X Beach (3rd). Moved forward to support trenches at Twelve Tree Copse 6 a.m. (6th) then on to firing line 2 p.m. To Geogheghan's Bluff (7th), positions between "X" and "Y" Beaches (9th). Lieutenant-Colonel Wilson left Battalion to command 32nd Brigade (11th Division) at Anzac (12th). To firing line – Worcester Flat (14th), Gully Beach (19th), "V" Beach (20th). Embarked for Suvla Bay 9.30 p.m. Arrived 2.30 a.m. (21st) and marched to Chocolate Hill. Moved forward to firing line – One Tree Gully – Kidney Hill (22nd). In support of 4th Worcestershire (25th) – 3 officers killed, 3 wounded; 3 other ranks killed, 30 wounded. Withdrew (29th) and sailed *Osmanieh* 9 p.m. (30th) for Imbros.

SEPTEMBER

Sailed *Osmanieh* for Suvla (7th). Moved forward to firing line (8th) – Scimitar Hill sector. Relieved (29th) and to reserve trenches.

OCTOBER

Second-Lieutenant W. Simpson killed by stray bullet (3rd). To West Beach (18th) and sailed Sarnia for Mudros. The Battalion had been replaced in the 29th Division by the Royal Newfoundland Regiment. Official History of the Great War records that the Battalion had received no drafts and weak in numbers could not be used effectively at the front.

1/7TH BATTALION (T.F.)

MAY

Larbert, Stirlingshire. Part of 156th Brigade, 52nd (Lowland) Division. Left in 2 trains for Liverpool (22nd). Train carrying Headquarters with "A" and "D" Companies (15 officers, 483 other ranks) left Larbert 3.45 a.m.

and in collision at Gretna 6.45 a.m. Total casualties for the disaster – 227 killed, 246 injured. To this day the worst ever railway accident. Casualties among Battalion – 3 officers, 207 other ranks killed; 5 officers, 219 other ranks injured. The uninjured – 7 officers and 57 men later continued journey, but next day the men together with a junior officer, were sent back home. Remainder of Battalion ("B" and "C" Companies) arrived Liverpool and embarked *Empress of Britain* (23rd). Sailed during evening. Strength – 20 officers, 477 other ranks. Called at Gibraltar (28th). Arrived Malta (31st).

JUNE
Sailed for Alexandria, Egypt 6 a.m. (1st). Arrived during evening (3rd). Disembarked (5th) and moved by train to Abukir. Returned to Alexandria (8th) and embarked *Empress of Britain.* Sailed for Lemnos 6 a.m. (9th). Arrived Mudros Harbour (11th). Transhipped to *Carron* (12th) and sailed for Gallipoli. Landed "V" Beach, Helles 1.30 a.m. (13th) and moved into camp. War Diary records camp being shelled from Achi Baba. Employed on digging divisional dug-outs and working on reserve and communication trenches. Moved forward to Eski Line in reserve (19th). Returned to camp (24th). To firing line east side of Gully Ravine (27th). Attack on trenches H12A and H12 (28th) – "C" Company charged and took first objective lying some 300 yards to their front. Most of the enemy running away before the troops reached H12A. Attack continued. Major John Ewing in his war history of the Royal Scots records that the enemy having had time to recover "delivered such a terrific fire that the Royal Scots fell literally in bundles." From 1/7th Battalion report (Lieutenant-Colonel W. Carmichael Peebles, Commanding) – "bombardment started at 0900 .... I reported through Brigade Headquarters that shells were bursting a little short a few minor casualties resulting. At 1045 troops on left (1/4th Royal Scots) advanced under very heavy fire. Promptly at 1100 Capt. Dawson gave the order to attack. Without hesitation or wavering the men sprang over the parapet and dashed forward. They appeared to have very few casualties when the first trench was reached H12A. The Turks cleared off to our right and offered little resistance. Rifle, machine gun and shrapnel fire was terrific." Advance continued – H12 taken and consolidated. Relieved 9.30 p.m., casualties – Major A.W. Sanderson, Captain J.B. Dawson, Captain D. Clark (H.L.I. attached), Lieutenants E.J. Thompson and A.S. Elliot and 7 other ranks killed; three officers, 114 other ranks wounded, 3 officers, 109 other ranks missing. Relieved during night and to Eski Line. Strength – 5 officers, 170 other ranks. Engaged in clearing battlefield (29th).

JULY
Relieved and to rest camp (2nd). Strength – 7 officers, 214 other ranks. To
firing line – Gurkha Bluff (4th). Formed composite battalion with 1/4th
Royal Scots, 1/7th Battalion providing "Z" Company. Relieved and to Eski
Line (9th), rest camp (10th). Orders for attack received (11th). War Diary
notes – "These orders were destroyed in conformity with an order that no
orders and maps were to be taken to firing line." Moved to Backhouse Post
and Eski Line in reserve to 155th and 157th Brigades early morning (12th).
Later advanced in support of attack by 1/4th Royal Scots Fusiliers on trench
E11. Objective rushed and cleared. Lieutenant-Colonel Peebles in his report
of the action specially mentions the work of the machine gun team, all six
men being mentioned by name and recommended for special awards.
Relieved from firing line and to Eski Line (14th). To rest camp (16th).
Casualties (12th-15th) – 1 officer, 13 other ranks killed, 1 officer, 29 other
ranks wounded, 9 men missing.

AUGUST
Temporary amalgamation with 1/4th Royal Scots discontinued (11th).
Strength – 9 officers, 159 other ranks. To Eski Line (13th), firing line – west
side of The Vineyard (16th). Relieved by 1/4th Royal Scots and to reserve
in No. 2 Australian Line (21st). Relieved 1/4th King's Own Scottish
Borderers in firing line just west of East Krithia Nullah (29th).

SEPTEMBER
To No. 2 Australian Line (2nd). Draft of 12 officers and 440 other ranks
arrived (3rd) and Battalion reorganised into 4 companies. To firing line just
west of East Krithia Nullah (6th), Eski Line (10th). War Diary records new
draft as "an excellent set of men and very keen. No. 1 Company are all men
left behind owing to injury or shock of Gretna." To firing line (15th).
Relieved by 1/4th King's Own Scottish Borderers and to rest camp (19th).
To firing line – Clunes Vennel sector (27th). War Diary records "Cheer
raised at 19.30 in honour of victories in France."

OCTOBER
Relieved and to rest camp (10th). To firing line on right of The Vineyard –
Nelson Avenue, Govan Road (17th). Contingent from 1/1st Lanarkshire
Yeomanry attached for instruction (20th).

NOVEMBER
To rest camp (1st). Formed composite battalion with 1/4th Royal Scots
(4th). To firing line (7th). Positions – west of East Krithia Nullah. War Diary

notes enemy having trebled their barbed wire in front of trench G 11 since Battalion last held this position. Men from 1/1st Ayrshire Yeomanry attached for instruction. War Diary records (10th) enemy fired 3 aerial torpedos "new to us" but did no damage. Positions in Renfield Street, Albion Road, and Clunes Vennel bombed (12th). Some 20 aerial torpedos fired by enemy (13th) – only half exploded. Attack on trench H11A opposite Russel's Loop (15th) – Nos 1 and 2 Companies charged and after bombing and hand to hand fighting captured objective. Trench H11A named Rosebery Street after Lord Rosebery, Honorary Colonel of 1/7th Battalion. Enemy rushed "A" Bomb Station about 9.27 p.m. (16th) – "gained a temporary footing but were eventually bombed out." Two more attacks repulsed. Casualties – 3 killed, 11 wounded. Relieved and to rest camp (21st). To firing line – Nelson Avenue and Main Street sector (28th).

DECEMBER
Relieved and to Eski Line (5th), rest camp (10th). To firing line – Rosebery Street to Rue de Paris (14th). War Diary records (17th) "Turks threw a few Broomstick bombs, two landing at Headquarters in Great Western Road. Good work was done by Catapult in No. 9 Bomb Sap, according to the groans which were heard in the Turkish front line." Relieved and to Eski Line (22nd) – position from Mule Trench to Krithia Nullah. To rest camp (26th), firing line (29th) – Achi Baba Nullah sector. Heavy shelling all day (30th) – 2 cook-houses destroyed. Casualties – 5 killed, 6 wounded, 1 missing.

JANUARY, 1916
Position extended to Hyde Park Corner (1st). Evacuated (8th) and to Mudros.

1st Garrison Battalion

OCTOBER
Stobs, Roxbergshire. Battalion had been formed for garrison duty from men unfit for active service. Commanding Officer – Colonel F.J. Brown. Entrained for Devonport (23rd) and sailed *Empress of Britain*. Called at Malta.

NOVEMBER
Arrived Mudros Harbour, Lemnos (4th). Party of 400 men under Major A.F. Douglas sent to Helles for labour duties (8th). In some notes written up for the war history of the Royal Scots, Colonel Brown puts on record his

reluctance to have his men used for anything other than garrison duties. Most were between 40 and 60 years of age, many of these being army pensioners, and the rest were men that had been wounded in France. He notes, however, that the Helles contingent worked right up to the evacuation suffering some 30 casualties.

DECEMBER
Colonel Brown notes the use of his men as an armed guard at the camp of the Egyptian Labour Corps. That formation at one time being on the verge of mutiny.

THE QUEEN'S (ROYAL WEST SURREY REGIMENT)

"Suvla" "Landing at Suvla" "Scimitar Hill" "Gallipoli, 1915"

2/4TH BATTALION (T.F.)

JULY
Bedford, Bedfordshire. Part of 160th Brigade, 53rd (Welsh) Division. Entrained for Devonport 12.30 a.m. (17th). Sailed *Ulysses* 8 p.m. Arrived Alexandria, Egypt (28th) then to Port Said (30th).

AUGUST
Sailed for Lemnos (4th). Arrived Mudros Harbour (7th) and from there sent straight to Gallipoli. Landed "C" Beach, Suvla during night (8th/9th). Strength 27 officers, 900 other ranks. Ordered forward to north-west slope of Chocolate Hill to assist 31st Brigade (10th Division) 6.40 a.m. (9th). Advanced over open ground south side of Salt Lake – several casualties from shell fire and rifle fire. Arrived Chocolate Hill 7.30 a.m. Lieutenant-Colonel Watney's diary (Commanding Officer) records then being ordered forward around northern slope of Chocolate Hill to support troops of 33rd Brigade (11th Division) who were "hard pressed." He mentions having no maps, but Scimitar Hill was pointed out and orders given to dig in, maintain a supporting position but under no circumstances advance – "don't go off into the blue!" Moved forward around northern spur of hill and then east to join 6th Royal Dublin Fusiliers. Advanced to top of Scimitar Hill but then forced to retire under heavy shell fire. Some, according to the records of the 53rd Division, "our own, which were firing short." Regained crest and position held until again forced to retire due to scrub catching fire. Casualties – 8 officers, approx. 250 other ranks killed, wounded or missing. Concentrated in former Turkish trenches and consolidated line 400 yards in length opposite Scimitar Hill. Relieved by 6th York and Lancaster during night (12th), returning to 160th Brigade on beach north-west side of Lala Baba. Returned to forward area (13th). Relieved by 1/5th Welsh and to Brigade Reserve (14th). Two companies to front line (18th) and supported with covering fire 87th Brigade (29th Division) attack on Scimitar Hill. Remaining two companies moved forward to front line (22nd). Employed on construction of fire, support and communication trenches. Front line position then held

north-west of Scimitar Hill. Relieved by 1/4th Cheshire during evening (31st) and to reserve positions eastern side of Hill 10.

SEPTEMBER
To front line – Kuchuk Anafarta Ova sector (4th), rest camp on "A" Beach (12th). Relieved 1/1st Herefordshire in firing line – Sulajik sector (16th). Small attack on Battalion's line (18th). Relieved by 7th Gloucestershire (19th) in trenches C52, C53, C54 and to reserve trenches south of Salt Lake. Began work digging winter quarters behind Lala Baba (20th). To "A" Beach (26th). Strength of battalion due to casualties and sickness by end of September – 5 officers, 335 other ranks.

OCTOBER
Moved to trenches near Salt Lake in reserve (2nd), dug outs eastern slopes of Lala Baba (4th). Employed digging trenches on and around Lala Baba. Formed composite battalion with 1/4th Royal Sussex (21st).

NOVEMBER
War Diary records location for November as southern slopes of Lala Baba. Draft of 100 men under Lieutenant P.C. Duncan arrived from England during month. Severe weather during November brought further casualties. Combined strength (with 1/4th Royal Sussex) 350.

DECEMBER
Captain E.G. Hewett and 3 men killed by shell (2nd). Embarked *El Kahirah* 7.15 p.m. (13th) and sailed for Mudros 1 a.m. (14th). Strength 14 officers, 224 other ranks. Total Gallipoli casualties – 4 officers, 78 other ranks killed, died of wounds or missing; 9 officers, 198 other ranks wounded; 4 other ranks died of disease; 16 officers, 400 other ranks invalided by disease.

THE KING'S OWN (ROYAL LANCASTER REGIMENT)

"Suvla" "Sari Bair" "Gallipoli, 1915"

6TH (SERVICE) BATTALION

JUNE

Blackdown, Surrey. Part of 38th Brigade, 13th (Western) Division. Entrained at Frimley for Avonmouth (13th). Embarked *Nile* – strength 28 officers, 891 other ranks. Steamed 2 miles down River Avon 7.30 p.m. and anchored for night. Sailed 6.15 p.m. (16th). Arrived Malta (23rd) and left for Egypt same day. Arrived Alexandria (26th). Remained in harbour. To Lemnos (27th). Disembarked (30th) and to camp eastern side of Mudros Bay. Records note that there were no tents and the men had to sleep on hard rough ground.

JULY

Sailed *Beagle, Bulldog* and *Basilisk* for Gallipoli (6th). Strength – 28 officers, 870 other ranks. Arrived "V" Beach, Helles, landing via beached *River Clyde*. Marched to bivouacs in Gully Ravine then to reserve line (Eski Line), 29th Division sector for instruction in trenches. To bivouacs in Gully Ravine (8th). Companies attached to battalions of 86th Brigade for instruction in front line trenches (9th). Relieved and to Eski Line (11th). Began tours in front line (14th). Relieved by 4th South Wales Borderers in trenches H12, H12A and H12B (17th) and to bivouacs south of Gully Ravine. Lieutenants C. Dowding, L.A.H. Dickenson and six men wounded by shrapnel. To reserve trenches – Brown House sector (19th). Relieved by 6th Lincolnshire (20th). Took over firing line from 1/6th Lancashire Fusiliers – Krithia Nullah sector (21st). Effective strength recorded in War Diary (25th) as 24 officers, 785 other ranks. Relieved and to reserve line (29th). To Mudros (31st).

AUGUST

Sailed *Abassieh* and *Sarnia* for Gallipoli (4th). Landed Anzac (5th) and to bivouacs at Victoria Gully. Strength – 22 officers, 722 other ranks. Heavy shelling (6th) – 4 killed, 40 wounded. Moved forward via Reserve Gully to Overton Gully about 12 noon (7th). Later moved forward in support of Australian troops at Damakjelik Bair. Lieutenant N.T. Worthington fatally wounded. Enemy attacked about 4.45 a.m. (9th) – came under heavy fire from Abdul Rahman Spur. Majors R.L. Carnegy, W. Sandbach, Lieutenant C.L. Mere and Second-Lieutenant R.D. Scolfield killed; Second-Lieutenants F.A.H. Freke-Evans and R. Marsden wounded. Turks driven back with heavy losses by 8 a.m.. War Diary notes casualties caused through trench not being deep enough and parapet not bullet proof. Heavy enemy machine gun fire and sniping kept up throughout day. Relieved 4 p.m. and to 39th Brigade Headquarters at Aghyl Dere. Soon after arrival, two companies sent back to Damakjelik Bair to assist 4th South Wales Borderers and Australians. Remaining two companies bivouacked in nullah south of Aghyl Dere. Moved forward to The Farm (10th). Enemy engaged – C.S.M. G.H. Jones noted in records for his leadership. At Damakjelik Bair enemy counter-attack held off. Captain H.E.P. Higgins, Lieutenants S.G. Jurgens (mortally wounded) and D.G. Lloyd-Williams killed. Other ranks casualties (9th/10th) – 45 killed, 150 wounded, 50 missing. Battalion collected in support trenches. Major H.W.C. Colquhoun assumed command (11th). G.O.C. 13th Division received letter from Brigadier-General J. Monash, Commander 4th Australian Brigade thanking him for Battalion's "valuable and effective" service. Relieved 5th Connaught Rangers in firing line – Chunuk Bair sector during night (12th). Position extended to the right as far as Aghyl Dere Gully (15th). Effective strength (16th) – 10 officers, 502 other ranks. Relieved by 6th South Lancashire (19th) and to bivouacs in Chailak Dere. Relieved 10th Hampshire in firing line – upper end of Damakjelik Bair (20th). Relieved by 1/5th Bedfordshire (29th) in positions near enemy's line at Sandbag Ridge and to bivouacs. Moved after dark to bivouacs at Lala Baba, Suvla (30th) – Captain D. Morrison fatally wounded by stray bullet during march.

SEPTEMBER
To bivouacs at "A" Beach, Suvla (3rd). Began shore fatigues. Numerous casualties, killed and wounded, from shell fire recorded. Moved inland to bivouacs (21st) and dug in. Working parties digging communication trench to firing line. Moved forward to trenches left of Chocolate Hill (30th).

OCTOBER
Working parties on new fire trench. Work began on Munster Avenue (12th). Took over section of trench from Birkenhead Road to about 50 yards to right of Inniskilling Sap (14th). Patrol led by Second-Lieutenant Burdekin engaged enemy (19th). Two casualties.

NOVEMBER
Construction work continued on new fire trench. Second-Lieutenant A.

Newsum (attached from 9th Lincolnshire) killed (10th). Began work on redoubt on Chocolate Hill (25th). Hackwood and Munster Avenues knee-deep in mud after 3 hours of torrential rain (26th). Many sick from frostbite.

DECEMBER

War Diary records (16th) – "2nd Lieuts. Tollemache, Saunders, Openshaw and Atkinson, Cpls. Mulvell and Windsor and 18 others had very successful patrol, killing 9 Turks." Relieved and to Chocolate Hill (18th). Battalion engaged in slitting sandbags. Eleven officers and 404 other ranks relieved and marched to Lala Baba. Embarked *Osmanieh* 7 p.m. and sailed for Mudros. Another party left Hackwood Park for Lala Baba 6.15 p.m. and sailed *Rowan* for Mudros.

THE NORTHUMBERLAND FUSILIERS

"Suvla" "Landing at Suvla" "Scimitar Hill" "Gallipoli, 1915"

8TH (SERVICE) BATTALION

JULY
Witley Camp, Godalming, Surrey. Part of 34th Brigade, 11th (Northern) Division. Moved by train to Liverpool (2nd). Embarked *Aquitania*, strength – 26 officers, 839 other ranks. Sailed (3rd). War Diary records attack by German submarine (4th). Torpedo fired but missed. Arrived Mudros Bay, Lemnos 7 a.m. (10th). Disembarked (11th) and to camp. Began fatigues – unloading stores and road making. Embarked *Grasshopper* and *Basilisk* (18th) and sailed for Imbros. Disembarked and to camp at Kephalos. Inspected by General Sir Ian Hamilton (24th). Draft arrived (3 officers and 114 other ranks) via *Lake Michigan* from England (25th).

AUGUST
To Suvla Bay (6th). Arrived about 11.30 p.m. under heavy shrapnel and rifle fire. Landed 3.30 a.m. (7th) under fire. Moved forward towards Hill 10. War Diary records ". . . took part in attack on Turkish trenches which was successful. Fighting continued until 7 a.m." Commanding Officer and 3 other officers wounded. Withdrew to beach in Divisional Reserve. Took over firing line (9th) – 3 officers killed, 1 missing, 4 wounded. Consolidated positions (10th). Relieved and to rest camp at Lala Baba (11th). To firing line during evening (12th). Relieved by 5th Dorsetshire (15th) and to reserve trenches. Relieved 5th Dorsetshire (18th) Heavy rifle fire during night – 4 other ranks killed, 11 wounded. Took part in attack (19th). War Diary records objective as being 700 yards in front of Battalion's line and 1,000 yards south of W Hills. Moved forward 4 a.m.- "X" and "Z" Companies in front, "W" and "Y" companies in support. War Diary records that the enemy's trenches were almost reached but were not entered due to heavy rifle and machine gun fire. ". . . occupied a gully and were caught in closed order at dawn by shrapnel." Casualties – 3 officers killed, 5 wounded, 3 missing; 23 other ranks killed, 141 wounded, 88 missing, 2 wounded and missing. Withdrew to reserve trenches south east of Chocolate Hill. Relieved by 6th East Yorkshire (20th) and to dug outs at Lala Baba Beach. Took over firing line near Susak Kuyu (23rd) and dug in under heavy fire during night.

Relieved by 6th Royal Dublin Fusiliers during night (24th) and to support line. Withdrew to beach (25th). To reserve trenches north of Karakol Dagh (28th).

SEPTEMBER
Relieved 6th York and Lancaster in front line – Jephson's Post (4th). War Diary records enemy snipers very active . . . "good shots, three men killed." Relieved by 6th Lincolnshire (21st) and to reserve trenches on beach. Relieved 8th Duke Of Wellington's in reserve lines – Karakol Dagh (29th). One company to fire trenches (30th).

OCTOBER
Relieved 11th Manchester in firing line – Jephson's Post (7th). Second-Lieutenant L.A. Coats (15th Battalion attached) killed by sniper (28th).

NOVEMBER
Relieved by 1/1st Royal Devon Yeomanry (3rd) and to Karakol Dagh. Moved to Long Gully in reserve to South West Mounted Brigade (7th). Two companies in support line, 2 in reserve. Relieved by 6th Lincolnshire (12th) and to West Beach. War Diary notes the heavy rain storm of (28th) and blizzard that followed ... "much frost bite among troops."

DECEMBER
"W" and "X" Companies with Machine Gun Section evacuated to Lemnos (17th). "Y" and "Z" Companies occupied loading ships on West Beach (18th). "Y" and "Z" Companies evacuated to Imbros (19th). "W" and "X" Companies with Machine Gun Section to Imbros (22nd).

THE ROYAL WARWICKSHIRE REGIMENT

"Suvla" "Sari Bair" "Gallipoli, 1915-16"

9TH (SERVICE) BATTALION

JUNE
Blackdown, Surrey. Part of 39th Brigade, 13th (Western) Division. Entrained Frimley station during night (17th). Arrived Avonmouth Docks and embarked *Royal Edward.* Sailed (24th).

JULY
Arrived Malta (1st). Sailed for Egypt (2nd). Arrived Alexandria (5th). Sailed for Lemnos (6th). Arrived Mudros Harbour (10th) and disembarked. Sailed for Gallipoli during night (13th). Landed "V" Beach, Cape Helles, strength – 26 officers, 728 other ranks. Relieved 4th Worcestershire in front line – Fusilier Bluff (15th). Relieved by 7th North Staffordshire and to Geogheghan's Bluff (18th). Casualties from first tour in front line – 2 killed, 7 wounded. Relieved 7th North Staffordshire in front line (20th). Lieutenant G.H. Grundy killed, Lieutenant J. Cattanach (Medical Officer) mortally wounded (22nd). Relieved by 7th North Staffordshire (22nd) and to Eski Line in Divisional Reserve. To Geogheghan's Bluff in Brigade Reserve (24th). Relieved 7th North Staffordshire in front line (25th). Commanding Officer – Lieutenant-Colonel C.H. Palmer killed by sniper. Relieved by 1st King's Own Scottish Borderers and 1st Royal Inniskilling Fusiliers in trenches facing Turkish line – J12 and Fusilier Bluff during night (28th). Sailed for Lemnos 9.30 p.m.

AUGUST
Sailed for Gallipoli (3rd). Landed Anzac Cove (4th) and moved into Divisional Reserve positions. Assembled at entrance to Aghyl Dere (7th). Moved forward for attack (8th). Crossed Bauchop's Hill and advanced to head of Aghyl Dere. Took part in attack on Koja Chemen Tepe. Crest gained but most of battalion later forced to fall back to The Farm. "D" Company dug new line in forward position on crest during night. Casualties – 4 killed, 28 wounded. War Diary records strength now as – 15 officers, 585 other ranks. "D" Company forced to retire to gully about 3.30 a.m. (9th) due to incompleteness of trenches and rifle and machine gun fire from above. Casualties – Second-Lieutenant F.H. Grigson and 4 other ranks killed, 2 officers and 9 other ranks wounded. Enemy attacked early morning

(10th) – War Diary records "Impossible to hold line with no supports immediately available . . . the trenches were enfiladed by machine gun fire and our men were mown down." Casualties – Majors A.G. Sharp, R.G. Shuttleworth (110th Mahratta. L.I. attached); Second-Lieutenants A.G. Kemp, E.N. Marson and 44 other ranks killed; 4 officers, 147 other ranks wounded; 1 officer, 117 other ranks missing. The following extract is taken from the report of a New Zealand officer who witnessed the Warwickshire in action – "They had immense difficulties to overcome. They were led the wrong way, and had to retrace their steps; they had to attack in full view of the enemy; their left was exposed to enfilading fire, and, in spite of all, they reached the Rhododendron Spur, and some the very ridge of 971 (Koja Chemen Tepe). They held on like grim death, held on when first one and then another unit retired. They asked for reinforcements, but were told none were available and still they stayed. They were now by themselves, and it was only when every officer save one was killed or wounded that three companies slowly retired. The fourth company, with its gallant major (Shuttleworth), held on to the farm near the ridge till all were killed. With their ranks terribly thinned they came back as from parade, parched and hungry, but still undaunted." Withdrew to Brigade Reserve camp. War Diary (11th) records effective strength as – officers nil, other ranks 288. Battalion under temporary command of Sergeant-Major Collicott. Command taken over by Major W.B. Gover (Cheshire Regiment) (12th). Moved to trenches on ridge to left of Farm Gully (14th). Took over second line trenches (15th). Relieved and to Overton Gully, Chailak Dere (19th). To Brigade Reserve camp (20th). Relieved 6th South Lancashire in trenches left of Farm Gully (24th). War Diary notes that battalion was responsible for area running from Farm Gully to top of spur connecting 39th Brigade Headquarters with Sari Bair. Effective strength now 10 officers, 353 other ranks. Relieved by 1/10th London and to Brigade Reserve (30th). To Salt Lake Line in reserve (31st).

SEPTEMBER
War Diary notes most days . . . "quietly occupied trenches." Some time spent digging winter quarters on beach. Relieved 2/4th Royal West Kent in fire trenches Sulajik sector (19th). Effective strength now 8 officers, 509 other ranks.

OCTOBER
"B" and "D" Companies moved back to reserve trenches (7th). "A" and "C" relieved by 7th North Staffordshire (10th) and to reserve trenches.

Relieved 9th Worcestershire in firing line (17th). Effective strength now 20 officers, 699 other ranks.

NOVEMBER
Second-Lieutenant L.H. Kay (12th Battalion attached) killed by shrapnel (18th). Trenches flooded after thunderstorm (26th). Parapets and kits swept away, dug-outs filled with water. War Diary noted (28th) "men in a critical condition through exposure. Several men dying of exposure."

DECEMBER
Effective strength (4th) – 13 officers, 297 other ranks. Began evacuation of trenches 7 p.m. (18th). Rearguard of 48 men under Captain E.S. Marshall and Second-Lieutenant P.J. Gething remained in firing line. Arrived Lemnos about 7 a.m. (19th) and to camp at Portianos. Rearguard party rejoined (24th). Sailed for Cape Helles (28th). Landed (29th) and to Geogheghan's Bluff. Effective strength – 13 officers, 551 other ranks. Relieved 1/1st West Kent Yeomanry in trenches – Essex Ravine (30th).

JANUARY, 1916
Evacuated from trenches (8th). Casualties since going into line – 6 killed, 11 wounded, 17 sick. Sailed for Mudros. Landed (9th) and to Portianos Camp. Effective strength – 11 officers, 481 other ranks.

THE ROYAL FUSILIERS (CITY OF LONDON REGIMENT)

"Helles" "Landing at Helles" "Krithia" "Suvla" "Scimitar Hill" "Gallipoli, 1915-16"

2ND BATTALION

MARCH

Coventry, Warwickshire. Part of 86th Brigade, 29th Division. Entrained for Avonmouth (15th-16th). Embarked *Alaunia* (16th). Strength – 27 officers, 962 other ranks. Sailed 6 p.m. Battalion transport and horses sailed *Mercian*. Arrived Malta (23rd). Sailed for Egypt 7.20 a.m. (25th). Arrived Alexandria noon (28th). Disembarked (29th) and to Mex Camp. War Diary records programme of exercises involving beach landings at night under fire.

APRIL

To Alexandria (8th) and embarked Alaunia. Transport – *Marquetta*. Sailed for Lemnos 10 a.m. (9th). Arrived Mudros Harbour (11th). War Diary records several periods of rowing practice and that great difficulty was experienced in getting boats – "The ships crew refused on one occasion to lower the boats and as they appeared to be neither under Military or Naval Law it was difficult to deal with them." "W" and "X" Companies, along with Machine Gun sections to *Implacable* to practiced getting into landing craft from ladders. Sailed for Gallipoli (25th). "W" and "X" Companies with Machine Gun Section landed "X" Beach, Helles from *Implacable* just after 5.15 a.m. – "sealed the cliff and took the top without any immediate opposition." "Y" and "Z" Companies followed with ammunition and tools. "W" and "X" Companies moved forward to attack Hill 114 and enemy trenches to the left – "They were met by heavy fire and suffered many casualties." "Z" Company joined "W" Company and by 11 a.m. had taken Hill 114 at point of bayonet. "X" and "Y" Companies took trenches to left with little opposition. Moving forward to enemy's second line met strong resistance and forced to retire. Entrenched for night south of Ridge 200. "W" and "Z" Companies advanced north east and east from top of Hill 114. Met opposition from enemy trenches on reverse slope – positions taken and consolidated. Enemy now 700 yards to the front. Counter attacks driven off during night. Enemy (estimated strength 1,500) attacked 2 p.m. (26th) and driven back. Another attack with reinforcements of

1,000 men also repulsed. Lieutenant-General Sir William Marshall (Commanding Officer of 87th Brigade) recalls in his book *Memories of Four Fronts* coming across the remains of a patrol sent out by the Royal Fusiliers. The men had first been taken prisoner, then shot in the head at point-blank range. Received orders to move into Divisional Reserve (2,000 yards in rear of firing line) 3 p.m. (27th). Battalion reduced to about half strength. First Battle of Krithia (28th). Moved back to firing line 8 a.m. In action throughout day supporting 88th Brigade. Retired to positions about one mile south of Krithia. Withdrew to Brigade Reserve line (29th).

MAY

Enemy (18,000 strong) attacked 10.30 p.m. (1st) – moved forward and counter attacked. Casualties – 5 officers, 32 men killed or wounded. War Diary records 250 prisoners taken and Turkish dead estimated at 2,000. A letter written by Major H.M. Farmer, DSO (86th Brigade-Major) recalls the action of the Royal Fusiliers during night of 1st May ... "they saved the situation with the bayonet." Withdrew to support trenches 7.45 a.m. (2nd). Later moved forward to support 1st Lancashire Fusiliers in front line at Fir Tree Wood but withdrew to support line during afternoon. Ordered back to reserve trenches 5 p.m. Reached reserve line 6.45 p.m. then 300 men ordered up to support positions in front line. War Diary notes total strength then 6 officers, 425 men. Whole battalion to front line (4th). Enemy attacked during night. War Diary notes Battalion's first use of flares and hand grenades. Also reorganisation of 86th Brigade due to heavy losses. Second Battle of Krithia: One company supported 2nd Hampshire around Gully Ravine (6th). About 700 yards gained in front of old line. Casualties – 51. New position entrenched under heavy fire. 1st Essex moved through 5 p.m. (7th) and took up positions 400 yards in front. New Zealand units passed through to positions 300 yards in front of Essex (8th). Relieved and withdrew to rest bivouacs 1 p.m. (10th). Men bathed on "X" Beach. Strength – 5 officers, 384 men. Returned to front line (17th). Attacked (22nd) – enemy trench taken but counter attack forced withdrawal. Casualties – 40. The Reverend O. Creighton (Church of England Chaplain to 86th Brigade) recalls the attack in his book *With the Twenty-Ninth Division in Gallipoli*. The leading company went forward at 8.30. "The men", he heard, "seemed to feel it was a counsel of despair" and that the officers "knew they could expect no support." With 3 officers hit – "the men rushed forward magnificently, almost officerless. There was a perfect hail of bullets, and then the Turks started throwing hand grenades, which did most of the damage, making ghastly wounds." Relieved by 4th Worcestershire in firing line between Twelve Tree Copse and Gully Ravine and to reserve line (23rd). Relieved 1st Essex in firing line (31st).

JUNE
Third Battle of Krithia (4th). "W" Company attacked and cleared enemy redoubt about noon. Regimental historian H.C. O'Neill records that this position was manned by Germans – the machine gun crew from the cruiser *Breslau.* He also points out that General Hamilton's despatch refers to the *Goeben,* but a statement made in June 1921 by R.S.M. Huband refers to captured ammunition boxes being marked "S.M.S. *Breslau.*" Casualties – 2 officers missing, one wounded, 20 other ranks killed, 52 wounded, 49 missing. Effective strength – 2 officers, 278 other ranks. Relieved and to Gully Beach 4 a.m. (7th). To reserve trenches near White House (12th). Relieved by 1st King's Own Scottish Borderers and to Gully Beach (17th). Relieved 1st King's Own Scottish Borderers in firing line (23rd) – strength: 14 officers, 662 other ranks. Relieved (27th) and to bivouacs near 86th Brigade dump. Moved forward from Geohegans Bluff 11.30 a.m. (28th). Attacked and captured Turkish trenches – J12 and J13. Positions consolidated – hand to hand fighting during night around area where enemy position joined those gained. Relieved (29th). Marched back to Gurkha Bluff then later to position near Eski Line. Casualties – 3 officers, 27 other ranks killed; 3 officers, 175 other ranks wounded; 3 officers, 57 other ranks missing. To bivouacs on beach near Gully Ravine (30th) – strength 3 officers, 412 other ranks.

JULY
To front line (3rd) – strength: 8 officers, 405 other ranks. Relieved by 6th King's Own (14th) and to reserve trenches near The Zig Zag. To bivouacs at Gully Beach (15th) then during evening embarked "V" Beach for Lemnos. Arrived and to billets about one mile from Mudros. War Diary records that this was the first day since 25th April that the Battalion had not been under fire. Returned to Gallipoli (21st) – landing "V" Beach and marching to Gully Beach during night. To front line (28th) – Essex Knoll to Worcester Flat. War Diary records that these were positions previously held and that they had not been maintained up to the standard of the Royal Fusiliers; either in sanitation or safety.

AUGUST
Stood by during 88th Brigade attack (6th). Withdrew to Eski Line 3.30 a.m. (7th) – casualties: 9 killed, 50 wounded, 2 missing. Two companies later moved forward to Brigade Reserve line, followed by a third 6.30 p.m. (8th).

Relieved 1st Border in front line – Fusilier Bluff (16th). Position on extreme left of British line running down to the sea – "W" Company hold side of cliff, "Z" in line turning back and running parallel to the sea. "Y" Company in close support, "X" in reserve at Trolley Ravine, Headquarters in Border Ravine. War Diary notes front line as being in some places within 15 yards of the enemy. Relieved and to Gully Beach (19th). To "W" Beach and sailed *Clacton* for Suvla Bay 9 a.m. (20th). Disembarked "C" Beach and marched to Chocolate Hill. Advanced in support of attack. Heavy casualties while moving forward down communication trench. New line dug. Retired behind Chocolate Hill (22nd) then to forward trenches – Kiretch Tepe Sirt sector.

SEPTEMBER
Relived and to reserve positions behind Hill 28 (1st). To West Beach (8th) and embarked *Osmanieh* for Imbros. War Diary notes this as being the first time the Battalion had not been under fire for six weeks. Casualties: from landing on 25th April – 279 killed, 954 wounded, 103 missing, 400 sick. Diary also notes that of the original members there remained no officers and just 166 other ranks. Sailed *Princess* for Suvla (21st). Relieved 2nd South Wales Borderers in front line – Kiretch Tepe Sirt (22nd). Relieved by 1st Essex (30th) and to rest area.

OCTOBER
Moved into support and reserve trenches – Kuchuk Anafarta Ova sector (2nd), front line (13th). Unsuccessful attack in front of Dublin Castle during night (16th-17th).

NOVEMBER
War Diary records in detail the great storm, and subsequent flood, of (26th) – "Water stood at 2 feet deep in the trenches after 1 hours rain. A tremendous flood of water then poured into our trenches from the hills behind the Turks, washing away our barricade completely and drowning several men. A mule, a pony, and 3 dead Turks were actually brought into our trench by the water." Diary also notes that Battalion's sector was turned into a lake within 2 minutes, those men that were not drowned stood on what high ground they could find. All were soaked to the skin and many without rifles and greatcoats. "Not a shot was fired on either side as the Turks must have been in an even worse state than we were . . . two orderlies (privates Frost and James) made their way to the Brigade with a message having to swim a part of the way." During the severe cold that followed it was necessary to send large numbers of men back suffering from exposure and frost bite. War Diary notes much sniping from the enemy and many men killed.

H.C. O'Neill records how two men of "W" Company were found near Salt Lake frozen stiff . . . "The younger of the two men could probably have got back to camp alone, but he would not leave his comrade . . . his arms round his companion, held a piece of broken biscuit in each frozen hand, and there were biscuit crumbs frozen into the moustache of the elder man." Second-Lieutenant Robert Gee, who was to win the Victoria Cross at Cambrai in 1917, recalled the great storm in *I Was There* (item No. 363). He heard a clap of thunder just after stand to, "it was worse than a bombardment of high explosive" he notes. "At 7 p.m. the barricade gave way and a solid wall of water seven feet high swept into the trench, carrying everything and every-body before it." Robert Gee noted insulated platoons of his company – No.3 were huddled together on a piece of high ground and with nothing to hold on to clung to each other. No. 4 were fighting for their lives in a maze of trenches. Whole battalion withdrawn (28th). Later Second-Lieutenant Camies and 12 men sent back to hold Dublin Castle. Just 350 men came out of the line – strength at 4 p.m. (29th) 105 men ... "of which 31 had been sent back from Ambulances in a state of semi-collapse" and 11 officers. Second-Lieutenant Camies's party relieved (30th) – all men sick. Roll call 4 p.m. – 10 officers, 84 men.

DECEMBER
To Dublin Castle sector (6th). Relieved (13th). Embarked *Barry* for Mudros (14th). Embarked *Brighton* for Helles (16th). Arrived (17th) and to camp about one mile in front of Sedd el Bahr. To camp at "X" Beach (18th). Provided working parties for Royal Engineers around Gully Beach area.

JANUARY, 1916
Embarked "W" Beach for Mudros (2nd).

THE NORFOLK REGIMENT

"Suvla" "Landing at Suvla" "Scimitar Hill" "Gallipoli, 1915"

1/4TH BATTALION (T.F.)

JULY
Watford, Hertfordshire. Part of 163rd Brigade, 54th (East Anglian) Division. Entrained for Liverpool (29th) and embarked *Aquitania*. Sailed (30th). Officers – Captains E.W. Montgomerie (in command due to illness of Lieutenant-Colonel J.R. Harvey, DSO), C.W.W. Burrell, S.D. Page, B.M. Hughes, W.H. Jewson, J.H.K. Fisher, B. Boswell; Lieutenants T.W. Flatt, V.C.C. Corke, W.V. Morgan, C.K. Bampton; Second-Lieutenants R.P. Caton, C.H.B. Elliot, H.J. Bradshaw, G.H.C. Culley, S.G. Steel, R.E. Burrell, R.B.C.M.T. de Poix, S.J.M. White, R.W. Thurgar, F.H. Collison, C.A. Wood, C.B.S. Spackman, J.H. Jewson; R.W. Moore (Quartermaster); J.C.F. Hosken (Medical Officer).

AUGUST
Arrived Mudros Bay, Lemnos (6th). Sailed *Osmanieh* for Imbros (9th). Landed "A" Beach, Suvla (10th). Moved forward to support trenches (11th). In support of attack on Kuchuk Anafarta Ova (12th). Followed 1/5th Suffolk on left of 163rd Brigade attack. Captain Montgomerie recalled reaching a hill and seeing the leading battalions of the Brigade (1/5th Norfolk, 1/8th Hampshire, 1/5th Suffolk) in difficulties. He held his position and noted that men separated from their units came in throughout the night. Position held (13th-14th) – enemy fire from left flank, men exhausted and with no food or water. Provided covering fire during relief of Brigade in front line (15th). Captain Montgomerie notes that the enemy used women snipers, their faces, arms, legs and rifles being painted green. Relieved by 1/4th Essex (16th) and to position near Kiretch Tepe Sirt. Relieved 5th Royal Inniskilling Fusiliers at Jephson's Post (17th). Relieved and to reserve trenches at Karakol Dagh (26th). Moved to Lala Baba during night (27th). Began fatigue duty at "A" Beach (30th). Strength at end of August recorded in regimental history as 13 officers, 580 other ranks. Losses had been mainly due to sickness.

SEPTEMBER
Moved to Anzac area (3rd). Relieved 1/5th Essex in firing line (5th). Position

held – Norfolk Street some 600 yards on right of Hill 60. Colonel Harvey arrived and took over command (10th). Relieved by 1/5th Suffolk and to reserve lines (15th). Further tours in trenches followed. Strength recorded at end of month – 14 officers, 376 other ranks.

OCTOBER
Tours in trenches – Norfolk Street area throughout month. Strength by middle of month recorded as 16 officers, 242 other ranks fit for duty.

NOVEMBER
Tours of duty in trenches throughout month.

DECEMBER
Evacuated to Mudros (7th-8th). Strength – 11 officers, 199 other ranks.

1/5TH BATTALION (T.F.)

JULY
Watford, Hertfordshire. Part of 163rd Brigade, 54th (East Anglian) Division. Entrained for Liverpool (29th) and embarked *Aquitania*. Sailed (30th). Officers – Colonel Sir H.G. Proctor-Beauchamp, Bart., CB (Commanding Officer); Majors W.J. Barton, T.W. Purdy; Captains A.E. Ward (Adjutant), F.R. Beck, A.D. Patterick, A.Wright, MVO, E.R. Cubitt, A.G. Coxon, A.H. Mason, E.R. Woodwark; Lieutenants T. Oliphant, E.A. Beck, G.W. Birkbeck, E. Gay, V.M. Cubitt, E.H. Cubit, A.G. Culme-Seymour; Second-Lieutenants R. Burroughes, M.B.G. Proctor-Beauchamp, A.E. Beck, A. Beck, A.R. Pelly, M.F. Oliphant, R.Adams, W.G.S. Fawkes, W.C. James, M.B. Buxton; Hon. Lieutenant S. Parker (Quartermaster); Captain R.G. Laden (Medical Officer).

AUGUST
Arrived Mudros Bay, Lemnos (6th) and remained in harbour. Transferred to *Osmanieh* (9th) and sailed for Imbros. To Suvla (10th), landing "A" Beach 5.30 a.m. Moved forward during evening. Nigel McCrery in his book *The Vanished Battalion* recalls how the advance was difficult, the men having to stop every 10 minutes for rest. Companies became separated and lost but eventually formed up during early hours of (11th) – the Battalion laying down in 2 ranks with bayonets fixed. Attack on the Kuchak Anafarta Ova (12th). Brigade advanced – 1/5th Norfolk on right, 1/8th Hampshire in centre, 1/5th Suffolk on left. 1/4th Norfolk in support. Nigel McCrery notes that Colonel Proctor-Beauchamp led his battalion, he was

smoking, waving a cane above his head and shouting encouragement to his men – "on the Norfolks on, come on my Holy Boys, forward the Hungry Ninth." The men, all from Norfolk villages and towns, were also calling out – "come on Yarmouth" "good old Sandringham" "forward the Lynns" "Come on Dereham show them the point." F. Loraine Petre in his history of the Norfolk Regiment records that an order to change direction half right was received soon after starting off. The Battalion then advanced quicker than those on its left, despite enfilading machine gun fire and shrapnel. War Diaries of 163rd Brigade record confused fighting, the several battalions becoming scattered and losing touch with each other. The following report is taken from Sir Ian Hamilton's despatch of 11th December, 1915 – "The 1/5th Norfolk were on the right of the line and found themselves for a moment less strongly opposed than the rest of the brigade. Against the yielding forces of the enemy Colonel Sir H. Beauchamp, a bold, self-confident officer, eagerly pressed forward, followed by the best part of the battalion. The fighting grew hotter, and the ground became more wooded and broken. At this stage many men were wounded, or grew exhausted with thirst. These found their way back to camp during the night. But the Colonel, with sixteen officers and 250 men, still kept pushing on, driving the enemy before them. Amongst these ardent souls was part of a fine company enlisted from the King's Sandringham estates. Nothing more was ever seen or heard of any of them. They charged into the forest and were lost to sight or sound. Not one of them ever came back." Some 122 bodies were found in 1919. War Diary gives casualties as 22 officers and about 350 men. Officers killed – Colonel Sir H.G. Proctor-Beauchamp, Bart., CB; Captains A.E. Ward, F.R. Beck, A.D. Patterick, E.R. Cubitt; Lieutenants E. Gay, V.M. Cubitt; Second-Lieutenants R. Burroughes, M.B.G. Proctor-Beauchamp, A.E. Beck, M.F. Oliphant, R.Adams. Both Captain A.G. Coxon and Second-Lieutenant W.G.S. Fawkes were taken prisoner. Relieved by 1/5th Essex (14th) and to reserve positions – Kiretch Tepe Sirt (16th). Relieved 6th Royal Munster Fusiliers in front line – Saddle Ridge near Jephson's Post (17th). F. Loraine Petre records much sickness (dysentery and jaundice) about this time. Captain E.W. Montgomerie of 1/4th Norfolk noted the strength of Battalion at this time as just 150 men under 1 officer – Lieutenant E. Beck. Captain E.R. Woodwark killed (21st). Relieved and to reserve trenches at Karakol Dagh (26th). Moved to Lala Baba during night (27th). Began fatigue duty at "A" Beach (30th).

SEPTEMBER
Moved to Anzac (3rd) and temporally attached to 162nd Brigade at

Gloucester Hill. Major Buxton records that the Battalion manned the forward area stretching along the brow of a ridge rising above Aghyl Dere alternatively with 1/10th London Regiment. Tours in front line normally about a week. Rest area was on other side of ridge, just 200 yards from front line.

OCTOBER
Tours in front line.

NOVEMBER
Organised into 2 companies due to high sickness rate (1st) and Lieutenant S. Parker died of wounds received. Relieved from trenches (30th).

DECEMBER
Evacuated to Mudros (4th). F. Loraine Petre notes that by this time only 3 of the original officers remained – Captains E. Cubitt, Birkbeck and Lieutenant Buxton.

THE LINCOLNSHIRE REGIMENT

"Suvla" "Landing at Suvla" "Scimitar Hill" "Gallipoli, 1915"

6TH (SERVICE) BATTALION

JUNE
Frensham, Surrey. Part of 33rd Brigade, 11th (Northern) Division. Entrained at Farnham for Liverpool (30th).

JULY
Sailed *Empress of Britain* (1st). Arrived Malta (8th). Sailed for Egypt (10th). Arrived Alexandria (12th) and then to Lemnos (16th). Arrived Mudros (18th). Transhipped to *Osmanieh* and *Elkatura* and to Helles (19th). Strength – 775 all ranks. Landed "V" Beach and concentrated around Sedd el Bahr. Attached to Royal Naval Division and moved forward to Eski Line, relieving 6th King's Own near Brown House. To front line across Achi Baba Nullah (21st). First casualties – 6 men wounded. Relieved by 6th Border and to Eski Line (27th). To front line (30th). Second-Lieutenant T.D. Overton killed (31st). Casualties since landing – 1 officer, 6 other ranks killed, 32 other ranks wounded.

AUGUST
Relieved (1st) and to Imbros. To Suvla (6th). Landed "B" Beach and to Divisional Reserve positions near Lala Baba. Advanced 5.30 p.m. behind 32nd Brigade. Moved across Salt Lake and came under heavy fire from northern side. Dug in near The Cut dawn (7th). Ordered forward for attack on Chocolate Hill 2 p.m. Advanced in extended order across northern side Salt Lake – "C" and "D" Companies leading, "A" and "B" in support. Major-General C.R. Simpson in his war history of the Lincolnshire Regiment records the Battalion's advance as being in "absolute parade ground order formation. A Magnificent spectacular admired by all that watched." Reached foot of hill. "D" and "B" Companies went forward through Royal Dublin Fusiliers, leading waves being cut down by heavy shrapnel, machine gun and rifle fire. Turkish trenches at top of hill rushed and taken. Casualties – Major D'A.M. Fraser, Major A.E. Norton, Lieutenant L. Webber killed; Lieutenant C.C. Downes later died of his wounds; 2 other officers wounded; approximately 84 other ranks killed, wounded, missing. Relieved (8th) and to Divisional Reserve at Lala Baba.

Advanced south of Salt Lake for attack on Ismail Oglu Tepe (9th). Halted at Chocolate Hill then at 5.15 a.m. continued forward. Came under heavy fire from Scimitar Hill and deployed – "A" Company on right with "D" behind, "B" on left supported by "C". Records show that attacking troops – 6th Border on right, 7th South Staffordshire in centre, 6th Lincolnshire on left, had been informed that Scimitar Hill was held by British troops. Scrub caught fire and withdrawal ordered by Commanding Officer – Lieutenant-Colonel M.P. Phelps at 12.15 p.m. Retired to trenches 300 yards to rear, many wounded being left in burning scrub. Line held running approximately from Hill 50 to Sulajik. Captain and Adjutant P.H. Hansen, with volunteers, made several journeys into the fire to bring back wounded. For his courage and leadership he was subsequently awarded the Victoria Cross. Relieved (12th) and to beach at Lala Baba. Casualties – Captains P.L. Browne, J.T. Lewis; Lieutenants T.G. Parkin, G.M. Hewart, K.J.W. Peake, R.L. Cooke, R.D. Foster, R.L. Hornsby killed; 4 other officers wounded or missing; 391 other ranks killed, wounded or missing. Many of the wounded had been burned alive in the scrub fire. Major-General Simpson records that none of the missing were ever seen again. Strength at beginning of attack – 17 officers, 561 other ranks. Formed composite battalion with 6th Border. Relieved 9th West Yorkshire at Fort Waller, Chocolate Hill (18th). In support during attack on Hetman Chair (21st). Casualties – 4 killed, 22 wounded, 6 missing. Relieved (22nd) and to Lala Baba. Formed composite battalion with 6th Border (24th). To Karakol Dagh (27th). Began tours of duty – Kiretch Tepe Sirt. Front line – Jephson's Post reserve lines – Karakol Dagh.

SEPTEMBER
Relieved (12th) and to rest camp at West Beach. Captain P.H. Hansen V.C. awarded Military Cross for reconnaissance work along coast. To forward area (20th). Relieved 8th Northumberland Fusiliers at Jephson's Post (21st). Separated from 6th Border (23rd). Relieved by 6th Border (28th).

OCTOBER
To front line trenches (7th). Relieved (20th) and to Corps Reserve at "A" Beach.

NOVEMBER
Relieved 8th Northumberland Fusiliers in support and reserve lines – Jephson's Post sector (12th). Relieved 9th Sherwood Foresters in firing line – Jephson's Post (24th). Major-General Simpson records that several men drowned during the storm and subsequent flooding of (26th). A number

were swept into the sea from their dug outs on cliff side. Some 100 men latter suffered from frost-bite.

DECEMBER
Relieved by 7th South Staffordshire in firing line – Grouse Butts (9th) and to Lone Tree Gully in Brigade Reseve. To front line (17th). Left Jephson's Post (20th) and embarked for Imbros.

THE SUFFOLK REGIMENT

"Suvla" "Landing at Suvla" "Scimitar Hill" "Gallipoli,1915"

1/5TH BATTALION (T.F.)

JULY

Watford, Hertfordshire. Part of 163rd Brigade, 54th (East Anglian) Division. Entrained (29th) for Liverpool; 2 trains – Headquarters, "A" and "C" Companies 6 a.m.; "B" and "D" Companies about 9.30 a.m. Strength – 29 officers, 978 other ranks. Embarked *Aquitania* and sailed 11 p.m. (30th).

AUGUST

Arrived Mudros Harbour, Lemnos 8 a.m. (6th). Remained in harbour. Transferred to *Fauvette* and sailed for Imbros (9th). Sailed for Gallipoli (10th), landing "A" Beach, Suvla and marching abut 2 miles inland to bivouacs. Moved forward during evening to trenches running from south face of Karakol Dagh to north-east edge of Salt Lake. Took up more forward position during morning (11th). Received orders 3.30 p.m. (12th) to advance 1,200 yards due east for attack. Attack on Kuchuk Anafarta Ova. In their war history of the 1/5th Suffolk, Captains A. Fair, M.C. and E.D. Wolton recall "The direction was pointed out, and the optimistic, if erroneous, information added that it was 'just a sniper drive to push back stray Turks.' We had just half an hour in which to plan and issue orders for an advance against an enemy whose position was not known." "A" and "C" Companies advanced 4 p.m.with "B" and "D" in support. After just a shot distance – "we came under most destructive fire from the concealed enemy, who from the nature of the ground and his intimate knowledge of it was able to bring machine-gun fire to bear on our flanks and rifle-fire from the front." One observer noted the Battalion moved forward "steadily and coolly as if they were still under training at Watford." Advance reached some 1,500 yards and position was held for an hour before orders were received to withdraw to a fenced ditch about 200 yards to the rear. This position occupied for 72 hours then relieved during evening (15th). Withdrew to reserve trenches. Casualties since attack – 11 officers, 178 other ranks killed, wounded or missing. Officers killed or missing – Lieutenant-Colonel W.M. Armes, Major R.H. Kendle, Captain G.W. Ledward, Second-Lieutenants C.W. Cory, T.S. Hinnell, G.K. Alston and O.B. Wolton. Officers wounded

– Lieutenants N. Rooke, G.G. Warnes, E.M. Ashton, A.S. Parker and F.H. Everett (R.A.M.C.). Battalion history notes that – "Only Second-Lieutenant G.K. Alson was known definitely to have been killed, all the remainder were missing. Only three men were afterwards reported prisoners, so all these officers, N.C.Os and men must be presumed to have been killed. It is thought that these fine men were the foremost and quickest to advance, and in their keenness had bravely rushed forward in isolated parties and without adequate support. They seemed to have completely disappeared." In support of attack (16th), returning to reserve trenches about 7 p.m. Moved forward in support of 10th (Irish) Division at Kiretch Tepe Sirt (17th). Relieved and to local reserve trenches (18th). Strength (21st) – 12 officers, 499 other ranks. Relieved and withdrew to Karakol Dagh (27th). Marched during night (28th/29th) across Salt Lake to Lala Baba. Here, Battalion historians record that a British aeroplane was forced to land, the enemy firing some 150 shells at it without success. Also, a bread ration was receive, the first since leaving the *Aquitania*.

SEPTEMBER
Moved to South Wales Borderers Gully (1st). "A" and "C" Companies attached to 3rd Australian Light Horse at Rhododendron Spur (2nd-11th). "B" and "D" Companies took over trenches on Hill 60 during night (2nd/3rd). Relieved by 1/4th Northamptonshire (5th) and to South Wales Borderers Gully. To Hill 60 (7th). Continued tours in Hill 60 trenches, resting at South Wales Borderers Gully. Battalion historians note trenches at Hill 60 as being no more than hurriedly made fire positions which required constant work by day and night. Precautions were made against surprise attacks, every man in the front line and one man in every six in the support trenches having to keep awake all night. Conditions were bitterly cold but greatcoats were not permitted to be worn as these would impede movement in case of attack. Wounded could only be removed in blankets, the trenches being to narrow for use of stretchers. Only the crest of the hill had been captured – the enemy being in places no more than 15 yards away. Many dead were buried in the parapets, and more lay in No Man's Land. Relieved and to bivouacs behind Norfolk Trench (13th). Casualties since (3rd) – 3 killed, 8 wounded, 32 to hospital. Relieved 1/4th Norfolk in Norfolk Street (15th). Came under heavy attack from artillery, rifle and machine gun fire during night (18th/19th) – 3 killed. Relieved (20th) and to bivouacs in Australian Gully West. Casualties since (15th) – 4 killed, Second-Lieutenant E.J. Kendle and 18 men wounded, 43 to hospital. First draft of officers arrived (21st) – Captain Coppinger Hill, Lieutenants A.A. Maris, P.W.B. Ashton; Second-Lieutenants H. Temple, F.E. Haynes and

D.C.W. Smith. Casualties since disembarkation – 7 officers, 78 other ranks killed or missing; 6 officers, 217 other ranks wounded; 4 officers, 80 other ranks sick. To Norfolk Street (25th). Australian bodies from fighting of 25th April found and buried. Relieved (30th). Casualties – 4 wounded, 1 officer and 51 other ranks to hospital.

OCTOBER
Further drafts of 6 officers and 57 other ranks arrived (4th, 7th and 8th). Battalion historians record that this draft of other ranks was the first and last to be received. Strength now – 21 officers, 380 other ranks. Garrisoned Norfolk Street (5th-10th). Casualties – 2 killed, 6 wounded, 1 officer and 27 men to hospital. Relieved 1/4th Northamptonshire at Hill 60 (15th). Relieved by 1/7th Essex (20th) and to bivouacs at Dixon's Gully. Further drafts of officers arrived. Strength (24th) – 23 officers, 328 other ranks. Losses since disembarkation recorded as 23 officers, 636 other ranks. Major H.M. Lawrence, Captain J.R. Rowley, Lieutenant E.D. Wolton and Lieutenant G. Kilnet being all that remained of the original officers. To Hill 60 (30th).

NOVEMBER
Relieved by 1/7th Essex and to Dixon's Gully (5th). A narrow escape for Second-Lieutenant G.G. Oliver recorded – the same bullet which had just killed a private slightly grazed his nose and knocked out several teeth. Relieved 1/4th Northamptonshire at Hill 60 (14th). Mines exploded in enemy's line (15th). Battalion under orders not to rush the crater but to remain in front line. One man killed, 8 injured by falling debris. Some men sent to hospital suffering from shock. Relieved by 1/7th Essex (16th), returned to Hill 60 (17th). An amusing incident is recorded in the history of the 1/5th Suffolk. Attempting to bring in a wire "knife rest" a bomb was attached to a rope and catapulted towards the rest. Over shooting the bomb landed in the Turkish trench and for a while a tug of war situation existed accompanied by laughter and shouts of encouragement from both sides. The days sport was eventually brought to an abruptly end, the Turks cutting the rope and the 1/5th men sprawling in the bottom of their trench. Another incident involved flocks of migrating geese moving south over Gallipoli. Both sides amusing themselves with target practice. Just one goose recorded as being hit, this falling into No Man's Land. Relieved by 1/7th Essex (20th).

DECEMBER
Embarked *Osmanieh* for Mudros during night (6th/7th). Strength – 19 officers, 249 other ranks.

THE PRINCE OF WALES'S OWN (WEST YORKSHIRE REGIMENT)

"Suvla" "Landing at Suvla" "Scimitar Hill" "Gallipoli,1915"

9TH (SERVICE) BATTALION

JULY
Witley Camp, Godalming, Surrey. Part of 32nd Brigade, 11th (Northern) Division. Entrained at Milford station for Liverpool (1st). Embarked *Aquitania* (2nd) and sailed 1.30 p.m. (3rd). Officers: Lieutenant-Colonel J.O'B Minogue (Commanding); Majors M.D. Wood, A.H. Cuthell; Captains W.B. Hore, C.E. Long-Price, R. Lupton, T.F. Fraser, E.A.T. Dutton, A.W. Browne, A.M. Pearkes; Lieutenants A.A. Adams, H. Curtis, O.V. Guy, L. Boston, F.E. Gent, R.O. Girling, C.A. Elliott, E. Worsnop; Second-Lieutenants C.Y. Coyne, H. Davenport, J.A.C. Spencer, C. Sanders, M.H. Miles, B.S. Evers, H.A. Gough, A.B. Gent. Captain A. Geary-Smith (Adjutant), Lieutenant A.W. Taylor (Quartermaster), Lieutenant N. Matthews (Medical Officer), Father T.J. Rigby (R.C. Chaplain). War Diary records "Alarm" sounded 5.45 p.m. (4th) – enemy torpedo reported to have passed astern. Arrived Lemnos 7 a.m. (10th). Disembarked 9 a.m. (11th) and to bivouacs western side of Mudros Bay. Sailed *Mosquito* and *Racoon* for Imbros (22nd). Arrived 8 p.m. and to "C" Area, Kephalos Camp. Inspected by Sir Ian Hamilton (24th).

AUGUST
To Gallipoli (6th). Leaving on Lighters "K5" and "K6" and landing "C" Beach 10 p.m. Attack on Lala Baba Hill. Moved forward in support of 6th Yorkshire. War Diary records advance as being in two lines – "B" and "A" Companies, "D" and "C" Companies, slow and over rough sandy ground. Ten snipers bayoneted en route. Everard Wyrall in his history of the West Yorkshire Regiment notes that conditions were pitch black and the country entirely unknown. Confusion arouse as the enemy were able to come right down on to the beach and fire on advancing troops from the rear. Captain Hore killed, Lieutenant Worsnop mortally wounded. Continued advance (7th) crossing Salt Lake then in support of 34th Brigade's attack on Hill 10. War Diary notes enemy holding strongly entrenched position surrounded with land mines. Part of Battalion moved north with 34th Brigade for attack on Kiretch Tepe Sirt, another accompanied 10th (Irish)

Division for its assault on Chocolate Hill. Battalion assembled at night in captured redoubt at Hill 10. Advanced (8th) and took up positions on Scimitar Hill. Enemy attacked (9th). Fell back to Sulajik Farm with heavy losses. Captains Long-Price and Fraser killed and 6 others wounded. Farm attacked and enemy driven off. Machine guns under Lieutenant Guy noted in War Diary as doing "excellent work." Farm held and line of road running north towards Kuchuk Anafarta Ova (10th). Moved back to reserve at Lala Baba 7 p.m. (11th). Casualties – 4 officers killed, 13 wounded, 6 missing; other ranks – 46 killed, 61 wounded, 88 missing. Majority of missing afterwards reported as killed. Moved around Salt Lake to Chocolate Hill (12th) and relieved 7th Royal Dublin Fusiliers at Fort Waller. Heavily shelled until relieved by 6th Lincolnshire 9 p.m. (18th). Moved to "C" Beach. Relieved 5th Dorsetshire in trenches southern slope of Chocolate Hill. Attack on Ismail Oglu Tepe (21st). Moved forward behind 6th Yorkshire and 6th York and Lancaster 3.05 p.m. – "D" Company in firing line, "A" and "B" in support, "C" in reserve. Attack held up and battalion ordered to fall back towards southern slopes of Green Hill and dig in. Relieved during night (22nd). Casualties – 1 officer and 11 other ranks killed, 4 officers, 142 other ranks wounded, 43 missing. Arrived "C" Beach. Roll call – 4 officers, 196 other ranks. Formed composite battalion (known as No. 1 Battalion) with 6th York and Lancaster. Relieved 1/4th Norfolk in front line – Jephson's Post (26th). Relieved and to support line (31st).

SEPTEMBER
Relieved and to rest camp on beach (4th). To front line right of Jephson's Post (12th). Strength – 4 officers, 268 other ranks. Relieved by 6th York and Lancaster and to support line (15th). Drafts arrived (19th) and (20th). New officers – Captain A.M. Phillips, Second-Lieutenants A. Benn, W. Bagnall and T.B. Sillers. Strength now – 10 officers, 724 other ranks. Major R. Isacks arrived from England (22nd) and took over command. "B" and "D" Company to front line (23rd). Relieved by 11th Manchester (28th) and to rest camp north of Karakol Dagh. Received draft of 10 officers and 100 other ranks (29th). Casualties for month – 2 other ranks killed, 12 wounded, 71 sick.

OCTOBER
To reserve positions – West Beach (2nd). Further drafts received. Second-Lieutenant P.R. Anderson killed by shrapnel (12th). To Karakol Dagh (19th). Strength – 26 officers, 901 other ranks. Constructed Toe Redoubt (22nd), Instep Redoubt (23rd) and Heel Redoubt (24th) on The Boot.

Casualties for month – 1 officer and 10 other ranks killed, 35 other ranks wounded.

NOVEMBER
War Diary notes (11th) second gully beyond the Toe to be called "Leeming Lane." Captain A.M. Philips killed by shell (11th). War Diary notes heavy damage and flooding to trenches during storm (26th) and subsequent severe weather conditions. Very hard work for rest of month but no casualties.

DECEMBER
First party of 9 officers and 502 other ranks began evacuated from Suvla 8.30 p.m. (18th). Sailed *Magnificent* for Imbros. Disembarked and to Kephalos Camp 6.00 a.m. (19th). Second party – 6 officers, 154 other ranks left via West Beach 10.30 p.m. Sailed *Redbreast* and arrived Kephalos 2 a.m. (20th). Headquarters, "A" and "C" Companies – 12 officers, 196 other ranks, embarked on "K" lighter 5.15 a.m. and arrived Kephalos 8.00 a.m.

THE EAST YORKSHIRE REGIMENT

"Suvla" "Landing at Suvla" "Scimitar Hill" "Gallipoli,1915"

6TH (SERVICE) BATTALION (PIONEERS)

JUNE
Witley Camp, Godalming Surrey. Pioneer Battalion, 11th (Northern) Division. To Avonmouth and embarked *Franconia* 1 p.m. (30th). Strength – 28 officers, 955 other ranks.

JULY
Sailed 8.45 p.m. (1st). Arrived Malta (8th). Sailed for Egypt (9th). Arrived Alexandria (11th). Sailed for Lemnos (13th). Arrived Mudros (15th). Disembarked (16th) and to West Camp. Began work on causeway to connect Turk's Head to island about 300 yards to north east, and road making. (17th).

AUGUST
Sailed for Imbros (2nd) – Headquarters, "A" and "B" Companies *Queen Louise*, "C" and "D" Companies *Orange Branch*. Arrived (3rd). Transferred to *Theseus* and sailed for Suvla (6th). Landed "C" Beach (7th). Entrenched south east slopes of Lala Baba. Received orders to join 32nd Brigade and attack position running Chocolate Hill to Sulajik 9 a.m. (8th). Advanced – "D" Company on right, "B" on left followed by "C" then "A". Reached Scimitar Hill – Captain A.S.C. Rogers killed. Halted and position entrenched. Ordered to retire 11.30 p.m. and concentrate in former Turkish trenches Sulajik area. Attack on Tekke Tepe Ridge (9th). Headquarters with "D" Company advanced with little opposition at first. Remaining companies, War Diary notes, followed and due to their being in an extreme state of exhaustion and without explicit instructions failed to keep touch with leading wave. Various reports by officers leading "A", "B" and "C" Companies record the exhausted state of the men. Also coming under heavy fire from side, front and rear which could not be located. "D" moved up lower slope – "the fire poured in from concealed Turkish trenches and our men were unable to hold their ground." Battalion withdrew and concentrated at The Cut on "A" Beach. Casualties – Lieutenant-Colonel H.G.A. Moore, Captain N.D. Pringle, Lieutenants H. Huggard, S. Jalland, Second-Lieutenant J.S. Newman, R.P. Wilson killed; Major C.L. Estridge, Captains

A. Grant, H.L. Willats; Second-Lieutenants Underhill, J.C. Banks wounded; Captain R.D. Elliot, Lieutenants R.A. Rawstorne, J. Still taken prisoner; 20 other ranks killed, 104 wounded, 28 wounded and missing, 183 missing. In his war history of the East Yorkshire Regiment, Everard Wyrall records how "D" Company became surrounded and cut off and were forced to surrender. Colonel Moore, having sat down exhausted, was then attacked by a single Turk and bayoneted in the back. He died almost instantly. The same individual also fired on Captain Elliot from about 10 yards, but missed. In his book *A Prisoner In Turkey* Lieutenant John Still records the advance as being over rough ground, some of the men getting lost among the prickly scrub. The enemy's fire, from the right and front, increased ... "In that hour my admiration for the splendid courage of the men rose to a pitch of exaltation. They were Yorkshire miners for the most part, dogged, hard men of the sturdiest breed on earth." John Still also notes how the wounded remained where they fell, those that were able moved on, their only complaint being that no enemy could be seen to fire on. John Still was later taken prisoner and was present when Colonel Moore was bayoneted. The Commanding Officer, Lieutenant Still recalls, did not seem to suffer pain but complained only of thirst – "They even allowed me to carry him on my back; and on my back the Colonel died.". War Diary records the following officers present (10th)- Major M.G. Cowper (in command), Captain E.A. Bray (Adjutant), Lieutenants H.F. Garrett, Mea, A.J. Dingle, A.J. Steele; Second-Lieutenant D. Hopkin. Marched to Nibrunesi Point during morning. Began work digging trenches south east of Lala Baba after dark. Reinforcements – 3 officers, 153 other ranks arrived from Imbros (13th). Parties began work on communication tench at Chocolate Hill (17th). Relieved 8th Northumberland Fusiliers in reserve trenches south east of Chocolate Hill (20th). Entrenched about 400 yards behind fire trench during night. In support of attack by 9th Lancashire Fusiliers and 5th Dorsetshire on trenches between Hetman Chair and Aire Kavak (21st). Moved forward to fire trench then advanced to captured Turkish line. Held some 300 yards of trench with Lancashire Fusiliers and Dorsetshire. Part of Azmak Dere on right also occupied and advance led by Lieutenant G.H. Mee attempted from there towards the orchard. Withdrawal ordered after heavy casualties. Enemy counter attack during night. War Diary notes "Nearly all our officers were killed during this period." Heavy enemy bombing attacks, rifle and shrapnel fire during morning (22nd) forced withdrawal to original firing line about 7.30 a.m. Relieved by 6th Royal Dublin Fusiliers during night and to Nibrunesi Point. Casualties – Captain A.J. Dingle, Lieutenants H. Garrett, G.H. Mee, A.J. Steel, Second-Lieutenant W. Hosken killed, 2 other officers wounded, 22 other ranks killed, 128 wounded, 49 missing. Began work on improving dug outs and mule lines. Moved to Suvla Point (27th). Began work on improving trenches and mule track.

SEPTEMBER
Worked on roads, light railway, construction of anti-aircraft gun emplacements West Beach area. Road at Karakol Gap, Cannon Street.

OCTOBER
Work as for September also Jephson's Post Road, Park Lane, Piccadilly Circus and Well Walk.

NOVEMBER
War Diary records (6th) considerable sniping and shelling as work moves closer to firing line. Majority of parties now operating at night. Began work on 2nd line defences and Karakol Redoubt (15th).

DECEMBER
Began work on communication trench to 29th Divisional Lines and at West Point. To West Beach (16th) and embarked *Barry* about 8.30 p.m. Disembarked Mudros about 2.30 p.m. (17th) and to camp south of Condia.

THE BEDFORDSHIRE REGIMENT

"Suvla" "Landing at Suvla" "Scimitar Hill" "Gallipoli,1915"

1/5TH BATTALION (T.F.)

JULY

St. Albans, Hertfordshire. Part of 162nd Brigade, 54th (East Anglian) Division. Entrained for Devonport (26th). Embarked *Braemar Castle* and sailed 5.30 p.m. Officers – Lieutenant-Colonel E. W. Brighten (Commanding); Captains J.E. Hill, W.K. Meakin, R.M. Smythe, B.C. Cumberland, R. Forrest, C.T. Baker, E.V. Andreini, E.T. Maier; Lieutenants C.R. James, C.R. Lydekker, W.S. Chirnside, F.S. Shoosmith, R.O. Clarke, F.W. Ballance, F.B. Hobbs, F.W.H. Nicholas, C.R. Day; Second-Lieutenants J.T. Yarde, F. Rising, P.R. Chaundler, R.D.J. Brighten, L.J. Hunter, E.L. Rawlings, H.E. Woodhouse, H.S. Toogood; Captain H. Younghusband (Adjutant), Lieutenant G.O. Lydekker (Quartermaster), Lieutenant F.C. Kempson (Medical Officer).

AUGUST

Called Malta (3rd). Arrived Alexandria, Egypt 2.30 p.m. (6th). Sailed for Lemnos 5 p.m. (7th). Arrived Mudros 9 a.m. (10th) and there received orders to proceed to Imbros. Arrived 3.00 p.m. Ordered to Suvla (11th). Arrived 5.30 a.m. War Diary records German aeroplane dropped bombs on shipping but hit nothing. Disembarked and moved inland to bivouacs. First casualties (14th) – Lieutenant Chaundler and Private Barton wounded. Moved forward for attack (15th) – "B" Company on right, "A" Company left, "C" and "D" in reserve. First objective taken with little loss. Advance on second objective, Kidney Hill, met with heavy shrapnel and rifle fire. In his history of the battalion, Captain F.A.M. Webster notes that during the advance, direction was lost, but good work by Major J.E. Hill and Captain H. Younghusband pushed the attack on. War Diary records . . . "attack arrived through with tremendous dash – hill taken and entrenched. Casualties – 14 officers & 300 men." Officers killed or died of wounds – Captain C.T. Baker, Captain B.C. Cumberland, Captain W.K. Meakin, Lieutenant F. Rising, Lieutenant C.R. Lydekker, Lieutenant R. Brighten (brother of commanding officer). One company is recorded as finishing up led by a private having lost all of its officers and N.C.Os. Trenches improved under constant shelling and sniping. Relieved by 1/11th London 8 p.m.

(20th) and to reserve (about 100 yards behind front line) at Lone Tree Gully. Lieutenant F.S. Shoosmith killed by sniper (21st). To rest camp (23rd), camp at Lala Baba (26th) and took over bivouacs from 1/4th Northamptonshire during night. Moved to Anzac (28th). Took over fire trenches from 6th King's Own near enemy's position at Sandbag Ridge (29th).

SEPTEMBER

Relieved by 1/11th London (4th) and to reserve positions at Finsbury Vale. War Diary notes (5th) Finsbury Vale "unsafe" and new sap made called "New Bedford Road." To front line trenches (11th). Continual sniping from Sandbag Ridge recorded (12th). Captain R.M. Smythe wounded (13th) and died of wounds (14th). Relieved by 1/11th London and to Finsbury Vale (17th). Draft of 9 officers arrived (21st). Strength now 16 officers, 461 other ranks. To front line (22nd). Relieved by 1/11th London and to Finsbury Vale (29th).

OCTOBER

To front line (7th). Draft of 5 officers arrived. Relieved by 1/11th London and to reserve bivouacs at Hay Valley (13th). "C" Company remaining in local support. Squadron of 1/1st Suffolk Yeomanry attached for 3-day period of instruction. "C" Company returned (16th). To front line (19th). Draft of 3 officers arrived. "D" Squadron, 1/1st Suffolk Yeomanry attached for 3 days. Strength recorded (22nd) as 236. War Diary notes (24th) that "Second-Lieutenant Woodhouse went out to cliff named after him and obtained some very useful information." Patrol occupied enemy post on Bulgar Bluff (25th). Captain Webster records that this position was occupied in turn by patrols from both sides and was regularly the scene of the most bloody hand-to-hand fighting. Relieved by "C" and "D" Squadrons, 1/1st Suffolk Yeomanry (26th) and to Hay Valley. To front line (31st). Strength – 21 officers, 235 other ranks.

NOVEMBER

War Diary records a bomb catapult being erected on left of line (4th). Captain Webster notes that the machine made such noise during arming that the Turks had ample warning of its intended use. Relieved (5th) and to Finsbury Vale. To front line (10th). War Diary records that Turkish deserter from Sandbag Ridge was interrogated and provided useful information. Relieved and to Finsbury Vale (15th). To front line (20th), Finsbury Vale (25th).

DECEMBER
Moved to Taylor's Hollow (2nd). Sailed *El Kahirah* for Mudros (3rd), arriving 8.30 a.m. (4th).

The Royal Irish Regiment

"Suvla" "Landing at Suvla" "Gallipoli,1915"

5th (Service) Battalion (Pioneers)

JULY

Basingstoke, Hampshire. Pioneer Battalion, 10th (Irish) Division. Officers – Lieutenant-Colonel Rt. Hon. B.A.W.P.H. the Earl of Granard, K.P., G.C.V.O. (in command); Majors G.M. Grogan, C. de W. Crookshank; Captains J. Fulda, V.M.B. Scully, W. Perry, S.R. Penrose-Welsted, E.G. Redway (Adjutant), L.K.V. Brown, J.D. Scott, E.C. Morel; Lieutenants T.A. Francis, J.N. More, W.P. Bewicke, E.F. Stephen, G. Harding, M.P. Pratt, G.W. Hawkes, J.R. Duggan, E.C. Beard, R. MacAndrew, F.C. Clements (Quartermaster); 2nd Lieutenants T.J. Comerford, P.L. McDermott, L.M. Lefroy, G.P. Costello, H.C. Stanley, H.G.V. Cunningham, R.A.F. Gill, N.M. Kerr, T.E.D. Byrne, D.L.N. Macartney-Filgate, C. Bewicke, A.P. Kelly. In his history of the 10th (Irish) Division, Bryan Cooper records that the men of 5th Royal Irish had received instruction in engineering work and road-making and were mostly miners and artificers. Entrained for Liverpool (less "A" Company and battalion transport) (7th). Strength – 23 officers, 730 other ranks. Embarked *Transylvania*. "A" Company entrained for Liverpool (8th) and sailed *Mauretania* (9th). Strength – 6 officers, 263 other ranks. *Transylvania* arrived Alexandria (17th) then to Mudros (18th). "A" Company arrived Mudros (16th) and to bivouacs at Pisperaghon (20th). Rest of battalion disembarked (22nd) and to Pisperaghon. Began work on roads.

AUGUST

Sailed for Gallipoli (6th). Strength – 27 officers, 749 other ranks. Landed Suvla (7th) and to bivouacs. Began work constructing shelters for Corps Headquarters and reserve line of trenches close to Ghazi Baba. In his book *Gallipoli Diary* General Sir Ian Hamilton recalls meeting the Royal Irish (9th) filling their water bottles at a well known as Charak Cheshme. Moving northwards with the men the General records a number of bullets falling (these were "overs") and notes this as the first time he had come under fire since the beginning of the war. Two officers and 156 other ranks joined from Mudros (14th). "A", "B" and "C" Companies moved forward to Kiretch Tepe Sirt (16th) and positions on extreme left of front line. Regimental historian – Brigadier-General Stannus Geoghegan, C.B. records that the line was almost untenable but held until withdrawal ordered by G.O.C. 30th Brigade. Casualties – Lieutenants MacAndrew and Duggan, 2nd Lieutenant Costello and 31 other ranks killed, 7 officers and 98 other ranks wounded, 18 missing. For remainder of month worked on construction of permanent defences, dug wells and employed on roads. Also manned trenches and outposts during night.

SEPTEMBER
Employed on construction of fire trenches, dug-outs for mules, incinerators and telegraph cable laying. Embarked for Mudros (29th/30th). Casualties in addition to those of 16th August – 9 killed, 37 wounded.

1ST GARRISON BATTALION

AUGUST
Wellington Barracks, Dublin. Embarked for Holyhead (28th) and then by train to Devonport. Embarked *Grampian*.

SEPTEMBER
Sailed (6th). Officers (from November, 1915 Army List) – Lieutenant-Colonel R.C.C. Cox; Major W.J.K. Dobbin; Captains T.F.W. Ricketts, T.R.B. Clifford, T. Tighe, J.P. Browne, F.T. O'Meagher, H. Bell (Adjutant), J.A. Millard, D.T.J. Sherlock; Lieutenants A.S. Machin, F.H. McCormack, A.B. Barclay; Second-Lieutenants J. Barbour, J.H.M. Redding, R.W. Steventon, B.S.F. Pickard, J.S. Mockler, P.O.E. Tuckey, R.W. Whyte, E.O. Humphreys, T.C. Kennedy. Lieutenant A. Reid (Quartermaster) and 944 other ranks. Arrived Lemnos and disembarked (24th). Went into camp at Mudros West. Battalion found working parties on transports (29th September-2nd October).

OCTOBER
One officer and 66 men to Suvla as guards over Turkish prisoners and 6 officers and 267 men detailed for special duty on communications and working parties (3rd). Guard details also found for *Aragon*, *Efi* and *Orange Branch*. Working parties used on road making, construction of dug-outs, carrying water to front line and unloading ships.

NOVEMBER
Many cases of frost-bite during severe weather conditions.

DECEMBER

Suvla detachment returned to Mudros (1st). Casualties from death, wounds and disease – 3 officers, 169 other ranks.

ALEXANDRA, PRINCESS OF WALES'S OWN (YORKSHIRE REGIMENT)

"Suvla" "Landing at Suvla" "Scimitar Hill" "Gallipoli,1915"

6TH (SERVICE) BATTALION

JULY

Witley Camp, Godalming, Surrey. Part of 32nd Brigade, 11th (Northern) Division. Entrained Milford for Liverpool (1st). Arrived early morning and embarked *Aquitania*. Strength – 30 officers, 944 other ranks. Officers – Lieutenant-Colonel E.H. Chapman (Commanding); Majors A. Roberts, W.B. Shannon; Captains J.C. Morgan, G.A. Heron, H. Chapman, W.R. Peel (Adjutant), R. Randerson, A.C.T. White, G.G. Currey, W.H. Chapman; Lieutenants B. Williams (Quartermaster), E.M. Worsley, W. Appleyard, N.M. Bruce, H. de C. Casley, I.McL. Wilson, A.E. Hall, C.H. Dawnay, M.B. Lambert; Second-Lieutenants A.M. Eadon, L.K. Gifford-Wood, E. Frank, J.F. White, M.Y. Simpson, C.E. Whitworth, S. Morris, T.W. Rutherford. Captain the Rev. F. King (Chaplain), Lieutenant E.W. Adcock (Medical Officer). Sailed 1.30 p.m. (3rd). War Diary records German submarine fired torpedo which passed close under stern. Arrived Mudros Bay, Lemnos 7 a.m. (10th). Disembarked (11th). Embarked *Happy* and *Savage* 5.30 a.m. (20th) strength – 24 officers, 772 other ranks. Arrived Imbros 12.30 p.m. and to bivouacs about 2 miles from Kephalos Harbour. Inspected by Sir Ian Hamilton (24th).

AUGUST

Embarked for Gallipoli (6th). Strength – 25 officers, 750 other ranks. In *The Green Howards in the Great War* Colonel H.C. Wylly records that troops wore a white patch sewn on the corner of their haversacks, two white armbands and triangular pieces of tin cut from biscuit boxes tied to the haversacks to act as unit identification. "A" and "B" Companies landed "B" Beach, south-east of Nibrunesi Point 11.00 p.m. and commenced attack on Lala Baba. *Official History of the Great War* records that the assault was the first to be made by any unit of the New Army. The attack being under conditions that would have "tried the mettle of highly experienced troops." "C" Company landed and under Major Shannon advanced on Turkish positions at Nibrunesi Point. "D" Company moved towards Salt Lake and set up piquet line. Under orders to use the bayonet only, "A" and "B" Companies advanced to top of hill in pitch dark. *Official History* records "officers and men fell thickly . . . most of the Turks scattered, but some lay low in their deep narrow trenches till the attacking troops had passed, and then sprang up to shoot them in the back." "C" Company cleared enemy from Nibrunesi Point and then advanced on Lala Baba Hill. Colonel Wylly includes the following account by Major Shannon in his history – "On arriving at the base of Lala Baba I ordered a charge and we ran up the hill. About three-quarters of the way up we came upon a Turkish trench, very narrow and flush with the ground. We ran over this and the enemy fired into our rear, firing going on at this time from several directions. I shouted out that the Yorkshire Regiment was coming, in order to avoid running into our own people. We ran on and about twelve paces further on, as far as I can judge, came to another trench; this we also crossed and again were fired into from the rear. I ordered the company to jump back into the second trench, and we got into this, which was so narrow that it was quite impossible for one man to pass another, or even to walk up it unless he moved sideways; another difficulty was that if there were any wounded or dead men in the bottom of the trench it was impossible to avoid treading on them in passing. There was a little communication trench running from right to left behind me, and whenever I shouted an order a Turk, who appeared to be in this trench, fired at me from a distance of apparently five or ten yards. I had some difficulty in getting anybody to fire down the communication trench in order to quite the enterprising Turk, who was endeavouring to pot me with great regularity, but eventually got him shot." Major Shannon pressed attack on over crest of hill . . . "A little way down the reserve slope we came to some groups of men (survivors of "A" and "B" Companies), several of whom were lying about apparently awaiting orders, and one group on the left was 'scrapping' with some Turks in a trench a few yards distant from them. In response to shouting I got an answer from two directions and picked up Lieutenant Whitworth and Second-Lieutenant Simpson. These were all the officers then present. I formed such of the Battalion as could be collected into a line facing north and we charged down to the base of the hill facing the further beach – afterwards known as "A" Beach. War Diary records "enemy driven north-east to Hill 10. Casualties – 16 officers, approx. 250 other ranks." Officers killed – Lieutenant-Colonel Chapman, Captains Morgan, Chapman, Randerson; Lieutenants Casley, Bruce, Wilson; Second-Lieutenants Frank and White. Major Roberts later died of his woundes. Took up outpost position on Hill 10 mid-day (7th). Advanced to line between Chocolate Hill and Sulajik 10.00 a.m. (8th). In action a mile to north of Scimitar Hill. Withdrew to Hill 10 4.00 a.m. (9th). Ordered forward again noon. Came under heavy rifle fire. Second-Lieutenant S. Morris killed

(10th). Withdrew to Lala Baba (11th). Moved forward to fire trenches eastern slopes of Hill 50 (12th). Withdrew to reserve positions on beach (18th). Took over fire trenches south of Hill 50 (20th). Attack on Ismail Oglu Tepe (21st). Advanced 3.30 p.m. under heavy shrapnel fire. Enemy's machine guns recorded as having a "clear target." Heavy casualties among officers. About 100 men under C.S.M. Green entered Turkish line on right which they held until next day. Captain Currey, Second-Lieutenants Rutherford and Appleyard killed, 6 other officers (3 presumed killed) wounded. Withdrew to beach (22nd). Strength 285. Formed composite battalion with 8th West Yorkshire. Took over trenches on extream left of line (26th). Positions on western slope of Kiretch Tepe Sirt running down to beach.

SEPTEMBER
Relieved and to reserve dug-outs (4th). Draft of 7 officers and 491 other ranks arrived (8th). To dug-outs south-west summit of Karakol Dagh (12th). To firing line – Jephson's Post (18th). Draft of 2 officers and 297 other ranks arrived (29th). Relieved and to reserve positions on beach north-east of Karakol Dagh.

OCTOBER
To reserve dug-outs (Oxford Circus) near Karakol Gap (19th). Machine gun section to fire trench near Jephson's's Post (20th). "A" Company moved forward to front line (27th) – one platoon at Jephson's Post, remainder in support trenches.

NOVEMBER
Releived 8th Duke Of Wellington's in front line (3rd) – Jephson's Post, Green Lane, Green Knoll. Lieutenant H.S. Opp, killed, Lieutenant B.S. Jennings mortally wounded (5th). Second-Lieutenant W.J. Kirkwood killed from shelling (11th).

DECEMBER
Enemy attack on Green Lane repulsed (15th). First party of 5 officers and 491 other ranks withdrew to beach for evacuation to Imbros (18th). Remainder followed, last man leaving trenches by 5.30 (20th). Battalion disembarked at Imbros same day.

THE LANCASHIRE FUSILIERS

"Helles" "Landing at Helles" "Krithia" "Suvla" "Landing at Suvla"

"Scimitar Hill" "Gallipoli,1915"

1ST BATTALION

MARCH

Nuneaton, Warwickshire. Part of 86th Brigade, 29th Division. To Avonmouth and sailed *Alaunia* for Egypt (16th). Strength – 26 officers, 932 other ranks. Transport sailed with 1 officer, 70 other ranks *Mercian*. Arrived Malta (23rd). Sailed for Egypt (25th). Arrived Alexandria (28th) and to Mex Camp.

APRIL

War Diary records exercises involving landing from ships and unloading of ammunition and stores. Sailed *Caledonia* for Lemnos (8th). Arrived Mudros (10th). To Tenedos (24th). Transhipped from *Caledonia* to *Euryalus* and *Implacable* ("D" Company) and to Gallipoli (25th). Transferred to boats (six per company) and moved off towards "W" Beach, Helles. Came under fire and all but two boats had to be abandoned. Captain H.R. Clayton (killed on 28th June) recalls the landing in a letter – "They let us off a lot, thank God, as they did not fire until the boats began to ground, and the rifles and machine guns poured into us as we got out of the boats and made for the sandy shore. There was tremendously strong barbed wire where my boat landed." Landed – rifles out of action from water and sand – impossible to return fire. Captain Clayton attempted to cut the wire, which he noted was "by now a thick mass of men, the majority of whom never moved again." Moved forward through enemy wire – "C" Company advancing on Hill 114. "D" Company landed below Hill 114 and soon cleared enemy from top. "A" and "B" Companies attacked and captured trenches and redoubt on Hill 138. The gallantry of 1st Lancashire Fusiliers during its storming of "W" Beach was recognised by General Sir Ian Hamilton in his official despatch of 20th May, 1915 . . . "The landing at W had been intrusted to the 1st Battalion Lancashire Fusiliers (Major Bishop) and it was to the complete lack of the senses of danger or of fear of this daring battalion that we owed our astonishing success . . . the Fusiliers literally hurled themselves ashore and, fired at from right, left and centre, commenced hacking their way through the wire. A long line of men was at once mown down as by the scythe, but the remainder were not to be denied." The following members of the Battalion were awarded the Victoria Cross – Captain C. Bromley, Captain R.R. Willis, Sergeant A. Richards, Sergeant F.E. Stubbs (killed), Corporal J.E. Grimshaw, Private W. Keneally. "W" Beach officially named "Lancashire Landing." After roll call, strength returned as 11 officers, 399 other ranks. First Battle of Krithia: Advanced (28th) – Fir Tree Wood taken with little loss.

MAY
Moved back to second line positions at Pink House (4th). Strength – 250 all ranks. To front line trenches – East Krithia road to Krithia Nullah (5th). Second Battle of Krithia: Attacked 11 a.m. (6th) – position reached east of Fire Tree Wood. No. 2 Company ordered forward to assist Australian troops (8th). Later retired to support line. To positions on "Y" Beach (13th). Moved forward to front line – Gurkha Bluff (19th). Relieved and to "Y" Beach (27th).

JUNE
To Gurkha Bluff (1st). Third Battle of Krithia: British bombardment (4th) recorded as falling short and causing high casualties. Machine gun section put out of action. "A" and "B" Companies attacked in centre on Gully Spur12 noon – heavy casualties from rifle and machine gun fire – most men hit while climbing parapet, few got forward not more than a few yards. "D" and "B" Companies followed and also swept by fire. Major-General J.C. Latter, C.B.E., M.C. in his 1914-1918 history of the Lancashire Fusiliers records how Captain H.R. Clayton was killed while leading "D" Company, his body being found in the Turkish wire two months later. Relieved and to Pink House in reserve (6th). Casualties – 14 officers, 500 other ranks. To Gully Beach (11th), trenches – Krithia Nullah (12th), bivouacs – West Gully Beach (17th), support trenches – Eski Line (23rd), bivouacs – White House, Achi Baba Nullah (27th). Attack at Gully Ravine (28th). Assembled at "Y" Ravine 10.15 a.m. Moved forward – "C" and "D" Companies in front, "A" in support, "B" in reserve. Leading companies met heavy fire and both lost touch with rest of battalion. "A" Company went forward and took enemy trenches in Gully Ravine. Private William Keneally, V.C. mortally wounded. Position consolidated and counter attacks driven of. Relieved and to Eski Line (29th) – casualties: 166 killed, 25 wounded. To Gully Beach (30th).

JULY
Moved forward to Krithia Nullah (4th). Relieved and to Lemnos (12th). To Gully Beach (22nd), trenches – Hampshire Cut, Krithia Nullah (27th).

AUGUST
Relieved and to Gully Beach (4th). To Eski Line (6th). "A" and "B" Companies in action at Hampshire Cut (7th). Releived in Hampshire Cut by 1st Essex (14th) and to Gully Beach. Sailed *Clacton* for Suvla Bay (19th). Moved forward to positions rear of Chocolate Hill (20th). Took part in attack on Hill 112 (21st) – moved forward 3.30 p.m. – heavy casualties from rifle and machine gun fire, also from burning scrub. War Diary records attack held up by 4.30 p.m. Report from "A" Company received stating that there were only 4 unwounded men remaining. Retired behind Green Hill – casualties: 12 officers wounded, 222 other ranks killed, wounded or missing. Relieved and to reserve at Salt Lake (22nd). To trenches – Kuchuk Anafarta Ova sector (31st).

SEPTEMBER
Relieved by 4th Worchestershire (9th) and sailed *Osmanieh* for Imbros. Sailed *Ermine* and *Redbreast* for Suvla Bay (21st) and to reserve at Lancashire Terraces. To support line (26th). Relieved 8th Cheshire in front line – Sulajik sector (30th).

OCTOBER
In support and front line.

NOVEMBER
In support and front line. In line near Dublin Castle during great storm (26th). War Diary records water entering trenches like a "tidal wave." Equipment swept away and several men drowned. Average depth of water noted as 4 feet (27th). Also noted the work of Sergeant C.A. Batham, who in command of stretcher bearers made numerous journeys waist deep in water to help the sick and wounded. He was awarded the Distinguished Conduct Medal. Casualties – 20 drowned, possibly no less than 19 frozen to death, 11 officers, 525 other ranks to hospital suffering from exposure. To reserve (28th).

DECEMBER
To front line (2nd), reserve (13th). Sailed *Barry* for Mudros (14th). Sailed *Southland* and *Brighton* for Helles (16th) and moved forward to Krithia Road. To rest area – "X" Beach (18th).

JANUARY, 1916
To "V" Beach (2nd) and sailed *Caledonia* for Egypt. Casualties for Gallipoli Campaign – 33 officers, 584 other ranks.

1/5TH BATTALION (T.F.)

JANUARY
Abbassia Camp, Ciro, Egypt. Part of Lancashire Fusiliers Brigade, East Lancashire Division which became 125th Brigade, 42nd (East Lancashire) Division in May.

MAY
To Alexandria (1st). Sailed *Menominee* for Gallipoli (4th). Landed "W" and "Y" Beaches, Helles (5th) and moved to forward to point above Gully Beach. Second Battle of Krithia: In support of 1/6th Lancashire Fusiliers (6th). Took part in attack on Gurkha Bluff (7th). Moved through line held by 1/6th Lancashire Fusiliers – some ground taken, but soon heavy rifle and machine gun fire forced withdrawal to start positions. Many casualties from both British and Turkish shells. Renewed attack during afternoon also failed. Withdrawal ordered and to "W" Beach during night. Casualties – 5 officers, 183 other ranks. To bivouacs in ruined fort just inland from Morto Bay (8th). Moved forward to reserve positions – Krithia Nullah (11th), support line Krithia (20th), reserve (23rd).

JUNE
Third Battle of Krithia: To front line and followed 1/6th Manchester into attack (4th) – three enemy lines captured and consolidated by "C" and "D" Companies on left flank, right of position at West Krithia Nullah above junction with East Krithia Nullah. Enemy counter attacked 3 a.m. (5th) – part of line taken around "D" Company's position at East Nullah. "A" and "B" Companies came forward from old British front line. "C" and "D" Companies surrounded by enemy during night and eventually withdrew. Some gains made during afternoon (6th). Positions held and consolidated. Relieved and to support line (11th). Casualties – 130. General Sir Ian Hamilton in his book *Gallipoli Diary* notes that the Battalion had been attached to 127th Brigade "and behaved with great bravery." To front line (17th), Redoubt Line (20th). Sailed *Prince Abbas* for Lemnos (23rd).

JULY
Sailed *Grampus* for Gallipoli (10th). Landed "V" Beach (11th) and to trenches – Krithia Nullah sector. To support line (16th), front line (18th),

reserve at Krithia (22nd), reserve – Eski Line (29th), support – Redoubt Line, Krithia Nullah (31st).

AUGUST
To front line (3rd). Took part in attack on The Vineyard (7th) – "C" and "D" Companies advanced 9.40 a.m. followed by "A" and "B". Enemy's first trench F12 taken. Second wave reached F12 after heavy casualties then charged forward. All officers became casualties and withdrawal to F12 ordered. This line recorded as being shallow, its hard ground making further digging a slow and difficult operation. Heavy casualties from shelling and enfilade fire. Enemy counter attack at 2 p.m driven off. Turks came forward again at 4 p.m. forcing Battalion to withdraw. Some ground retaken latter. Heavy fighting recorded for subsequent 2 days, but gains held. Relieved and to support line (9th). To reserve – "X" Beach (13th), trenches – Gully Ravine (19th), reserve – "X" Beach (22nd), Gully Beach (25th).

SEPTEMBER
To trenches – Fusilier Bluff (2nd), Gully Beach (18th), trenches – Gully Ravine (24th).

OCTOBER
To Gully Beach (1st), support – "Y" Ravine (6th). Relieved 1/4th East Lancashire in front line – Gully Ravine (15th), Gully Beach (29th). Battalion temporally amalgamated with 1/8th Lancashire Fusileers due to casualties and sickness.

NOVEMBER
To trenches – Gully Ravine (12th), "Y" Ravine (26th).

DECEMBER
To trenches – Gully Ravine (10th), Eski Line East (24th), Gully Beach (27th) then to "W" Beach. Sailed *Ermine* for Mudros during night. Casualties for Gallipoli Campaign – 9 officers, 234 other ranks.

1/6TH BATTALION (T.F.)

JANUARY
Cairo, Egypt. Part of Lancashire Fusiliers Brigade, East Lancashire Division which became 125th Brigade, 42nd (East Lancashire) Division in May.

MAY
Embarked Alexandria for Cape Helles (4th). Landed "W" Beach (5th) and to firing line – Gully Spur relieving 1st King's Own Scottish Borderers. Second Battle of Krithia (6th). Led advanced on extreme left of attack. Gained Turkish position 400 yards to front with high casualties then forced to halt. Held and consolidated gains. Relieved (7th) and withdrew to "W" Beach. To bivouacs just inland from Morto Bay, near ruined fort (8th).

JUNE
To front line – Krithia Nullah sector (3rd). Took part in fighting near The Vineyard (4th). In front line, support and reserve lines till (23rd) then to Lemnos.

JULY
Sailed for Cape Helles (10th). Landed "V" Beach and began tours of front line trenches – Krithia Nullah sector, support positions – No. 2 Australian Line and reserve at Eski Line.

AUGUST
Left trenches – Krithia Nullah (4th) and to No. 2 Australian Line. To trenches – West Krithia Nullah (6th). Took part in fighting at The Vineyard (7th). Objectives taken with hand to hand fighting and enemy counter attacks repulsed. To reserve – No. 1 Australian Line (9th), Eski Line (13th), front line – Gully Ravine (19th), reserve line – Gully Ravine (22nd), Gully Beach (25th).

SEPTEMBER
To front line near Western Birdcage (1st), Relieved by 1/5th East Lancashire and to Gully Beach (17th). To front line (24th).

OCTOBER
To Gully Beach (1st), Gully Spur (15th), reserve line – Gully Ravine (29th). Temporarily amalgamated with 1/7th Lancashire Fusiliers due to casualties and sickness.

NOVEMBER
To Geogheghan's Bluff (2nd), support and reserve trenches – Broughton Street, Essex Street, East Street, Fusilier Street (11th), front line (16th), Eski Line (26th).

DECEMBER
To support line (10th), front line (17th), Eski Line (24th). To "W" Beach (27th) and sailed *Ermine* for Mudros. Casualties for Gallipoli Campaign – 13 officers, 188 other ranks.

1/7TH BATTALION (T.F.)

JANUARY
Cairo, Egypt. Part of Lancashire Fusiliers Brigade, East Lancashire Division which became 125th Brigade, 42nd (East Lancashire) Division in May.

MAY
Sailed *Nile* for Gallipoli (1st). Landed "W" Beach (5th) and moved to area between Gully Ravine and the sea above Gully Beach. Second Battle of Krithia: In support of attack by 1/6th Lancashire Fusiliers (6th). Moved forward through captured line (7th) but forced to retire after 2 attempts (10 a.m. and 4 p.m.) to take Gurkha Bluff. Relieved and to "W" Beach at sundown. Moved to bivouacs near ruined fort just inland from Morto Bay (8th). To front line Krithia Road sector (11th). Relieved and to Eski Line (16th). To support trenches Krithia Nullah (29th).

JUNE
To front line Krithia Nullah (4th). Engaged in fighting around junction of East and West Krithia Nullahs. Relieved and to support line (11th). Casualties – 179. To front line (20th), Redoubt Line (23rd), support (26th), front line (29th).

JULY
To support line (2nd), front line (5th), Eski Line (7th). Sailed for Imbros (8th). To Cape Helles (13th) and moved forward to Redoubt Line in support. Took over front line east of Krithia Nullah (16th). To Redoubt Line (19th), Eski Line (22nd), Redoubt Line (27th), front line Achi Baba Nullah (30th).

AUGUST
To Redoubt Line (4th), front line Krithia Road (7th). Took part in attack on The Vineyard. Objectives taken and held against numerous counter attacks. Position consolidated and improved on western side. Relieved and to No 2 Australian Line (9th). War Diary notes the men as being "thoroughly worn out" and that out of a strength of 410 N.C.Os and men, only

139 returned. To Eski Line (12th), reserve line, Gully Ravine (19th), front line, Gully Ravine (21st). Relieved and to Gully Beach (22nd).

SEPTEMBER
To front line west of Gully Ravine (1st), Gully Beach (18th), Gully Spur (24th).

OCTOBER
To Gully Beach (1st), reserve line, Gully Ravine (15th), front line east and west of Gully Ravine (18th). Enemy mine blown at Crawley's Crater (29th) – several men buried. Relieved and to Geogheghan's Bluff. Temporally amalgamated with 1/6th Lancashire Fusiliers due to casualties and sickness.

NOVEMBER
To front line (12th), Eski Line West (26th).

DECEMBER
To front line (10th). Enemy mine-shaft located in The Gridiron near Cawley's Crater during patrol (14th). In his history of the 42nd (East Lancashire) Division, Frederick P. Gibbon records that Cawley's Crater was occupied by the Battalion and just 6 yards from The Gridiron. Party led by Captain A.W. Boyd successfully laid and exploded charge in mine-shaft (15th). Mine exploded in The Gridiron, 2.15 p.m. (19th). Party led by Captain Boyd charged forward and occupied crater and surrounding trenches. Enemy counter attacked 9.40 p.m. and regained line. Captain Boyd organised another charge and re-took gains by 9.55 p.m. Telegraph received from Lieutenant-General Sir Francis Davies (Commanding VIII Corps) officially naming position "Boyd's Crater." To Eski Line West (24th), Gully Beach (26th). To "W" Beach (27th) and sailed *Ermine* for Mudros. Casualties for Gallipoli Campaign – 7 officers, 242 other ranks.

1/8TH BATTALION (T.F.)

JANUARY
Abbassia Camp, Cairo, Egypt. Part of Lancashire Fusiliers Brigade, East Lancashire Division which became 125th Brigade, 42nd (East Lancashire) Division in May. To Mustapha Barracks, Alexandria (19th).

MARCH
To Heliopolis (19th).

APRIL
To Abbassia (19th), Alexandria (30th).

MAY
Sailed *Karoa* for Cape Helles (3rd). Landed "W" Beach (5th) and to forward area Gully Ravine. Took part in attack (6th) – one company on extreme left in support, another advancing with 88th Brigade on right of Gully Ravine. Later moved into and held captured line. Relieved and to "W" Beach (7th). Moved to bivouacs near ruined fort just inland from Morto Bay (8th). To front line Krithia Road sector (11th). Relieved and to Princes Street, Krithia Nullah (16th).

JUNE
To forward trenches – Krithia Nullah sector (2nd). In action (4th) – "C" and "B" Companies advancing to trenches east of The Vineyard 2.45 p.m. and taking part of enemy's line. Forced to withdraw at 6.30 p.m. Lieutenant-Colonel J.A. Fallows (Commanding) and Major E.L. Baddeley (Second in Command) killed during capture of enemy redoubt near junction of East and West Krithia Nullah (6th). Relieved and to support – No. 1 Australian Line (10th). To front line (14th), support (17th), reserve – Eski Line (24th), front line (26th), support (29th).

JULY
To front line (2nd), Princes Street (7th). Embarked "V" Beach for Imbros (9th). Arrived (10th) and to Kephalos Camp. To Cape Helles (14th) and moved forward to support – No. 1 Australian Line. To front line Krithia Nullah (16th), support (18th), Eski Line (22nd), front line Krithia Road (28th).

AUGUST
To support – No. 1 Australian Line (1st), front line Krithia Nullah (4th). Took part in attack on trenches near The Vineyard (7th). Moved forward in 3 lines and gained enemy's first line. Heavy counter attack later forced withdrawal – casualties reducing strength in firing line to just 7 officers and 73 other ranks. Relieved and to Redoubt Line (8th). To front line – The Vineyard (9th). Relived and to bivouacs near "W" Beach (12th). To reserve line – Gully Ravine (18th), front line (22nd), reserve (25th).

SEPTEMBER
To Trolley Ravine and "Y" Ravine (2nd), front line – Border Trench (5th),

Trolley Ravine and "Y" Ravine (8th), Border Trench (11th), Trolley Ravine and "Y" Ravine (14th), Eski Line West (27th).

OCTOBER
To "Y" Ravine (1st), front line – Border Trench (8th), Geogheghan's Bluff (15th), Gully Beach (22nd), Gully Ravine (29th). Temporally amalgamated with 1/5th Lancashire Fusiliers due to casualties and sickness.

NOVEMBER
To Gully Beach (7th), support lines – Gully Ravine (12th), front line (15th), support (19th), front line (23rd), Geoghehgan's Bluff (26th).

DECEMBER
To front line – Border Trench (10th), support line (14th), front line (18th), Gully Beach (24th), Eski Line West (25th). Moved to "W" Beach and sailed *Ermine* for Mudros (27th). Casualties for Gallipoli Campaign – 15 officers, 238 other ranks.

9TH (SERVICE) BATTALION

JULY
Witley, Surrey. Part of 34th Brigade, 11th (Northern) Division. Commanding Officer – Lieutenant-Colonel H.M. Welstead. Entrained to Devonport (4th). Sailed *Ionic* for Alexandria, Egypt (5th). Arrived (19th). To Lemnos (21st). Sailed *Grasshopper*, *Basilisk* and *Snaefell* to Imbros (23rd). Arrived (24th).

AUGUST
Embarked for Gallipoli 5.30 p.m.(6th) – Headquarters and "W" Company in lighter "K2" towed by *Bulldog*, rest of Battalion in lighter "K1" towed by *Grampus*. Lighters went aground some 1,000 yards south of intended landing area – "A" Beach. Enemy opened fire as men began to wade ashore. "Z" Company under Major C.E. Tristram moved forward to edge of Salt Lake. "X" (Captain E.M. Elwell) and "Y" (Captain F.R.L. Lowth) Companies followed. Lieutenant-Colonel W.J. Woodcock (Second in Command) moved forward with part of "W" Company and cleared enemy which had force their way between "Z" and "Y". Heavy casualties among "Z" Company – all officers hit. Enemy attacked at daybreak (7th) and driven off. Lieutenant-Colonel Welstead killed by sniper on beach. Advanced on Hill 10 in support of 8th Northumberland Fusiliers and 5th Dorsetshire. Hill taken together with surrounding trenches after heavy fighting. Gains con-

solidated under Captain M.C. Ferrers-Guy now senior officer. Casualties among officers so far – 7 killed, 7 wounded. In support of 5th Dorsetshire during attack (8th), advancing to position 250 yards behind Hill 28. Retired to Hill 10 during night. Attack on enemy trenches south of Karakol Dagh (9th). Advanced on right of 5th Dorsetshire – 2 companies in front, 2 in support. Halted soon after attack began and remained in support. Withdrew (10th) and dug in on right of 5th Dorsetshire then entrenches on Karakol Dagh. Relieved and to rest area behind Lala Baba (12th). Casualties – 14 officers. Other ranks casualties not recorded. To support positions (14th). Releived 11th Manchester in firing line – Azmak Dere sector (15th). To support line (18th), front line – Dead Man's House sector (20th). Attacked enemy trenches 3 p.m. (21st). Objective taken by 3.10 p.m. In his war history of the Lancashire Fusiliers, Major-General J.C. Latter, C.B.E., M.C. records how the Battalion held gallantly to its gains for 19 hours, there being no response to repeated requests for support. With just 100 men, no officers or warrant officers, a withdrawal to the start line was eventually forced. Out of the 29 officers that sailed for Gallipoli in July just 4 remained unhurt. Later formed composite battalion with 8th Northumberland Fusiliers and known as No. 1 Battalion, 34th Brigade. No 9th Battalion War Diary exists for period 21st August – 1st October. According to that of the 8th Northumberland Fusiliers, No. 1 Battalion occupied reserve dug-outs on the north side of Karakol Dagh overlooking the sea from (28th).

SEPTEMBER
34th Brigade took over support and fire trenches – Jephson's Post (4th). Line recorded as quite but with continuous sniping. Relieved and to reserve positions on West Beach (21st). War Diary of 5th Dorsetshire records a move with No.1 Battalion (8th Northumberland Fusiliers, 9th Lancashire Fusiliers) to sector around Jephson's Post during evening (28th).

OCTOBER
Trenches, Lone Tree Gully.

NOVEMBER
Releived by 1/1st West Somerset Yeomanry (3rd) and to reserve positions north of Karakol Dagh – Leather Lane (7th). Relieved by 7th South Staffordshire (12th) and to rest camp.

DECEMBER
To West Beach (13th). Evacuated to Mudros (18th) Casualties for Gallipoli Campaign – 11 officers, 242 other ranks.

THE ROYAL SCOTS FUSILIERS

"Helles" "Gallipoli,1915-16"

1/4TH BATTALION (T.F.)

MAY
Stirling, Stirlingshire. Part of 155th Brigade, 52nd (Lowland) Division. Entrained for Liverpool (19th) and embarked *Mauretania*. Strength – 30 officers, 952 other ranks. Sailed (21st). War Diary records (22nd) No. 6344 Sergeant T. Ashton "drowned at sea." Arrived Mudros Bay, Lemnos (29th).

JUNE
Two companies and Machine Gun Section embarked *Renard* (6th) and to Gallipoli. Landed "V" Beach, Cape Helles. 7 p.m. Two companies sailed *Rowan*. Moved to rest camp and dug in. Camp shelled (7th) – Medical Officer Major James Craik Taylor mortally wounded. Relieved 4th Worcestershire in trench H11 (10th). War Diary records trenches in need of considerable improvement – drainage, thickening of parapet, cutting of fire steps and new communication trench between firing line and support. Trenches heavily shelled (11th) – Captain A. Logan and 3 other ranks killed, 21 others wounded. Relieved by 1st Essex (13th) and to rest camp. War Diary records (18th) – 1 killed, 4 wounded from "stray rifle bullets." Camp heavily shelled (19th) – Lieutenant H.M. Lewis mortally wounded; 1 man killed, 12 wounded. Relieved 1/5th East Lancashire and 1/9th Manchester in trenches – Krithia Nullah sector (22nd). Relieved and to reserve line on "stand bye" (27th). Enemy aeroplane dropped bomb on camp (29th) – 1 killed, 4 wounded.

JULY
Relieved Anson Battalion in forward trenches – Gully Ravine sector (6th). Relieved and to bivouacs (9th). Later, at 7 p.m., "A" and "C" Companies sent to take over French line (Parsons Road). "B" and "D" Companies joined "A" and "C" (10th). Attack on Trench E11 (12th) – moved forward in 4 waves on right of 155th Brigade 7.35 a.m. – "D" Company (1st wave), "A" Company (2nd and 3rd waves), part of "B" (4th wave). *Official History of the Great War* records that the men of the Battalion found themselves engulfed in a maze of half-obliterated trenches . . . "Enormous execution had been done in the Turkish lines, and some of their shallow trenches were filled with dead." War Diary notes attack as "quite successful" – 2 enemy

trenches taken and consolidated. Several counter attacks repulsed. "C" Company renewed attack in afternoon – another trench gained and held. Casualties – Major W. Stewart; Captain A. Kenneth; Lieutenants J. Barnett, G. Sturrock; Second-Lieutenants G.H. Kyle, M.B.W. McCail and 49 other ranks killed; all other officers except 3, 150 other ranks wounded; 62 missing. Strong enemy counter attack repulsed (13th). Relieved by Chatham Battalion (14th) and to support trench. To rest bivouacs (15th) – "B" Company remaining forward in reserve line. "B" Company joined battalion (16th). Began work on communication trenches around Mule Track (17th).

AUGUST
Relieved 1/9th Manchester in trenches east of Krithia Nullah to The Vineyard (13th). Private D.R. Lauder distinguished himself while with a bombing party, placing his foot on a bomb that had failed to clear the parapet. He was later awarded the Victoria Cross. Captain N. Jamieson killed by sniper. Relieved by 1/5th King's Own Scottish Borderers (17th) and to support and Redoubt Line. Relieved 1/5th King's Own Scottish Borderers in firing line (21st). War Diary notes (23rd) . . ."quality of sand bags supplied to firing line poor and to small." Relieved by 1/5th King's Own Scottish Borderers (25th) – 1 company to support line, 1 in reserve at No. 1 Australian Line and Redoubt Line. Took over firing line from 1/4th Royal Scots – Vineyard sector (26th). Relieved by 1/7th Scottish Rifles (29th) and to Eski Line east of Krithia Nullah.

SEPTEMBER
Relieved 1/7th Scottish Rifles in firing line (2nd). Relieved and to Redoubt and Eski Lines (6th). To firing line (10th). Relieved by 1/7th Scottish Rifles and to rest camp (14th). To firing line (19th). War Diary notes first use by enemy of rifle grenades. Relieved and to rest camp (26th).

OCTOBER
Moved to forward area – right sub-section (3rd). Came under shrapnel fire (7th) – 1 officer wounded, 2 men killed. War Diary notes latter established that French battery were responsible. Relieved and to rest camp (17th). To firing line – Hope Street, Argyle Street, St. Vincent Street, Queen Street, Renfield Street (24th). 1/1st Ayrshire Yeomanry attached for instruction. Casualties for October – 3 other ranks killed; 1 officer, 5 other ranks wounded; 2 officers, 83 other ranks to hospital sick.

NOVEMBER

Relieved and to rest camp (7th). To firing line west of Achi Baba Nullah (14th). Relieved and to Eski Line in Divisional Reserve (21st). To rest camp (28th). Casualties for November – 1 man killed; 4 wounded; 4 officers, 56 men to hospital sick.

DECEMBER

To firing line Krithia Nullah (5th). War Diary notes new kind of rocket bomb in use by enemy. Approximately 100 land nightly but most do not explode. Just 1 casualty from this source. War Diary records (19th) party led by Lieutenant C.M. Laing successfully took in wire in front of Cathedral Street then cut Turkish wire in front of trench G12. In action (20th) during 157th Brigade arrack on G12 and G11A. Casualties – 2 killed, 18 wounded. Relieved and to rest camp (21st). To firing line east of Krithia Nullah to No. 3 Grenade Post, support line – Krithia Nullah to "C" Avenue (26th). Mines exploded under G11Y and H11A. Consolidating party went forward to assist subsequent attack by 1/5th Royal Scots Fusiliers. Relieved by 1st Essex and to rest camp (31st). Casualties for December – 12 killed, 44 wounded, 47 sick.

JANUARY, 1916

Began evacuation to Mudros. Last men leaving during night (8th).

1/5TH BATTALION (T.F.)

MAY

Stirling, Stirlingshire. Part of 155th Brigade, 52nd (Lowland) Division. Entrained for Liverpool (19th) and embarked *Mauretania*. Sailed (21st). Arrived Mudros Bay, Lemnos (29th).

JUNE

Embarked *Basilisk* and *Immingham* (6th) and sailed for Gallipoli. Landed "V" Beach and to rest camp. Camp heavily shelled (7th and 8th). Relieved 1/5th Royal Scots in firing line near Fir Tree Wood during night (9th). Relieved by 1/5th Royal Scots and to rest camp (13th). To reserve trenches at Clapham Junction (19th).

JULY

Returned to rest camp (6th). To firing line (10th), support trenches – Brown House Line (11th). In reserve during 155th Brigade's attack (12th). "A" Company moved forward and held original firing line. "C" with half of "D" dug communication trenches to captured lines. "B" and other half of "D" reinforced 1/5th King's Own Scottish Borderers in captured trenches (13th). War Diary records that companies digging communication trenches suffered over 50% losses but completed their task. "B" Company lost all of its officers. "D" Company held off fierce counter attack (13th). War Diary records " . . . not one of the enemy survived." Casualties (12th-13th) – 6 officers, 61 other ranks killed; 1 officer, 139 other ranks wounded; 8 missing. To support trenches – Mercer Road (15th) then to rest camp. Total casualties since landing – 7 officers, 71 other ranks killed; 4 officers, 224 other ranks wounded; 9 missing; 8 officers, 141 other ranks to hospital sick. Effective strength (31st) – 10 officers, 498 other ranks.

AUGUST
To firing line west of Krithia Nullah (12th) – trenches H11and H10. Major J. Russell killed (26th). Relieved by 1/4th Royal Scots (29th) and moved back to support and Redoubt Lines. Casualties for August – 1 officer, 8 other ranks killed; 12 wounded; 1 missing; 4 officers, 53 other ranks sick. Effective strength (31st) – 20 officers, 489 other ranks.

SEPTEMBER
Relieved 1/4th Royal Scots in firing line (2nd). To rest camp (6th), firing line (10th). Relieved by 1/4th Royal Scots (14th) and to support and reserve line. To firing line (19th), rest camp (26th). War Diary records (26th) that since 8th August there has been practically no activity from either side and that our front had been considerably thinned. The enemy had also reduced his numbers and . . . "he has fallen of in morale." There had been much sniping, in which the Battalion had "obtained complete mastery" and trench mortars had been used with great effect. Jaundice had made an appearance and there had been difficulty in obtaining ordnance supplies . . . "the condition of the men's clothing is disgraceful." Casualties for September – 6 killed, 1 wounded, 45 sick. Effective strength (30th) – 17 officers, 415 other ranks.

OCTOBER
Relieved 1/6th Highland Light Infantry in firing line (3rd). War Diary notes that enemy snipers active for first 24 hours but soon "subdued by bombers and snipers." Moved back to support and Redoubt Line (9th). To firing line (11th), Redoubt Line (15th), Eski Line in Divisional Reserve (18th). Began fatigues clearing Krithia and Achi Baba Nullahs of weeds and dirt. To firing line (24th). Captain J. Vivers of "B" Company killed by sniper (27th). Casualties for October – 1 officer, 5 other ranks killed; 12 wounded, 54 sick.

NOVEMBER

"C" and "D" Companies successfully pushed forward "B" Bomb Station 70 yards. Now just 20 yards from enemy trench H11A. Relieved and to rest camp (7th). Relieved 1/5th Highland Light Infantry in firing line (14th). Assisted 1/7th Scottish Rifles in their attack on enemy trenches H11A and G11B. Relieved by 1/5th King's Own Scottish Borderers (21st) and to Redoubt Line in reserve. To rest camp (28th). Casualties for November – 9 wounded; 2 officers, 35 other ranks to hospital sick.

DECEMBER

To firing line, support and Redoubt Line east of East Krithia Nullah (5th). Took part in attack on G11B (19th) – 2 new bombing posts set up and connecting trench dug between G11B and G12. Also assisted 1/5th Highland Light Infantry in attack on G12. Casualties – 2 killed, 13 wounded. War Diary records that these were mainly caused by falling debris from exploded mines. Relieved by 1/6th Highland Light Infantry and to rest camp (20th). Relieved 1/5th Highland Light Infantry in firing line (26th). War Diary notes "trenches a sea of mud." Attack on G11A (29th). Two mines blown at 1 p.m. then assault led by Lieutenants McIntosh and McNaughton. Objectives taken within half hour. Gains – G11A, 40 yards of G11Y and G11Z. Also communications trenches. Four enemy counter attacks repulsed after dark. Casualties – Second-Lieutenant J.C. Austin and 6 other ranks killed; 5 officers, 31 other ranks wounded. Trenches heavily shelled for over 4 hours (30th). War Diary records 50 shells landing per hour. Casualties – Lieutenant A.N. Mitchell, Second-Lieutenant S.S. Anderson killed; Lieutenant W.J. McNaughton mortally wounded; 16 other ranks killed, 30 wounded. Relieved by 1st Essex (31st) and to rest camp. Ordered to move to "V" Beach for evacuation 7 p.m.

JANUARY, 1916

Embarked *Prince Abbas* (1st) and sailed for Mudros.

THE CHESHIRE REGIMENT

"Suvla" "Sari Bair" "Landing at Suvla" "Scimitar Hill" "Gallipoli,1915"

1/4TH BATTALION (T.F.)

JULY
Bedford, Bedfordshire. Part of 159th Brigade, 53rd (Welsh) Division. To Devonport and sailed *Euripides* (16th). Called Gibraltar (20th), Malta (24th). Arrived Alexandria (27th). Sailed for Port Said (30th).

AUGUST
Sailed for Lemnos (4th). Arrived Mudros Harbour (7th). *Euripides* went to ground on edge of reef. Men transferred to another ship and sailed for Gallipoli (8th). Landed "C" Beach, Suvla and bivouacked on beach. To positions on north west slope of Lala Baba 4.30 a.m. (9th). Attached to 34th Brigade and later in support of 32nd Brigade during attack on Anafarta Sagir. Advanced and took over firing line at Sulajik. Attacked during after-noon (10th). War Diary records attack failed due to lack of support. Casualties – 9 officers killed, 7 wounded; 20 other ranks killed, 117 wounded, 289 missing. Withdrew to support line (11th). In support of attack by 1/5th Norfolk (12th). Took over front line trenches from 1/5th Welsh (17th). Began work digging new forward line and communication trench during night (18th/19th). Reinforcement of 3 officers, 167 other ranks arrived (22nd). Strength now – 17 officer, 521 other ranks. Relieved by 1/1st Herefordshire (27th) and moved back to rest area at Hill 10. Relieved 2/4th Queen's in forward trenches – Sulajik sector (31st).

SEPTEMBER
Relieved by 1/1st Herefordshire (7th) and to rest camp. To firing line – left sub section, "C" Sector (12th). Relieved by 8th Royal Welsh Fusiliers (20th) and to reserve positions north west slope of Lala Baba. Began beach fatigues.

OCTOBER
Reserve line Lala Baba. Beach fatigues.

NOVEMBER
Reserve line Lala Baba. Beach fatigues and work under 53rd Divisional Engineers. War Diary of 159th Brigade records (10th) – no further beach

fatigues to be found by Brigade. Units now at disposal of C.R.E. 53rd Division. Work to consist of roadworks and defences – right section Lala Baba up to and including crossroads leading to Chocolate Hill. To forward trenches (29th). War Diary of 159th Brigade notes severe weather and casualties (20th-30th) – 1 officer wounded, 2 sick. 1 other rank killed, 7 wounded, 212 sick.

DECEMBER
Holding left of Brigade line. Condition of trenches noted as bad due to recent storm. Some sections 2 feet deep in mud and slush, parapets in bad state of repair. Moved from left of line to Cater's House (5th). Relieved and to reserve line – Lala Baba (9th). To "C" Beach (12th) and embarked *Ermine*. Sailed for Mudros (13th).

1/7TH BATTALION (T.F.)

JULY
Bedford, Bedfordshire. Part of 159th Brigade, 53rd (Welsh) Division. To Devonport and sailed for Egypt. Arrived Alexandria then to Port Said for 6 days.

AUGUST
To Mudros (4th), Gallipoli (8th). Landed "C" Beach, Suvla then moved forward to line south of Sulajik. Strength – 24 officers, 750 other ranks. Took part in attack on Scimitar Hill (10th). War Diary records operation as unsuccessful and that the Battalion "suffered somewhat severely." Enemy attack at 7 .p.m. repulsed. Many Turks seen dressed as Gurkhas. Casualties – 9 officers wounded, 2 missing; 18 other ranks killed, 145 wounded, 286 missing. Moved position north (11th). Line pushed forward 100 yards on right, 150 yards left (17th). Reinforcement arrived (21st) – 3 officers, 190 other ranks. Relieved by 1/5th Royal Welsh fusiliers (27th) and to rest camp near Hill 10. To front line trenches – Sulajik sector (31st). Casualties since landing – 16 officers, 363 other ranks.

SEPTEMBER
Relieved and to rest camp (8th). To Brigade Reserve line (12th), firing line (16th). Second-Lieutenant E. McKay killed with wiring party. War Diary records trench mortar blew up (18th) – 2 men killed, 1 wounded. Relieved and to beach at Lala Baba (20th).

OCTOBER
Lala Baba. War Diary records Battalion rearmed with short rifles and long bayonets (19th).

NOVEMBER
Lala Baba. Worked beach fatigues and construction of defences. Battalion ordered to be in "a state of constant readiness" (9th). Relieved from state of constant readiness (18th). Began tours of duty in Lala Baba defenses. Attached to Highland Mounted Brigade (27th) and to Brigade Reserve trenches – South Area. Two companies remained at Lala Baba attached to 1/4th Cheshire, then to forward trenches (29th).

DECEMBER
Second-Lieutenant H.A. Seal killed (7th). Relieved and to Lala Baba (9th). Began work on defences. To "C" Beach and embarked *Ermine* (12th). Sailed for Mudros (13th).

8TH (SERVICE) BATTALION

JUNE
Pirbright, Surrey. Part of 40th Brigade, 13th (Western) Division. To Avonmouth and embarked *Ivernia* (26th).

JULY
Arrived Malta (3rd), departed (4th). Arrived Alexandria (7th), departed (8th). Arrived Mudros (10th) disembarked (14th). Embarked *Whitby Abbey* (16th). Landed "V" Beach, Cape Helles and to Gully Beach. Moved forward to reserve positions – Eastern Mule Trench – rear of Eski Line. Relieved 8th Royal Welsh Fusiliers in firing line – Worcester Flat (19th). Relieved and to Eski Line (20th). Relieved 8th Royal Welsh Fusiliers at Worcester Flat (25th). Relieved and to Gully Beach (28th). To "W" Beach (30th) and sailed for Mudros. Arrived (31st). Casualties since 16th – 2 killed, 20 wounded, 1 accidently drowned.

AUGUST
To Anzac (4th) and to reserve positions rear of Walker's Ridge. Moved forward to Russell's Top 3 a.m. (7th). In support during failed attack by Australian Light Horse on The Nek. Two companies also in support of unsuccessful attack by 8th Royal Welsh Fusiliers from Monash Gully. Relieved during night and to support trenches – half battalion behind Walker's Ridge, half Quinn's Post. Moved along beach to No. 2 Post (9th).

Later received orders to return – half battalion behind Russell's Top, half in Monash Gully in support of Quinn's Post and Courtney's Post. To Chailak Dere (13th) taking over reserve at The Apex during night. Took over firing line east ridge of Chailak Dere (14th). Moved to positions – The Apex and Rhododendron Spur (24th). Relieved by New Zealand troops (28th) and to Divisional Reserve line – Kaiajik Dere. Position just east of Arpa Oran. Casualties for August – 9 killed, 66 wounded, 2 missing.

SEPTEMBER

To dug outs in cliffs south end Suvla Bay (1st). Began work on Lala Baba defences – north east side. War Diary records sickness (mainly dysentery) during period (1st-20th) reducing strength from 652 to 471. To forward area (20th) relieving 159th Brigade Sulajik sector. Relieved by 1st Lancashire Fusiliers (30th) and to reserve line. Casualties during September – 2 killed, 18 wounded, 352 sick. Strength – 18 officer, 407 other ranks.

OCTOBER

Relieved 6th Royal Munster Fusiliers in forward trenches B58 and B59 (1st). War Diary records a patrol (6th) led by Second-Lieutenant R.H. Gwyn-Williams leaving a letter from Turkish prisoner in front of enemy's tenches. Relieved and to Brigade Reserve lines (28th). Casualties for October – 2 killed, 13 wounded, 132 sick. Strength – 21 officers, 503 other ranks.

NOVEMBER

Relieved 8th Royal Welsh Fusiliers in fire trenches B61 and B62 (12th). Heavy bombardment from Turkish guns on right at Chocolate Hill (16th). War Diary notes (18th) – no blankets allowed for men in fire trench, just ground sheets and greatcoats. Casualties for November – 1 officer wounded, 5 sick, 3 other ranks killed, 10 wounded, 341 sick. Strength – 17 officers, 354 other ranks.

DECEMBER

"D" Company to Lala Baba defences (10th). Remainder withdrew to Salt Lake Line (19th) then to Lala Baba at midnight. Left South Pier (20th) and embarked *Osmanieh* for Imbros. Last party under Captain Boote left Salt Lake Lines 2.50 a.m. and left by *Princess Ena*. Embarked *Huntsgreen* 5 p.m. and sailed for Mudros. Disembarked (22nd) and to Portianos Camp. To North Pier (30th) and embarked *Princess Alberta* for Gallipoli. Landed "V" Beach, Helles and to Brigade Reserve at Gully Beach. Casualties for

December – 2 killed, 3 wounded, 282 sick. Strength – 15 officers, 386 other ranks.

JANUARY, 1916

To dug outs about 200 yards below Eski Line (1st). Began work on new road from Zig Zag to Gully Beach. To Frith Walk in support of 4th South Wales Borderers (7th). Withdrew to dug outs during evening. To Eski line – Artillery Road to Gully Ravine 5.30 a.m. (8th). Later moved back to "W" Beach and embarked *Ermine*. Sailed about 9 p.m. for Mudros.

THE ROYAL WELSH FUSILIERS

"Suvla" "Sari Bair" "Landing at Suvla" "Scimitar Hill" "Gallipoli,1915-16"

1/5TH (FLINTSHIRE) BATTALION (T.F.)

JULY
Higham Ferrers, Northamptonshire. Part of 158th Brigade, 53rd (Welsh) Division. Entrained at Irchester for Devonport (13th). Embarked *Caledonia* and sailed (14th). Arrived Gibraltar (17th). Sailed (18th). Arrived Malta (21st). Sailed for Egypt (22nd). Arrived Alexandria (25th). Sailed for Lemnos (26th). Arrived Mudros (28th). Disembarked and to bivouacs (30th).

AUGUST
Embarked *Rowan* and sailed for Imbros (8th). Strength – 26 officers, 811 other ranks. To Suvla 4.30 a.m. (9th). Landed "C" Beach 6 a.m. and to bivouacs at Lala Baba. One company detailed to take equipment up to front line. Moved forward 4.45 a.m. (10th). Advanced across Salt Lake under heavy shrapnel and rifle fire. Passed through entrenched battalions of 159th Brigade 11.30 a.m. *Official History of the Great War* records that the 1/5th was gallantly led by Lieutenant-Colonel B.E. Philips and penetrated to within a few hundred yards of Scimitar Hill. Opened fire on enemy about 200 yards from Turkish front line. Later ordered to withdraw to 159th Brigade lines. Further attempts to take enemy positions during afternoon also failed. All reports of 158th Brigade's advance refer to lack of maps and confusion. Casualties – Lieutenant-Colonel B.E. Philips, Lieutenant H.O. Williams, Second-Lieutenants R.C. Walton, J.H.F. Leland, F.P. Synnott, R.M. Mocatta and 13 other ranks killed, 6 officers, 116 other ranks wounded; 39 missing. Moved to positions in Sulajik sector facing Scimitar Hill (11th). Began work improving trenches, 2 men killed during night. War Diary (12th) records "Impossible to work on trenches by day owing to enemy rifle fire." Major B. Head killed by sniper (13th). Relieved by 1/4th Royal Sussex 10 p.m. and to Azmak Dere. Took over trenches in "C" Sector (16th). First reinforcements – 2 officers, 115 other ranks arrived (17th). Relieved during night (22nd) and to rest camp near "A" Beach. Casualties since 16th – 11 killed, 29 wounded. Relieved 1/7th Cheshire in trenches Kuchuk Anafarta Ova sector (27th). War Diary notes to date about 160 men to hospital with dysentery and diarrhoea.

SEPTEMBER

Relieved and to rest camp near "A" Beach (4th). Relieved 1/5th Welsh in trenches – Sulajik sector (8th). Relieved and to rest camp at Hill 10 (16th). Moved to camp near West Beach (21st), north side of Karakol Dagh (25th). Began work on roads and beach fatigues. War Diary records about 180 men to hospital during September suffering from dysentery.

OCTOBER

Strength – 18 officers, 355 other ranks. Temporarily amalgamated with 1/6th Royal Welsh Fusiliers (9th). Camp shelled between 10-11 a.m. (26th) – 3 killed, 1 wounded. Took over reserve trenches south west of Chocolate Hill (31st). War Diary notes position as extending from Susak Kuyu on right to De Prees Sap, 50 yards short of Azmak Dere, on left. total length, 775 yards.

NOVEMBER

Relieved 1/1st Lovat's Scouts in front line (1st). War Diary records Turkish prisoner captured in Patterson's Sap (9th). Work began on new Battalion Headquarters in Oak Tree Sap (10th). Much work by enemy on trenches at West Hill noted. Artillery "more active" (13th) – some shrapnel over Poplar Sap, about 12 H.E. shells landed 200 yards in rear of support line – only 4 burst. Headquarters moved to Oak Tree Sap (21st). Heavy thunderstorm (26th). Area flooded – barricade across Azmak Dere washed away, communication with Brigade Headquarters cut off. Trenches flooded 2-3 feet deep, all regimental documents and papers lost. War diary notes enemy positions also flooded – "many Turkish dead floated down." No Mans Land flooded 3-4 feet deep in places. Relieved by 1/1st Lovat's Scouts (27th) and to bivouacs on hills north of Welsh Field Ambulance camp. Strength – 11 officers, 344 other ranks. Many men to hospital (28th) suffering from frost bite and exposure after blizzard. To Lala Baba (29th). Strength just 88 other ranks.

DECEMBER

Began work on Lala Baba defences (1st). Bombed by enemy aeroplane (8th) – no casualties. To "C" Beach (12th) and embarked *El Kahirah*. Disembarked Mudros West (13th) and to bivouacs.

1/6TH (CARNARVONSHIRE & ANGLESEY) BATTALION (T.F.)

JULY

Rushden, Northamptonshire. Part of 158th Brigade, 53rd (Welsh) Division. Lord Silsoe in his book *Sixty Years A Welsh Territorial* records how his battalion was at first passed unfit for overseas service. The problem being mainly the state of the men's teeth. Last minute arrangements were made for mass extractions and dentures ordered. The latter arriving on the Suez Canal some twelve months later. He was also responsible for making up the nominal roll and he notes that out of a strength of about 800, some 200 of the men were named Jones. Entrained at Irchester for Devonport (13th). Embarked *Caledonia* and sailed (14th). Arrived Gibraltar (17th). Sailed (18th). Arrived Malta (21st). Sailed for Egypt (22nd). Arrived Alexandria (25th). Sailed for Lemnos (26th). Arrived Mudros (28th). Disembarked and to bivouacs (30th).

AUGUST

Sailed for Suvla via Imbros (8th). Lanced "C" Beach (9th) and marched to Lala Baba. Moved forward on left of Brigade attack (10th). Lord Silsoe recalls receiving orders to capture Green Hill and that the Battalion set off in broad daylight. Crossing Salt Lake the men sunk in above the ankles. The lake being covered by a crust of salt. Came under heavy shrapnel fire during crossing. Battalion passed through 11th Division front line on Chocolate Hill and advanced on Green Hill. Forced to withdraw from Green Hill during evening and took up support positions to first line trenches. Lord Silsoe recalls reaching the crest of Green Hill with his platoon – some 25 – 30 men. After heavy bombardment from British naval ships he noted that only his party were present. The remainder of the Battalion being then behind on the slopes between Chocolate and Green Hills. Took over front line (12th). Relieved and to Azmak Dere (15th). To front line – Kiretch Tepe Sirt sector (17th). Relieved by 2nd Royal Fusiliers during night (22nd/23rd) and to rest camp "A" Beach. Commanding Officer – Lieutenant-Colonel T.W. Jones records in War Diary . . . "nothing but sand and shrapnel . . . 1st rest we have had since we landed." Relieved 1/4th Welsh in front line – Kuchuk Anafarta Ova sector (27th). War Diary records (31st) sickness (diarrhoea) had broken out while at camp. Most of the senior officers had been lost (killed or wounded) . . . "Of the 30 officers that came out from England at present I have only 12 left."

SEPTEMBER

Relieved and to rest camp on "A" Beach. To forward area – Sulajik sector (8th). Relieved and to rest camp at Hill 10 (16th). Moved to camp at West Beach (21st), north side of Karakol Dagh (25th). Began beach and water fatigues and road making.

OCTOBER

Strength – 21 officers, 354 other ranks. Temporarily amalgamated with

1/5th Royal Welsh Fusiliers (9th). Camp shelled between 10-11 a.m. (26th) – 3 killed, 1 wounded. Took over reserve trenches south west of Chocolate Hill (31st). War Diary notes position as extending from Susak Kuyu on right to De Prees Sap, 50 yards short of Azmak Dere, on left. total length, 775 yards.

NOVEMBER
Relieved 1/1st Lovat's Scouts in front line (1st). War diary records Turkish prisoner captured in Patterson's Sap (9th). Work began on new Battalion Headquarters in Oak Tree Sap (10th). Much work by enemy on trenches at West Hill noted. Artillery "more active" (13th) – some shrapnel over Poplar Sap, about 12 H.E. shells landed 200 yards in rear of support line – only 4 burst. Headquarters moved to Oak Tree Sap (21st). Heavy thunderstorm (26th). Area flooded – barricade across Asmak Dere washed away, communication with Brigade Headquarters cut off. Trenches flooded 2-3 feet deep, all regimental documents and papers lost. War diary notes enemy positions also flooded – "many Turkish dead floated down." No Mans Land flooded 3-4 feet deep in places. Relieved by 1/1st Lovat's Scots (27th) and to bivouacs on hills north of Welsh Field Ambulance camp. Strength – 20 officers, 335 other ranks. Many men to hospital (28th) suffering from frost bite and exposure after blizzard. To Lala Baba (29th). Strength – 8 officers, 102 other ranks.

DECEMBER
Began work on Lala Baba Defences (1st). Bombed by enemy aeroplane (8th) – no casualties. To "C" Beach (12th) and embarked *El Kahirah*. Disembarked Mudros West (13th) and to bivouacs.

1/7TH (MERIONETH & MONTGOMERY) BATTALION (T.F.)

JULY
Rushden, Northamptonshire. Part of 158th Brigade, 53rd (Welsh) Division. "A" Company (Captain E. Lloyd-Jones) and "D" Company (Captain W. Williams) to Devonport (14th) and embarked *City of Edinburgh*. Sailed (15th). Remainder to Devonport (16th) and sailed *Huntsend* and *Ulysses*. Arrived Alexandria (28th).

AUGUST
Sailed for Port Said (1st), Lemnos (4th). Arrived Mudros (7th). To Suvla via Imbros (8th). Landed "C" Beach during morning (9th) then marches to bivouacs west side of Lala Baba. Ordered (10th) to relieved 159th Brigade

in forward area then advance on enemy positions at Scimitar Hill. Moved forward across Salt Lake 5 a.m. in centre of Brigade attack. Came under heavy shrapnel fire then rifle and machine gun. War Diary records . . . "engaged all day. Fighting ceased 7.30 p.m." Withdrew to 1st and 2nd line trenches. Casualties included 15 officers. Took over front line (11th). War Diary notes heavy fighting to left on 159th Brigade front. Relieved by 1/1st Herefordshire (13th) and withdrew to reserve trenches just east of Azmak Dere. To "C" Beach (14th) and embarked for Mudros. Sailed *Barry* (15th). Strength – 10 officers, 446 other ranks. Casualties (9th-14th) – Captains E.W. Lloyd-Jones, A.G. Reed, B.H.E. Beadon; Lieutenant J.W. Beanland; Second-Lieutenants B.B. Silcock, R.H. Jones, A.E.P. Grant and 13 other ranks killed. Captain E.G. Harries and Second-Lieutenant E.M. Buckley mortally wounded. Seven other officers and 138 other ranks wounded, 74 men missing.

SEPTEMBER
Occupied unloading and loading stores and guarding Turkish prisoners.

OCTOBER
Embarked *Sarnia* (14th) and sailed for Suvla. Strength – 29 officers, 496 other ranks. Rejoined 158th Brigade in reserve trenches at Karakol Dagh. To reserve – Salt Lake Line (31st).

NOVEMBER
Began work digging communication trenches (1st). Moved forward to local reserve trenches – "A" Section (5th), Brigade Reserve (12th). took over right subsection firing line – Susak Kuye to Glenmohr (21st). Severe flooding in trenches after storm (26th). Relieved by 1/2nd Lovat's Scouts (27th) and to Lala Baba. War Diary records 105 men to hospital suffering from exposure and trench foot (29th-30th).

DECEMBER
Strength (1st) – 19 officers, 287 other ranks. Employed on Lala Baba defences and beach fatigues. To "C" Beach (12th) and embarked for Mudros. Sailed (13th). Arrived 9 a.m. and to Tower Hill Camp.

8TH (SERVICE) BATTALION

JUNE
Pirbright, Surrey. Part of 40th Brigade, 13th (Western) Division. Entrained at Brookwood for Avonmouth (28th). Sailed *Megantic* (29th).

JULY

Reached Malta (5th), Alexandra (8th). To Lemnos (10th) arriving Mudros (12th). Sailed for Gallipoli (15th). Arrived Cape Helles (16th) and to Gully Beach in Divisional Reserve. Relieved 6th South Lancashire in front line – trenches H11, H12, Worcester Flat sector (17th). Relieved by 8th Cheshire and to Brigade Reserve – Eski Line (19th). Returned to front line (20th). Relieved and to Eski Line (25th). Relieved (30th). Embarked *Beagle* from "V" Beach and sailed for Mudros.

AUGUST

Embarked *Abassieh* (4th) and sailed 3 p.m. for Anzac Cove. War Diary records that no kits, coats or blankets were taken. Landed about 9 p.m. and marched to bivouacs in White Gully. Headquarters, "A" and "B" Companies moved forward to Russell's Top, "C" and "D" Companies to Monash Gully (5th). Battalion attached to Australians: "C" and "D" Companies – No. 3 Section, "A" and "B" Companies – No. 4 Section. "C" Company to front line – Quinn's and Courtney's Posts. Lieutenant T.D. Daly noted an enthusiastic welcome from the Australians, distance from enemy trenches just 5 – 10 yards, smell from dead bodies lying in No Man's Land and that the front line was the safest place – "all movement behind the front line was fatal." There was also a shortage of water (4 pints per man per day), the heat melted the bully beef and swarms of flies covered everything. "A" and "B" Companies moved from Russell's Top to Monash Gully 3.30 a.m. (7th). In support of Australian attack on The Nek – "A" and "B" companies advanced up Monash Gully – "A" Company moving to right, "B" to left. "A" Company reached the ridge then came under attacked from crest. War Diary notes steep slopes on both sides thick with scrub – "casualties occurred at once and the men falling back knocked over the men coming up behind." Leading platoons of "B" Company swept with machine gun fire. Ordered to fall back and remain under cover in Gully. Both companies moved back to Russell's Top in evening. Casualties – 4 officers, 61 other ranks killed or wounded. Headquarters, "A" and "B" companies to No. 3 Section (8th). Battalion to Bridges Road in Army Corps Reserve (9th). To bivouacs in Chailak Dere during morning (10th). Moved forward to Apex 8 p.m. and entrenched. One company sent forward to reinforce Australians at Rhododendron Spur. Returned to bivouacs (11th). To front line at The Apex (15th). Party under Lieutenant E.A. Allen took part in raid on enemy position 5 a.m. (16th). Came under fire from Chunuk Bair and forced to fall back. Lieutenant Allen and 5 men missing. Another attempt led by Lieutenant Mc. C. Jones at 9.30 p.m. also failed. Lieutenant Jones went out again 2 a.m. (17th). Reached Turkish line but again bombs and machine gun fire forced withdrawal. Relieved by New Zealand troops 2 p.m. and returned to bivouacs. To The Apex (20th). Relieved by 8th Cheshire (24th) and to Cheshire Ridge.

SEPTEMBER
Relieved by New Zealand Mounted Rifles (4th) and marched to Lala Baba. Took up reserve positions on No. 4 Beach. Began work on defences, winter quarters and unloading ships. Marched across Salt Lake (20th) to fire trenches – left sub section, "C" Sector. Private A.W. Priddle killed by stray bullet. One man killed, 4 wounded during heavy shelling (22nd). Draft of 100 men arrived during evening. Second-Lieutenant A de C. Spencer (8th Welsh attached) killed while leading patrol (25th). Relieved by Newfoundland Regiment (30th).

OCTOBER
Took over reserve trenches – "B" Section (1st). Draft of 8 officers, 203 other ranks arrived (5th). War Diary records (6th) heavy shelling from ships on The Pimple . . . "the firing appeared to be very accurate." Lieutenant (Quartermaster) W. Hill, DCM accidentally killed from bomb explosion on Lala Baba Beach (11th). Took over fire and support trenches – B59, B60, B61, B62 (14th). War Diary records (20th) R.A. experimented at cutting enemy's wire on Scimitar Hill. Draft of 2 officers, 130 other ranks arrived from England (30th). Casualties for October – 1 officer, 4 other ranks killed; 29 other ranks wounded; 52 sick.

NOVEMBER
Relieved by 8th Cheshire in trenches B61 and B62 (12th) and to reserve trenches. Began work at night on new redoubt on Chocolate Hill. Trenches flooded during thunderstorm (26th). War Diary notes "The men suffered the greatest discomfort the majority having no shelter of any description." Took over fire trenches – B58, B59 from 4th South Wales Borderers (30th). Casualties during November – 6 other ranks killed, 13 wounded; 6 officers, 130 other ranks sick.

DECEMBER
Received orders for evacuation (17th). Relieved from front line (18th) and moved to beach at Lala Baba. Sailed for Imbros (20th).

The South Wales Borderers

"Helles" "Landing at Helles" "Krithia" "Suvla" "Sari Bair" "Scimitar Hill" "Gallipoli,1915-16"

2ND BATTALION

MARCH

Rugby, Warwickshire. Part of 87th Brigade, 29th Division. Entrained for Avonmouth (16th) and embarked *Canada*. Transport on *City of Edinburgh*. Sailed (17th). Passed Gibraltar (21st), Arrived Malta (24th). Sailed for Egypt (26th). Arrived Alexandria (29th) and to Mex Camp (30th).

APRIL

To Alexandria (8th) and embarked *Alaunia*. Strength – 25 officers, 929 other ranks. Sailed (9th). Transport sailed *Manitou* and on voyage was intercepted by Turkish torpedo boat off Skyros. Crew and passengers were then given 8 minutes to leave the ship before it was torpedoed. Three torpedos were then fired, unsuccessfully, and Turks left. Most of the men rejoined *Manitou* which continued to Lemnos. Some 50, however, were drowned, 1 man – Private H. Hogg being from 2nd South Wales Borderers. Arrived Mudros (11th). Sailed for Tenedos (23rd). Arrived early (24th) and transhipped to *Cornwallis*. Sailed 10 p.m. for Gallipoli. Three companies landed "S" Beach, Helles early (25th). "D" Company, the first to land, climbed cliff in shirt sleeves and without packs and made for De Tott's Battery which was quickly taken. "B" and "C" companies made for trench in front of beach. C.T. Atkinson in his war history of the South Wales Borderers records that objective was promptly taken . . . "most of the Turks bolted, but "B" and "C" were too quick for others and shot and bayoneted several, while about a dozen surrendered." Major G.C. Margesson, Lieutenant R.P. Behrens and 12 other ranks killed; 2 officers, 40 other ranks wounded. Another 6 men were missing, presumed drowned during landing. Gains consolidated by 8 a.m.- "D" and part of "C" Company held De Tott's, "B" with "C" established firing line along ridge facing north. Remained in support near beach. Message received from General Hunter-Weston "Well done S.W.B. Can you maintain your position for another 48 hours?" Relieved by French troops (28th) and to "X" Beach. "A" Company landed "Y" Beach (25th) and attached to 1st King's Own Scottish Borderers advanced inland. Later dug in and held line (constructed from the men's packs) under heavy fire. Strong enemy attack (26th) forced withdrawal to beach. Casualties – Captain R.G. Palmer and 26 other ranks killed; 1 officer, 42 other ranks wounded. Effective strength – 17 officers, 639 other ranks.

MAY

Holding trenches near White House running east to Morto Bay (1st). Enemy attacked 10.30 p.m. – War Diary records . . . "did not come closer than 100 yards." "A" Company in support of attack by 1st Border dawn (2nd). War Diary (3rd) notes Turks putting out burying parties under white flag. Battalion also assisted – some 150 Turkish dead counted just in front of right flank. Relieved by 1st Border 8.30 p.m. and to Gully Beach. "A" Company remained in support. C.T. Atkinson records that the men were so exhausted that they slept most of the day and could not even be roused for diner. "A" Company rejoined (4th). Moved forward up Gully Ravine in reserve (5th). Took over forward trenches from 42nd Division (7th). Took part in attack (8th) – "C" and "D" Companies went forward 5.40 p.m. and immediately encountered cross fire, C.T. Atkinson records that casualties were especially heavy in the second line . . . "which was mown down wholesale as it crossed the parapet." Relieved by 1st King's's Own Scottish Borderers and withdrew to support trenches near White House. Casualties – Second-Lieutenant G. Bruce killed; Second-Lieutenants C.H. Heal, W.J. Stanborough morally wounded; 14 other ranks killed, 83 wounded, 34 missing. War Diary notes – "There is not much doubt that the missing are all killed." To Gully Beach (9th). Began fatigues unloading stores at "W" Beach and road making. Moved forward (22nd) – "A" and "B" Companies in support of 1st Inniskilling Fusiliers at Gurkha Bluff and "C" and "D" up Gully Ravine to assist 14th Sikhs. Returned to Gully Beach (23rd). War Diary records (30th) – causalities 2 killed, 19 wounded – "mostly caused by spent bullets."

JUNE

Moved forward (4th) and relieved 1st Royal Dublin Fusiliers in trenches near Geogheghan's Bluff. In action around trench J10 and The Boomerang – 12 casualties. Two brothers were in action – Lieutenant R.C. and Second-Lieutenant H.J. Inglis who were noted as showing great gallantry and determination. Both were wounded – Lieutenant R.C. Inglis dying on 29th June. Relieved (12th) and to Gully Beach. To firing line – Turkey Trench (17th). Enemy attacked (18th) and forced line back at north west end. Lieutenant J. Jordan mortally wounded and most of his men killed or wounded. Battalion cut off from 1st Royal Inniskilling Fusiliers on right. Severe hand to hand fighting followed – Turkish bombers eventually clearing Turky Trench. Later 3 platoons led by Lieutenant Cass charged, but almost all became causalities. Mixed party of Borderers and Inniskillings eventually regained losses. Casualties – Lieutenants H.L. Cass, J. Jordan; Second-Lieutenant B.I.L. Jones killed; 3 other officers wounded; almost 80 men killed, wounded or missing. Relieved by 1st King's Own Scottish Borderers (20th) and moved back to Eski Line near White House. Moved back to Gully Beach (23rd). Moved forward to firing line (27th). Took part in attack on trenches J9 and J10. Began assault west of Gully Ravine – "A" Company on right came under heavy fire but soon cleared both objectives. Held and consolidated gains while 1st Inniskillings and 1st King's Own Scottish Borderers passed through to (28th). Moved forward to new firing line between J11 and J12 (29th). War Diary records "The whole place was littered with dead and the stench almost unbearable."

JULY

War Diary records (2nd) that Turks were seen massing in gully at eastern end of J13. Artillery and machine gun fire was then turned on them – "it was observed that the Turkish commanders had considerable difficulty in persuading their men to advance." When they did come forward machine guns "simply mowed them down." Enemy losses estimated at 4,000 killed, 10,000 wounded. Successful attack led by Lieutenant P.H. Turner (6th) who was killed. Lieutenant D. Kerr (14th Cheshire, attached) and 13 other ranks also killed and 30 wounded. Captain H.F. Elgee killed by sniper 7.30 p.m. Relieved (8th) and to Gully Beach. Sailed for Imbros from "V" Beach (10th). War Diary records that Battalion was not expected and at 4 p.m. sailed for Lemnos. To Australian Pier (21st) and sailed *Rowan* for Gallipoli. Landed "W" Beach and marched to Gully Beach in reserve. Moved forward to "Y" Ravine (28th), firing line at Border Barricade (30th).

AUGUST

Moved to reserve – Eski Line, J10 and Bruce's Ravine (12th). Relieved (16th) and to Gully Beach. Embarked "V" Beach 4.30 a.m. (17th) for Suvla. Landed and to rest camp near beach. Moved forward 8 p.m. to Hill 10 and attached to 53rd Division. Relieved and to rest camp (19th). To Chocolate Hill (20th). Attack on Scimitar Hill (21st) – "C" and "D" Companies led assault who from Battalion Headquarters could be seen charging over the crest of the hill. Later forced to withdraw. Casualties over 300. War Diary notes that most of these were "missing." Withdrew to reserve line (22nd). Relieved 4th Worcestershire in firing line Kiretch Tepe Sirt (29th).

SEPTEMBER

Relieved by 2nd Royal Fusiliers (22nd) and to "A" Beach. Later to "W" Beach and sailed *Prince Abbas* for Imbros.

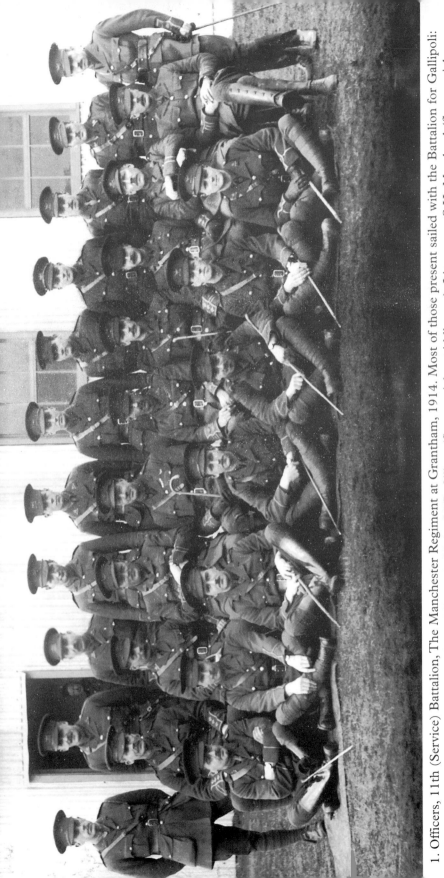

1. Officers, 11th (Service) Battalion, The Manchester Regiment at Grantham, 1914. Most of those present sailed with the Battalion for Gallipoli: Major H.C. Bates (second from left, middle row); Major J.J.D. Sillery (first on right, middle row); Lieutenant S.H. Marsland (first on right, front row); Second-Lieutenant R.S. Innes (second from right, front row); Second-Lieutenant T.A.E. Evanson-Jones (third from right, front row) all being killed on 7 August, 1915. Second-Lieutenant E.V. Bell (fourth from left, back row) was mortally wounded on 13 August. Lieutenants E.H.K. Smithers (fourth from right, back row) and G.M. Sproat (fifth from right, back row) both survived Gallipoli only to be killed on the Somme in July, 1916.

6. Lieutenant-Colonel Francis Hercules Walker, Commanding Officer, 7th (Service) Battalion, The Prince of Wales's (North Staffordshire Regiment). Colonel Walker had served in the Tirah Campaign of 1897-8 and was killed at Fusilier Bluff, Cape Helles on 7th January, 1916. *(Courtesy Peter Lead)*.

7. Second-Lieutenant Alfred Victor Smith, 1/5th Battalion, The East Lancashire Regiment (T.F.). He was awarded the Victoria Cross (posthumously) for gallantry during the night of 22/23 December, 1915.

8. Roll of Honour prepared by Trooper W.H. Regan 1/1st Welsh Horse. *(Welch Regiment Museum)*.

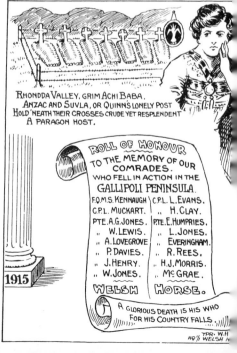

OCTOBER
Sailed *River Fisher* and *Viceroy* to Helles (1st). Disembarked and to reserve lines near Pink Farm. Moved forward to Eski Line and Brown House (14th), front line east of Achi Baba Nullah – Parsons Road, Central Street, Backhouse Road (15th). Relieved and to reserve positions west of Krithia Road (23rd). To firing line – trench E11 and The Horseshoe (31st).

NOVEMBER
Relieved by 1st Border (4th) and to White House, Brown House and Eski Line. One company in support at Parsons Road. Relieved by 1st Royal Inniskilling Fusiliers (9th) and moved back to winter quarters. Relieved 1st King's Own Scottish Borderers in Brigade Reserve at Brown House (17th). War Diary records Oxford Street and Central Street flooded (18th). Relieved 1st Border in firing line – Horseshoe sector (20th). Relieved and to rest camp (25th).

DECEMBER
Relieved 1st King's Own Scottish Borderers in firing line – trench E11 (2nd). Relieved by 1st Border and to Brown House (6th). To rest camp (10th). Took over firing line – Fusilier Street, Essex Knoll, Worcester Barricade from 1st King's Own Scottish Borderers (18th).

JANUARY, 1916
Relieved by 1st King's Own Scottish Borderers and to Eski Line (2nd). Position just on Mule Trench east of Krithia Road. Evacuated to Mudros (8th).

4TH (SERVICE) BATTALION

JUNE
Woking, Surrey. Part of 40th Brigade, 13th (Western) Division. Embarked *Megantic* at Avonmouth (28th) – officers: Lieutenant-Colonel F.M. Gillespie (Commanding); Major M.J. de la P. Beresford (Second in Command); Captain H.P. Yates (Adjutant); Lieutenant J.A. Mellsop (Quartermaster); Lieutenant W.N.V. Bickford-Smith (Machine Gun Officer); Lieutenant S. Hemmingway (Transport Officer). "A" Company – Major Sir W.Lenox. Napier, Bart, Captain A.W. Hooper, Lieutenant N.Y. Tessier, 2nd Lieutenants E.P. Bury and D.A. Addams-Williams. "B" Company – Major F.W. Birch, Captain J. Fairweather, 2nd Lieutenants L.H. Stockwood, D.S. Phillips, A. Buchanan and G.M. Owen. "C" Company – Captain C.E. Kitchin, Lieutenants J.H. Miller and

T.C.M. Austin, 2nd Lieutenants L.G. Cooper, E.G. Staples and C.M. Lucas. "D" Company – Captains P.R.M. Mundy and J.B. Blaxland, Lieutenant J. Farrow, 2nd Lieutenants A.F. Bell, T.M. Jenkins and J.W.L. Napier. Other ranks – 970. Sailed 9 p.m. (29th).

JULY
Arrived Malta (5th), Alexandria (8th) – one officer and 31 men left in charge of animals, then to Lemnos (10th). Arrived Mudros (12th). Party under Captain A.W. Hooper sent ashore to act as reinforcements. Remained in harbour then to Gallipoli (15th). Landed "V" Beach, Helles then to Gully Beach. Strength – 26 officers, 875 other ranks. Moved forward up Gully Ravine to support line west of Twelve Tree Copse (16th). Relieved 6th King's Own in front line – trenches H12, H12A, H12B (17th). Distance from enemy recorded as between 150 and 15 yards. The Royal Dublin Fusiliers had recently been in action and their dead were noted all around the area. Releived by 5th Wiltshire (19th) and to Gully Beach. Returned to front line (21st). Enemy attacked 39th Brigade on left (23rd) – "B" Company opened fire driving Turkish flank driven back. Withdrew to Brigade reserve (25th) then to Mudros during night (30th). Casualties at Helles – 4 killed, 30 wounded. The dead included R.S.M. G. Halford.

AUGUST
To Anzac (3rd). Strength – 25 officers, 750 other ranks. C.T. Atkinson in his war history of the South Wales Borders records the trip being made in a small vessel that had previously been used on the ferry service between Ardrossan and Belfast. The steamer also carried 7th North Staffordshire and was overcrowded, the men being told to keep still in case they capsized. Landed Gaba Tepe around 10 p.m. and to White Gully. There had been some casualties from sniper fire before disembarkation. Action at Damakjelik Bair (6th). Moved forward 8 p.m. – rifle and machine gun fire from Bauchop's Hill and Table Top. Passed through Chailak Dere. Came under fire near mouth of Aghyl Dere. "D" Company charged forward and cleared enemy from their trenches. Advanced on Damakjelik Bair. Position captured by 1.30 a.m. C.T. Atkinson records that "D" Company were mainly engaged, their casualties – 8 killed, 17 wounded. Sir Ian Hamilton wrote: "The rapid success of this movement was largely due to Lieutenant-Colonel Gillespie, a very fine man, who commanded the advanced guard, consisting of his own regiment . . . a corps worthy of such a leader . . . Here was an encouraging sample of what the New Army under good auspices could accomplish. Nothing more trying to inexperienced troops can be imagined than a night march exposed to flanking fire, through a strange

country, winding up at the end with a bayonet charge against a height, formless and still in the starlight, garrisoned by those spectres of the imagination, worst enemies of the soldier." Gains consolidated – "D" Company to high ground 400 yards to left guarding flank. Heavy fighting noted both to left and right (7th). Sixty casualties from sniper and shrapnel fire. Moved position to right after withdrawal of 5th Wiltshire – "A" Company on left, "C" in centre, "B" on right, "D" in reserve. Enemy attacked between 4.30 – 5 a.m. (9th) and driven back – Lieutenant-Colonel Gillespie, Lieutenant Miller and 2nd Lieutenant Cooper killed. Another attack at 7 p.m. also repulsed – War Diary records – "Turks again hotly attacked, "C" Company under Captain C.E. Kitchin with part of "D" Company counter attacked with bayonet, driving enemy back about 200 yards." Casualties 44 killed, 6 officers and 72 men wounded. Lieutenants Austin, Farrow and Bell; C.S.M. Bush, Sergeant Myles, all noted as distinguishing themselves during the fighting. Position officially named "Gillespie Spur." Enemy attack repulsed (10th). Casualties – 3 killed, 19 wounded, 5 missing. Attack on Kabak Kuya (11th). Covering party moved forward 6 p.m. – objective gained and new line consolidated. Enemy counter attack beaten off during evening. Lieutenant Bell and 2nd Lieutenant Addams-Williams mortally wounded. Major Sir William Lennox Napier killed by sniper (13th). Attack on Hill 60 (21st-22nd). "A" Company advanced and consolidated positions captured by 5th Connaught Rangers. "C" Company went forward to assist New Zealand troops – 60 casualties while moving up. Placed on N.Z. right. Carried out bombing attack on Turkish communication Trench – Lance Corporal M. Beary gained Distinguish Conduct Medal. Fought off several counter attacks throughout night. Lieutenant O.S. Phillips killed. Relieved during night (22nd) and to reserve lines at Rhododendron Ridge. Casualties – 16 killed and missing, 71 wounded. To Divisional Reserve positions just west of Old No. 3 Post (24th). Moved to Brigade Reserve in rear of The Apex, Chunuk Bair (25th). Relieved New Zealand troops – Old No. 3 Post, Big Table Top (28th).

SEPTEMBER
To Suvla (3rd) and Corps Reserve positions at Lala Baba. Occupied constructing defensive positions and unloading ships. To Front line west of Anafarta Sagir (19th), Chocolate Hill sector (30th). War Diary notes much sickness, strength by end September – 10 officers, 211 other ranks.

OCTOBER
To fire and support trenches (14th). Drafts received. Strength by end October – 22 officers, 378 other ranks.

NOVEMBER
War Diary records that during tour in firing line "complete ascendency was obtained over enemy's snipers." It was also noted that the Turks dug constantly in front of Battalion's lines – "as their working parties constantly re-appear shortly after having been dispersed by our machine guns, it seems probable that they consist of forced labour." High casualties from trench feet and frost bite as a result of blizzard (26th-29th). Relieved by 8th Royal Welsh Fusiliers in trenches B58 and B59 (30th) and to reserve lines. Strength at end of month – 15 officers, 236 other ranks.

DECEMBER
Relieved 5th Wiltshire in firing line opposite Scimitar Hill just south of Sulajik Farm (15th). Began evacuation (19th). Last battalion of 40th Brigade to leave trenches. Embarked from Lala Baba, last men leaving for Imbros 3 a.m. (20th). Left camp 2.40 p.m. and embarked *Huntsman*. Sailed for Mudros (21st). Embarked *Princess Alberta* (30th) and sailed for Gallipoli. Disembarked "V" Beach, Helles during night and marched to Gully Beach. Moved forward to trenches (31st). Took over line – Northern Barricade to junction of New Cut and Rue de Paris.

JANUARY, 1916
Evacuated to Mudros (8th).

THE KING'S OWN SCOTTISH BORDERERS

"Helles" "Landing at Helles" "Krithia" "Suvla" "Scimitar Hill"

"Gallipoli, 1915-16"

1ST BATTALION

MARCH

Rugby, Warwickshire. Part of 87th Brigade, 29th Division. Entrained for Avonmouth (17th) and embarked *Dongola* for Egypt. Officers – Lieutenant-Colonel A.S. Koe (Commanding); Majors D.R. Sladen, D.S.O., W.H.S. McAlester; Captains A.J. Welsh, R.D. Whigham, C.A. Antrobus, A.S. Cooper, E.A. Marrow (Adjutant), J.B. Hartley, M.A.N. Becher, A.J. Sanderson, G.M.H. Ogilvy, P.N. Sanderson; Lieutenants A.G. Paterson (Machine Gun Officer), C.S. Stirling-Cookson, W.J.N. Cheatle, J.A. Ainslie, C.S. Renny, F.H. Deighton, R.M. Shorter, T.A.G. Miller, E.W.T. Agar, W. Simpson (Quartermaster); Second-Lieutenants J.R. Redpath, J.R. Keltie (4th Scottish Rifles attached), F.A. Williamson (4th Scottish Rifles attached). Lieutenant W.N. Rishworth (R.A.M.C., Medical Officer), The Rev. D.A. Cameron Reid (Chaplain). Other ranks – 998. Transport – Lieutenant J.C. Grogan and 90 other ranks embarked *Marquette*. Sailed (18th). Arrived Alexandria (30th) and to Mex Camp.

APRIL

"D" Company and Machine Gun Section to Alexandria (13th). Remainder arrived (15th) and embarked *Southland*. Strength – 28 officers, 957 other ranks. Sailed for Lemnos (16th). Arrived Mudros Harbour (18th). Remained on board practising descending rope ladders into small boats. "A" and "B" Companies transferred to *Amethyst*, Headquarters with "C" and "D" to *Sapphire* during afternoon (24th). Proceeded to point 4 miles of "Y" Beach, Cape Helles 7 p.m. Transferred into 4 trawlers about 2.30 a.m. (25th) and moved towards shore 4.45 a.m. Transferred to rowing boats – "A" and "B" Companies landed first, followed by "C" and "D". War Diary records scouts sent up cliff but no enemy was sighted. Battalion assembled at top of cliff 6.20 a.m. and took up positions in line – "B", "C", "A" Companies with "D" in support. Captain Stair Gillon in his war history of the King's Own Scottish Borderers records the line being constructed under heavy and increasing rifle fire from the men's packs. Two men of "A"

Company killed by shell. Captain Stair Gillon notes shell as being a naval short. Enemy sighted 9 a.m. and began shelling 11.30 a.m. Series of attacks on left of position commenced 2.30 p.m. Enemy withdrew around 7 p.m. under shell fire from sea. Attack renewed 7.30 p.m. and continued throughout night. War Diary records 4 main assaults coming from the left which worked towards the centre and right – "several times the enemy approached within ten yards of our position . . . so close did the enemy reach our lines, that in one place a German officer, walked up to out trench and said 'you English surrender, we ten to one' He was thereupon hit on the head with a spade." In one section where the line was broke, the enemy were seen calmly bringing along a machine gun mounted on a pony. The party, Captain Gillon records, was dealt with by Lieutenant Miller and his revolver. Naval bombardment reopened 5.45 a.m. (26th) – 2 shells from *Goliath* falling short into 1st K.O.S.B. lines. Enemy attack opened 6 a.m. – War Diary records heavy casualties from rife fire at very close range and hand grenades. Right of line broke 7 a.m. and withdrawal down cliff forced. Troops holding the centre followed, but left remained fast. Counter attack soon organised on right and positions regained. War Diary records this counter attack as being the cause of heavy casualties among the officers. Centre also counter attacked with success. Order received to evacuate and withdrawal down to beach commenced 3 p.m. Taken out to sea by *Goliath*, *Amethyst* and *Sapphire* and then transferred to *Ansonia*. Casualties – 296 killed and wounded. Officers killed – Lieutenant-Colonel Koe; Captains Antrobus, Cooper, Becher, Marrow, A.J. Sanderson (died of wounds 2nd May), P.N. Sanderson; Lieutenants Cheatle, Miller; Second-Lieutenants Redpath, Williamson (died of wounds 4th June). Memorial Service held on board 6.30 a.m. (27th). Battalion inspected 6 a.m. (28th). War Diary records hardly a man had a pack. Landed at "W" Beach during morning and moved forward to firing line about 900 yards opposite Krithia 1 p.m. Retired to support line about 800 yards to the rear 4.30 p.m. and dug in. Casualties during day – 35 other ranks, Major McAlester wounded. Position moved 500 yards west 4 p.m. (29th). 1st Lancashire Fusiliers on right, 2nd South Wales Borderers on left. Relieved and to reserve lines near Gully Beach (30th).

MAY

Relieved 1st Border in left sector firing line 1,000 yards south-west of "Y" Beach (1st). Enemy attacks throughout night. Enemy began retreat 5.30 a.m. (2nd). Machine guns fired on party of enemy dug in some 400 yards to the front of 1st Royal Inniskilling Fusiliers – 132 prisoners taken. "B" Company moved forward 500 yards. "D" Company advanced but forced to retire due to heavy machine gun fire. "B" Company also forced to retire. Casualties – 22 other ranks, Major Welch and Second-Lieutenant Keltie wounded. Enemy attack 9 a.m. repulsed. Relived by 1/6th Lancashire Fusiliers at Gully Spur during night (5th) and to reserve at Gully Beach. Advanced up Gully Ravine 10 a.m. (7th). Took over support trenches. Moved towards firing line 4.45 p.m. Retired to support trenches during evening. Casualties – 9 other ranks. Moved forward to line astride Gully Ravine (8th) – "A" and "B" Companies in support of attack by 1st Royal Inniskilling Fusiliers on right, "C" and "D" behind 2nd South Wales Borderers on left. Moved forward in support 6 p.m. Held firing line until relieved (9th). Moved back to positions 1,000 yards south of Pink Farm. Casualties 12 other ranks, Lieutenant Ainslie wounded. War Diary records (11th) trench collapsing – 5 men of "D" Company buried – 1 man died. Provided fatigue parties at "W" Beach and Pink Farm. One officer per company and all platoon sergeants began instruction in bomb throwing at Gully Beach (15th). First draft arrived (16th) – 1 officer, 45 other ranks. Fatigue parties began work road making at Gully Beach (23rd) and digging communication trenches in rear of firing line. Several contingents from other battalions attached for instruction throughout month.

JUNE
Moved forward to fire trench Twelve Tree Copse (3rd). Attached to 88th Brigade for attack – 2nd Royal Fusiliers on right, 4th Worcestershire on left. British bombardment ceased 11.20 a.m. (4th). War Diary records . . . "the men cheered and fixed bayonets." "A" and "B" companies attacked 12 noon. Leading waves soon enfiladed by fire, the majority of men being killed close to parapet. Few managed to take shelter in reach a small nullah some 100 yards from Turkish line. "C" and "D" Companies moved forward from support trenches into firing line then with a number of platoon rushes advanced quickly over the enemy's lines. Trenches H11 and H12 taken and consolidated. "D" Company charged 7 p.m. and cleared enemy massing in communication trench to H14. Enemy counter attacked during night and gained 100 yards of H14 communication trench. Part of message sent by C.O. to 88th Brigade (5th) "K.O.S.Brs are at present holding a portion of H12 . . . I would again like to point out that in my opinion it would be a mistake to evacuate H12. The other trenches in rear of it and also original firing line are all connected up by communication trenches. We have had 7 officers killed and 3 wounded. If it could be managed could the Battn. be withdrawn from firing line tomorrow to re-organise." Message from "C" Company (5th) – "Could we have some sand-bags sent up. We are loosing good men owing to lack of head cover. Also some entrenching tools." War

Diary (6th) records Turks appearing in large numbers on left flank of H12 at 3.30 a.m. party holding H11 did not fire as it was thought they were Indian troops – some of the Turks were wearing Sikh puggaris. Relieved from firing line (12th) and to bivouacs between Gully Beach and Gurkha Bluff. Lieutenant-General Sir William Marshall, Commanding Officer of 87th Brigade, recalls in his book *Memories of Four Fronts* . . . "I brought back my shattered K.O.S.B. into reserve; there were only two officers left . . . " Began fatigues on "X" and "W" Beaches. Moved forward to reserve trenches near White House (17th). Began work assisting Royal Engineers at Eski Line. "C" Company moved forward into support trenches (18th). "D" Company relieved "C" (19th). Front and support trenches bombarded – 4 killed, 8 wounded. Remainder of Battalion took over firing line from 2nd South Wales Borderers (20th). Began work burying Turkish dead – 32 bodies buried from Turkey Trench. Relieved by 2nd Royal Fusiliers (23rd) and to Gully Beach. War Diary notes Battalion Parade (26th) – the first since leaving Egypt. Moved forward up Gully Ravine (27th) and assembled at rear of firing line. Attack on enemy trenches (28th). "A" and "B" Companies advanced and captured J11. "C" and "D" followed and Battalion situated in J11 from junction of J10A, the ravine from J11 to H11. Casualties – 8 officers, 223 other ranks. Relieved (29th) and withdrew to reserve in trench J8. To support and front lines (30th).

JULY
Relieved by 1/5th Royal Scots (7th) and to Gully Beach. Embarked "V" Beach (11th) and sailed for Imbros. To Australian Pier (21st) and sailed for Gallipoli. Arrived "W" Beach and to dug outs South Gully Beach. Began fatigues – improving dug outs and road making in Gully Ravine. Moved forward to firing line (28th). Relieved 9th Royal Warwickshire in positions on west of Gully Ravine facing Turkish trench J12. Left of line on The Birdcage. War Diary records (30th) a *Feu de Joie* followed by 3 cheers at receipt of news of recent victory in the Persian Gulf.

AUGUST
Relieved and to "Y" Ravine (4th). One company to trench J10. Began work on Gully Ravine road. To firing line (8th). Mine exploded under enemy line 11.30 p.m. (10th). Attempt to occupy crater failed. Casualties – 9 killed, 30 wounded, 1 officer, 8 men missing. War Diary records "The shock of the explosion apparently did more harm to our trench than to the Turks." Relieved and to "Y" Ravine (12th). One company in trench J10. Began fatigues in Gully Ravine. Relieved 3 a.m. (16th) and to South Gully Beach. During evening to "W" Beach and embarked for Suvla Bay. Landed "A"

Beach during morning (17th) and to bivouacs about 500 yards north of Kangaroo Pier. Moved forward to firing line between Chocolate and Scimitar Hills (20th). Supported attack on Scimitar Hill with rifle and machine gun fire (21st). Casualties – 1 officer and 25 other ranks. Relieved by 6th Royal Inniskilling Fusiliers (22nd) and withdrew to reserve bivouacs. Began work on 2nd line defences. To firing line (29th).

SEPTEMBER
Began work on advance line. Began sending half companies for 24 hours rest at "A" Beach (5th). Band heard in enemy lines playing a British march (9th). Relieved by 1st Royal Dublin Fusiliers (22nd) and to reserve bivouacs. Casualties for month – 1 officer, 3 other ranks killed, 21 other ranks wounded. 101 to hospital sick. Embarked *Prince Abbas* for Imbros (24th).

OCTOBER
Embarked for Cape Helles (1st). Arrived "W" Beach and moved to 52nd Divisional Reserve Area – Eski Line. Began work on new winter quarters. Two officers killed by shell (15th). Began work digging new quarters on cliff south of "X" Beach (16th). "C" and "D" Companies attached to 1st Royal Inniskilling Fusiliers in firing line (23rd). "A" and "B" Companies began work on Boundary Road and trenches in front of Eski Line east of Achi Baba Nullah. "A" and "B" Companies to firing line (27th) relieving 1st Royal Inniskilling Fusiliers in positions trench E11 and The Horseshoe. Relieved by 2nd South Wales Borderers (31st) and to Corps Reserve lines.

NOVEMBER
Began work on light railway, making terraces on cliff south of "X" Beach. Relieved 2nd South Wales borderers in firing line (8th). Relieved by 1st Royal Inniskilling Fusiliers (12th) and to Brigade Reserve at Brown House and Parsons Road. Began work on improving Central Street and new trench in front of Brown House. Relieved by 2nd South Wales Borderers (17th) and to Corps Reserve lines. Began work on new winter quarters on cliff just south of "X" Beach. "D" Company to camp at "W" Beach (20th). "A" Company attached to 1st Royal Inniskilling Fusiliers in front line – trench E11 (24th). "B" and "C" Companies to Brown House (25th). Began work on draining Central and Oxford Streets. Relieved 1st Royal Inniskilling Fusiliers in firing line (28th) – right on P3 next to French, left on Achi Baba Nullah.

DECEMBER

Relieved by 2nd South Wales Borderers (2nd) and to Eski Line. Relieved Hood Battalion in firing line (10th) – Rue de Paris. Support trenches held – Essex Knoll, Worcester Flat, Munster Terrace. Relieved by 2nd South Wales Borderers (18th) and to Eski Line. Casualties since 10th – 3 killed, 8 wounded. To firing line (23rd). Support trenches held – Russell's Loop, Weavers Vennel, Mayfair, Worcester Flat, Munster Terrace. Relieved and to Eski Line (30th). Casualties since 23rd – 3 killed, 11 wounded.

JANUARY, 1916

Relieved 2nd South Wales Borderers in firing line (2nd). Began withdrawal to Eski Line (5th). Evacuated to Lemnos during night (8th/9th).

1/4TH (THE BORDER) BATTALION (T.F.)

MAY

Stirling, Stirlingshire. Part of 155th Brigade, 52nd (Lowland) Division. Entrained for Liverpool (21st). Sailed *Empress of Britain* (23rd). Officers – Lieutenant-Colonel J.M. McNeile (Commanding); Majors W.E.A. Cochrane, J. Herbertson, D.R. Taylor (Medical Officer); Captains J.C. Lang (Adjutant), A. Wallace, M.G. Jobson, H. Sanderson, C.E. MacDonald, W.T. Forrest, D. Elder, R.W. Shape, P.L.P. Laing, Lieutenants E.H. Follis (Quartermaster), J.M. Dun, T.M. Alexander, J. Harrison, A. Bulman, G. Dun, R.R.M. Lumgair, J.B. Innes, Second-Lieutenants A.H.M. Henderson, P. Woodhead, W.K. Innes, A. Galloway, J.B. Patrick, A. Fairgrieve, J. Elder, J.B. Stewart, R.P. Smith. Called Gibraltar (28th), Arrived Malta (31st).

JUNE

Sailed for Egypt (1st). Arrived Alexandria (3rd), disembarked and entrained for camp at Abukir (4th). To Alexandria (8th) and embarked *Empress of Britain.* Sailed (9th), arrived Mudros (11th). Transferred to *Abbas* and *El Kahirah* (13th) and sailed during evening for Cape Helles. Landed "V" Beach early (14th) and moved inland. Came under shell fire. Dug in about 1 mile from beach. Casualties by (18th) – 1 man killed, 1 officer, 16 other ranks wounded. To front line – Gully Ravine sector (22nd). Relieved and to rest camp (27th). Casualties – 3 killed, 11 wounded.

JULY

To reserve lines on right of Achi Baba Nullah (9th) – "A" and "B" companies Backhouse Road, "C" and "D" Companies Brown House Road.

Moved forward to Parsons Road (front line) and Trotman Road (support) (11th). Attacked 7.35 a.m. (12th) – leading waved charged forward and gained first objectives – trenches E10 and E11. Advanced on enemy's third line trench E12, which records indicate did not exist, but heavy fire and casualties forced to withdraw to E11. Gaines held during enemy counter attacks (13th). Captain Forrest records ..."Suddenly, about 100 Turks appeared from behind a small ridge. They were charging in a half-left direction, and they simply disappeared when our machine guns and rifles opened fire. Not a man of them got back." He also noted that in a subsequent attack, the Turks were hesitant, moving forward a few yards then halting. At this an officer was seen first to hit one man from behind with a rifle butt, then shoot another. Relieved (14th) then to rest camp. Killed or mortally wounded – Lieutenant-Colonel McNeile; Majors Herbertson, Taylor; Captains Lang, Sanderson, Wallace; Lieutenants Alexander, Innes, Bulman; Second-Lieutenants Henderson, Woodhead, Partick and 319 other ranks. Wounded – 6 officers, 203 other ranks. Taken prisoner – 13 other ranks. Battalion reorganised and began fatigue duties.

AUGUST
Carried out tours in forward area – Krithia Nullah sector and fatigues at "W" Beach. Releived in firing line just west of East Krithia Nullah by 1/7th Royal Scots (29th).

SEPTEMBER
Shared duty with 1/4th and 1/7th Royal Scots in firing line throughout month – in line (2nd-6th), (10th-14th), (19th-26th). Carried out work on extention to Clunes Vennel.

OCTOBER
Tours in trenches – The Vineyard sector Took part in succesfull operation to advance bombing station (12th).

NOVEMBER
Tours in trenches. Releived (28th) and to rest camp near Krithia Road.

DECEMBER
To front line (5th) – Argyle Street, Wigan Road. Headquarters – St. Vincent Street. Lieutenant W. Sorley Brown joined the Battalion in December and in his book *My War Diary (1914-1919)* he recalls the jouney from rest camp to the front line as taking 2 hours, 20 minutes. He went into the support line which was about 100 yards from the Turkish front line. Releived (21st) and

to rest camp. To firing line (25th). Second-Lieutenant J.A.G. Cairns killed (29th). Releived and to rest camp (31st). W. Sorley Brown recalls that the New Year was seen in during a halt in "C" Avenue.

JANUARY, 1916
Began fatiuges on "W" Beach. First party evcuated to Mudros (2nd). Last contingent to "W" Beach and sailed *Prince Abbas*, *Prince George* for Mudros during early morning (8th).

1/5TH (DUMFRIES & GALLOWAY) BATTALION (T.F.)

MAY
Stirling, Stirlingshire. Part of 155th Brigade, 52nd (Lowland) Division. Entrained for Liverpool (19th). Sailed *Mauretania* (21st). Arrived Lemnos (29th) and remained in Mudros Harbour.

JUNE
"D" Company sailed *Immingham*, remainder *Harpy* for Helles during night (6th). Landed "V" Beach under heavy shelling and to camp. Strength – 28 officers, 929 other ranks. To support line (29th Division sector) near Twelve Tree Copse (9th). Retired to reserve positions at Backhouse Post (13th). First casualties – 2 killed, 19 wounded. "A" Company took part in attack with Hawke Battalion (18th). Battalion historian Captain G.F. Scott Elliot records that the company was only intended as support – the order for "A" Company to attack being intended for "A" Company, Hawke Battalion. Captain Scott Elliot in his history of the Battalion provides much information regarding bombing. He notes the general high efficiency of the Turks who's German manufactured bombs often were slow to explode and could be thrown back. Our own bombs were few, some 30 assorted devices only being available in one week for training. Referring to "Jam Tin" bombs, Captain Scott Elliot provides a detailed account of how these were manufactured by the men. They were crude missiles, he records, and on one occasion only 80 out of 123 thrown exploded. But these "were better than nothing." "C" Company relieved "A" Company in support trenches (19th). Two companies in support during French attack (21st). Battalion relieved and to rest camp (22nd). Held French sector fire trenches during night (29th-30th).

JULY
To front line (4th), relieved (10th). Action of Achi Baba Nullah: Moved forward to positions at rear of front line (11th) – Mercer Road and

Backhouse Road. Followed 1/4th K.O.S.B. into attack 7.35 a.m. (12th) – Captain Scott Elliot noted . . . "sunlight sparkled on the bayonets and on the little slips of tin which every third man carried on his back as a guide to our artillery." Heavy casualties passing over Mercer Road, Trotman Road (support trench) and Parson Road. The latter being the front line and according to War Diary some 200 yards from enemy. Private Nixon, who was taken prisoner by the Turks, recalled . . . "men fell like corn below the scythe. Major Herberston, lying on his side, was waving his revolver and urging us on." He also records his experience after reaching Turkish lines. After a period of heavy fighting he became unconscious only to awake covered by his dead comrades. He was bayonets six time in the back while lying there. Captain Scott Elliot gives a detailed and vivid description of the attack in his history and of the Battalion's gallant fighting in captured trenches. Withdrew during (14th-15th) and to rest camp (16th). Casualties – 6 officers killed, 5 wounded, 76 other ranks killed, 183 wounded. Began work (17th) – improving communication trenches, unloading boats. Note dropped by German aeroplane giving 24 hours to leave Gallipoli (22nd). Rest camp bombed on three occasions.

AUGUST
Ordered to Divisional Reserve trenches (6th). Moved forward (13th) relieving 1/6th Manchester in Wigan Road and Redoubt Line. Turkish snipers noted (17th) as "peculiarly enterprising" during tour in line from Sap 8 to Krithia Nullah – eight periscopes hit. Snipers of the Battalion are also recorded as being active. An experienced shot watching a particular gap in the Turkish parapet would hit every man that passed. Captain Scott Elliot mentions that a sign put up by the enemy advising men to crawl past this vulnerable spot only caused more casualties when they stopped to read it. Tours in forward area are recorded by Captain Scott Elliot as 15 days during August.

SEPTEMBER
Relieved 1/7th Scottish Rifles in firing line (2nd). Relieved by 1/7th Scottish Rifles (14th). An entry in the diary (15th) of one member of the Battalion records how he slept under cover for the first time in over 100 nights. The shelter consisting of sheets of corrugated iron. Tours in forward area during month – 18 days.

OCTOBER
All 3 battalions of the King's Own Scottish Borderers at Gallipoli held front line together (26th). Tours in forward area during month – 21 days.

NOVEMBER

Heavy Turkish casualties recorded during counter attacks (21st). Tours in forward area – 26 days. Releived by 1/1st Ayrshire Yeomanry in Main Street (28th).

DECEMBER

Battalion severely effected by cold weather and noted as being "lame and unfit for duty" upon return to line left of Shrapnel Nullah (5th). December tours in front line recorded as being constantly under shell fire and bombing attacks. In support during attacks on West and East Nullahs (18th-19th). Relieved from front line (20th). Christmas dinner: bottle of beer, an orange and apple, two bars of chocolate, one spoonful of plum pudding provided by Dumfries Comforts Committee. Returned to front line near Krithia Nullah (26th). Attack on enemy lines (29th) – Sergeant Byers and party charged and gained trench G11A after explosion of mine. Work of Private L. McGuffie noted during subsequent enemy counter attack. He was later awarded the Victoria Cross (posthumously) for gallantry near Wytschaete in Belgium on 28th September, 1918. Relieved (31st) and to rest camp. Evacuation ordered: Battalion ordered to move about to suggest "business as usual."

JANUARY, 1916

Moved to "V" Beach 7 p.m. (6th). Embarked *Partridge* for Lemnos. Three officers and approximately 100 men remained on beach duties. Lieutenant A. Tweedie wrote – "The last three days on the Peninsula were about the worst. Most of our Battalion departed a few days before the evacuation but Captain Watson, Lieutenant Murdoch, and myself were left as a working party to ship stores, and only embarked on the last night (8th) . . . The Turks never yet re-took any of the posts we captured. I honestly believe that they were glad to let us get away quietly!" Gallipoli casualties: Original strength plus drafts – 50 officers, 1,082 other ranks. Strength on evacuation – 20 officers, 322 other ranks.

THE CAMERONIANS (SCOTTISH RIFLES)

"Gallipoli, 1915-16"

1/7TH BATTALION (T.F.)

MAY
Grangemouth, Stirlingshire. Part of 156th Brigade, 52nd (Lowland) Division. Entrained for Liverpool (21st). Arrived (22nd). Sailed *Empress of Britain* (23rd). Called Gibraltar (28th). Arrived Malta (31st).

JUNE
Sailed for Egypt (1st). Arrived Alexandria (3rd) and to camp at Abukir. To Alexandria (8th). Embarked *Empress of Britain* and sailed for Lemnos (9th). Arrived Mudros (11th). Headquarters, Machine Gun Section and 533 other ranks embarked *Whitby Abbey* (13th) and to Helles. Remainder of Battalion – 320 all ranks, left and arrived (14th). Began work digging trenches. First casualties – 1 officer wounded, 1 man killed, 8 wounded (15th). Moved forward during evening (19th) and bivouacked near Pink Farm. Later relieved 2nd Hampshire in reserve trenches. Relieved by 1st Essex (24th) and to rest camp. Moved forward to reserve trenches (27th). Took over firing line (28th) and in support of attack by 1/4th Royal Scots, 1/7th Royal Scots and 1/8th Scottish Rifles on trenches H12A and H12. Later relieved by 2nd Hampshire in H12A and H12. Formed composite battalion with 1/8th Scottish Rifles.

JULY
Relieved 1/4th Royal Scots in firing line – Gurkha Bluff (9th). Relieved and to Divisional Reserve at Backhouse Post (11th). To Eski Line (12th) then firing line. Relieved (13th) and to Backhouse Post. Began beach fatigues and digging communication trenches. Battalion under orders to be in a state of constant readiness for move forward. War Diary notes that men became very weak from continuous work and that general condition of feet was bad due to fact that boots were required to be kept on at all times.

AUGUST
Continued beach fatigues and digging. Moved forward to Eski Line (13th). Strength – 15 officers, 496 other ranks. Relieved 1/6th Highland Light Infantry in firing line (16th). Relieved by 1/4th Royal Scots (21st) and took over support positions – Wigan Road and reserve – Redoubt Line. War

Diary records position moved a little to left (25th). Took over firing line from 1/4th Royal Scots Fusiliers – Krithia Nullah – Krithia Road (29th).

SEPTEMBER
Relieved by 1/5th King's Own Scottish Borderers and 1/4th Royal Scots Fusiliers (2nd) and to Eski Line. To firing line (6th). Relieved and to rest camp (10th). Relieved 1/5th King's Own Scottish Borderers and 1/4th Royal Scots Fusiliers in firing line (14th). Two companies holding support trenches – Argyle Street and Queen Street. Relieved (19th). To firing line (26th).

OCTOBER
Relieved from forward area (10th) and to rest camp. To front line (17th), rest camp (31st).

NOVEMBER
To firing line – Russel's Loop sector (7th). Took part in successful attack on enemy trenches H11A and G11B (15th). Relieved and to rest camp (21st). To firing line (28th).

DECEMBER
Relieved (5th) and to Redoubt Line. To rest camp (10th), firing line north side of Krithia Nullah (14th). Relieved and to Eski Line (21st). To rest camp (22nd), Redoubt Line west of Small Nullah (28th).

JANUARY, 1916
Moved forward to Parsons Road in support (1st). Relieved 1/4th Royal Scots in firing line between Achi Baba Nullah and Small Nullah (2nd). To "V" Beach (8th) and evacuated to Mudros.

1/8TH BATTALION (T.F.)

MAY
Falkirk, Stirlingshire. Part of 156th Brigade, 52nd (Lowland) Division. Left for Devonport in 2 trains (17th). Arrived (18th) and embarked *Ballarat*. Officers – Lieutenant-Colonel H. Monteith Hannan (Commanding), Major J.M. Findlay (Second in Command), Captain C.J. Bramwell (Adjutant), Captain A. Bankier Sloan (R.A.M.C., Medical Officer), Lieutenant H. Bowen (Quartermaster), Lieutenant E. Maclay (Machine Gun Officer), Second-Lieutenant T. Stout (Signals Officer). Arrived Mudros (29th) and remained in harbour; No. 1 Company – Captains H.A. MacLehose, C.J.C.

Mowat, Lieutenants A.D. Templeton, G.A.C. Moore, Second-Lieutenants J.Wood Scott, O.T. Sloan; No. 2 Company – Captains J.M. Boyd, W. Campbell Church, Lieutenant W.N. Sloan, Second-Lieutenants T.L. Tillie, R.M. Pattison; No. 3 Company – Captains C. Dunn Macindoe, R.C. B. Macindoe, Lieutenants R. Humble, D.S. Carson, Second-Lieutenants A.F. Rogers, R.B.H. Roberston; No. 4 Company – Major R.N. Coulson, Captain E.T. Young, Lieutenants J.T. Findlay, Hew McCowan, Second-Lieutenant W.S. Maclay.

JUNE
Two officers – Lieutenant W.N. Sloan, Second-Lieutenant R.M. Pattison and 100 men sent ashore to act as Police Piquet. Colonel J.M. Findlay, D.S.O. records in his history of the Battalion, that the Camp Commandant at Mudros was "having great difficulty in guarding the wells, keeping the Australians in hand, and preventing the Greeks pilfering around generally." Sailed for Cape Helles (13th) – part of Battalion in *Osmanieh*, part in trawler No. 328. Landed "V" Beach during night and to Torres Lines. Attached to 29th Division. Heavily shelled from Asia Minor (15th) – several casualties. Relieved 1st Essex in front line – Rue de Paris during night (18th/19th). Colonel Findlay records the journey from Torres Lines being via Pink Farm, Southern Mule Track, Krithia Nullah, which he recalls was full of croaking frogs, into the Eski Line then via communication trench to front line. Lieutenant-Colonel Hannan killed by sniper (21st). Relieved and to Torres Lines (24th). Lieutenant Sloan, Second-Lieutenant Pattison and party rejoined Battalion from Mudros (25th). To front line (27th). Took part in attack on Trenches H12 and H12A (28th) – Nos. 1 and 3 Companies advanced followed by No. 2 Company 11 a.m. Colonel Findlay records – "Five minutes after they had started they were practically wiped out." Few men reached the enemy's line, those that did were either killed or wounded. No. 4 Company in support also suffered heavily while moving towards firing line. Relieved – casualties – 14 officers and 334 other ranks killed, missing or mortally wounded; 11 officers, 114 other ranks wounded. Strength of Battalion on morning of (29th) – Captain A.B. Sloan, Lieutenants E. Maclay, H. Bowen and 70 other ranks. Later formed composite battalion with 1/7th Scottish Rifles.

JULY
To Backhouse Post in Divisional Reserve (11th), Eski Line (12th). Moved into firing line 11 a.m. No. 1 Company took part in attack during afternoon and gained part of enemy's line. Three counter attacks repulsed during night. Relieved and to Backhouse Post (13th). Carried out further tours in

firing line to right of Krithia Nullah, support – Redoubt Line, reserve – Eski Line.

NOVEMBER
Took part in successful attack by 156th Brigade (15th). Colonel Findlay records Brigade casualties as – 5 officers, 107 other ranks – more than half of these being from the Battalion. Relieved and to rest camp (21st). To front line (29th).

DECEMBER
Draft of 3 officers and 78 other ranks arrived (1st). Some 15 officers had arrived during July and August, but this was the first reinforcement of other ranks. Relieved and to rest camp (22nd). Began evacuation (8th) – moved to "V" Beach and sailed *Prince George* for Lemnos. *Prince George* hit by torpedo which failed to explode. Arrived Sarpe Pier, West Mudros (9th).

THE ROYAL INNISKILLING FUSILIERS

"Helles" "Landing at Helles" "Krithia" "Suvla" "Landing at Suvla"

"Scimitar Hill" "Gallipoli,1915-16"

1ST BATTALION

JANUARY
Arrived Avonmouth from India (10th) and to Rugby. Joined 87th Brigade, 29th Division. Entrained for Avonmouth (16th) and embarked and sailed *Andania* (17th). Strength – 26 officers, 884 other ranks. Arrived Malta 7. 30 a.m. (24th), leaving 8a.m. (26th). Arrived Alexandria 5 p.m. (28th). Disembarked and to Mex Camp. War Diary records water supply at Mex "insufficient" and sanitary arrangements "poor." Transport (1 officer and 115 other ranks) arrived on *City of Edinburgh* from Avonmouth (31st).

APRIL
Left Mex Camp for Alexandria (8th) and embarked *Andania*. Strength – 26 officers, 929 other ranks. Sailed for Lemnos 5.45 a.m. (10th). Arrived Mudros Harbour 7 a.m. (12th). Sailed for Gallipoli 5 p.m. (24th). Landed "X" Beach, Helles 9 a.m. (25th). Moved about 600 yards inland 4.30 p.m. and dug in. In his book *History Of The Royal Inniskilling Fusiliers in the Great War*, Sir Frank Fox recalls an order issued by officers upon landing directing that any man hit was to empty his pouches, if able to do so, in order that others could pick up his ammunition. This instruction being complied with by the Battalion's first casualty Sergeant Smalls. Came under attack during night. Moved forward (27th). Attack on Krithia (28th). Advanced on eastern side of Gully Ravine. War Diary records – objectives almost gained in centre, but withdrawal forced due to failure of troops on left (French) to advance. Fell back and dug in at White House.

MAY
Enemy attacked in force during night (1st). Sir Frank Fox records that the Turks came on with determination and shouting "Eeneeskeeling, Eeneeskeeling, do not fire." The enemy's first line comprised bombers, and these were killed by the bayonet. Main waves repulsed by rapid fire at range of 20 to 30 yards. 132 prisoners captured. Commanding Officer – Lieutenant-Colonel F.G. Jones mortally wounded by shell (2nd). "A" and

"C" Companies in support of 88th Brigade and 1st Lancashire Fusiliers (4th). In reserve for attack on Achi Baba (6th). In action (7th) – two companies sent to reinforce 1st Lancashire Fusiliers during attack. War Diary records "The attack is entirely held up by cross fire from enemy's machine guns which cannot be located. Neither 88th Brigade or Lancashire Fusiliers can advance." Entrench on left rear of 88th Brigade for night. Covered left flank during New Zealand Brigade attack on Krithia (8th). Advanced 10.30 a.m. – some 400 yards gained and dug in. One company advanced and extended left of New Zealand line 7 p.m. Relieved by 89th Punjabis 7 p.m. (9th) and to reserve positions near Pink Farm. Attached to 29th Indian Brigade. Moved forward in support of 1/6th Gurkhas and 14th Sikhs (13th). Relieved 1/6th Gurkhas in firing line – Gurkha Bluff (15th). Line advanced about 100 yards (16th). Enemy attacked 2 p.m. (22nd) – advance post taken along with part of 1st and 2nd lines. Sir Frank Fox records fierce hand-to-hand fighting in the trenches for almost 4 hours. Enemy eventually driven back. Casualties – 1 officer, 36 other ranks killed, 1 officer, 59 other ranks wounded, 14 missing. Relieved by 1/6th Gurkhas (23rd) and to support line. War Diary records (25th) sinking of the *Triumph* by enemy torpedo which could be seen from Gurkha Bluff. To Brigade Reserve near White House (25th). To firing line – Gurkha Bluff (27th).

JUNE
Relieved by 1st Lancashire Fusiliers (1st) – 2 companies to "Y" Beach, 1 to Geogheghans Bluff in Brigade Reserve, 1 in support line. Company in support to "Y" Beach (2nd). Moved forward (less company at Geogheghans Bluff) for attack 10.15 a.m. (4th). Remained in close support of 1st Lancashire Fusiliers. Company at Geogheghans Bluff advanced in support of 14th Sikhs 6.15 p.m. Withdrew to "Y" Beach (5th) then rejoined 87th Brigade at White House. In support of 88th Brigade during day (6th). "C" and "D" Companies in support of 2nd South Wales Borderers and 1st King's Own Scottish Borderers during day (11th). Withdrew to Gully Beach in Divisional Reserve (12th). Relieved 1st Lancashire Fusiliers in fire trenches – Krithia Nullah (17th). "B" Company came under bombing attack and forced to withdraw some 30 yards (18th). Line later regained with help of "A" Company. Bombing party under Captain G.R. O'Sullivan attacked and forced enemy from sap 4.30 a.m. (19th). War Diary records enemy shot down by "A" and "B" Companies while evacuating the sap and retiring across open ground. Captain O'Sullivan wounded and recommended for Victoria Cross. Relieved by 1st Border (20th) and into support trenches. Relieved and to Divisional Reserve dug outs near Gully Beach (22nd). To Gurkha Bluff (27th). Attacked enemy positions in Gully Spur

11.10 a.m. (28th) – "A", "B" and "C" Companies advancing over open ground took 2nd objective by 11.20 a.m. Gains consolidated. Sir Frank Fox records that the attack was met with little resistance, the captured trenches being almost on the outskirts of Krithia and containing the enemy's breakfasts of biscuits and hard-boiled eggs. Bodies of men from 1st Royal Dublin Fusiliers killed on 27th April found still unburied. Heavy enemy counter attack repulsed 8.30 p.m. Attacks continued throughout night and next day.

JULY
Enemy counter attack during night (1st/2nd) gained some ground in 2/10th Gurkha trenches. "D" Company under Captain H.S. Edden and 2 platoons of "A" Company under G.R. Captain O'Sullivan sent up to retake positions. War Diary records "these companies, headed by bombing parties covered by men with fixed bayonets, three times drove the Turks out . . . being successful in holding the trench after 3rd attempt." Casualties 1 officer, 5 other ranks killed; 4 officers, 33 other ranks wounded. The wounded officer, Captain O'Sullivan, was awarded the Victoria Cross – "For most conspicuous bravery during operations south-west of Krithia, on the Gallipoli Peninsula. On the night of the 1st-2nd July, when it was essential that a portion of a trench should be regained, Captain O'Sullivan, although not belonging to the troops at this point, volunteered to lead a party of bomb-throwers to effect the recapture. He advanced in the open, under a very heavy fire, and in order to throw his bombs with greater effect, got up on the parapet, where he was completely exposed to the fire of the enemy occupying the trench. He was finally wounded, but not before his inspiring example had led on his party to make further efforts, which resulted in the recapture of the trench." (*London Gazette*). Also awarded Victoria Cross – Sergeant J. Somers . . . "Sergt. Somers remained alone on the spot until a party brought up bombs. He then climbed over into the Turkish trench, and bombed the Turks with great effect. Later on he advanced into the open under very heavy fire, and held back the enemy by throwing bombs into their flank until a barricade had been established. During this period he frequently ran to and from our trenches to obtain fresh supplies of bombs. By his gallantry and coolness Sergt. Somers was largely instrumental in effecting the recapture of a portion of our trench which had been lost." (*London Gazette*). Moved back to support line 4 p.m. (2nd). To firing line – Fusilier Bluff (5th). Relieved by 4th Worcestershire and to Gurkha Bluff 10 a.m. (7th). To Gully Beach 4 p.m. and bivouacked on side of road leading from Gully to "X" Beach. Employed on road mending and digging terraces on side of cliff (8th-10th). Moved (less "C" Company) to "V" Beach 1 a.m. (11th). Embarked and sailed for Imbros 4 a.m. Strength – 16 officers,

440 other ranks. War Diary records no preparations having been made at Imbros to accommodate 87th Brigade which should have gone to Mudros. Re-embarked 5 p.m. and sailed 8 p.m. Arrived 8.30 a.m. (12th) and via Australian Pier marched to bivouacs one and half miles along Mudros-Romanos road. "C" Company later arrived. Sailed *Queen Victoria* for Gallipoli (21st). Landed "V" Beach 2 a.m. (22nd) and marched to dug-outs on Gully Beach-"X" Beach road. Relieved 9th Royal Warwickshire at Fusilier Bluff (28th). Left of firing line on sea. War Diary records 5 p.m. (30th) "Whole firing line from R.N.D. on right to Inniskillings on left, stood to arms, gave 3 cheers and fired *Feu-de-Joie* in celebration of victory at Nasirryas."

AUGUST

Relieved (1st) and to Brigade reserve at "Y" Ravine. War Diary records Battalion receiving its second anti-cholera inoculation. Relieved 1st King's Own Scottish Borderers in firing line (4th). War Diary records (6th) "A" and "D" Companies withdrawing into ravines during night where they spread out sheets and moved about in order to deceive enemy Taubs flying overhead. Clouds of dust were created by dragging brushwood and blankets along by a rope. This being "to represent strong reinforcements arriving." When 88th Brigade and 42nd Division attacked at 4.30 p.m., . . . "87th Bde. fixed bayonets, cheered and moved about in trenches, showing tips of bayonets above parapet to represent preparation for attack and so draw off fire from 88th Bde." Enemy mine exploded 6.50 p.m. (14th). War Diary records the mine not being far enough forward and only giving The Birdcage "a severe shaking." "A" Company, supported by "C", engaged enemy during night while repairs were carried out to parapets and buried men excavated. Releived by 1st Essex and to former dug outs between Gully and "X" Beaches (16th). Battalion ordered to Suvla. Began move by sea from "V" Beach 8.30 p.m. Strength – 25 officers, 814 other ranks. Moved forward to 87th Brigade bivouacks in Corps Reserve. Moved forward across Salt Lake to Brigade Reserve positions 7.30 p.m. (20th). Attack on Scimitar Hill (21st). "A", "B" and "D" Companies advanced through 1st K.O.S.B. 3.30 p.m. Sir Frank Fox records that for the first 400 yards the Battalion had few casualties. Soon, however, "officers and men were swept down as by an invisible scythe." First trench taken approx. 3.40 p.m. War Diary records – 3.45 p.m. "Part of front line fell back, half way down the hill in disorder, suffering heavy casualties: but it was rallied within 150 yards of the top of the hill. The Borders and S.W.Bs then came up in support. A second charge advanced was made up the hill but did not get home, the enemy standing on their parapets and firing from the hip and throwing hand grenades."

Heavy and accurate shrapnel fire also noted. "A" and "B" Companies attempted further assault at 7 p.m. but forced back by enemy counter attacks. Captain O'Sullivan, V.C. was reported as having led one of the final charges calling "One more charge for the honour of the Old Regiment." Battalion ordered to withdraw 11 p.m. Strength on going into action – 21 officers, 723 other ranks. Roll call (22nd) – 4 officers, 230 other ranks. Communication trench to firing line dug (22nd). Relieved by 5th Royal Inniskilling Fusiliers and to reserve lines during evening. To "A" Beach (27th), reserve lines (28th).

SEPTEMBER
Embarked *Ermine* (22nd). Strength – 10 officers, 332 other ranks. Sailed for Imbros. Arrived 6.30 a.m. (23rd). War Diary (28th) records casualties for action of 21st August – Officers: Captain H.S. Edden, Second-Lieutenants P.A.X.M. Thompson and P.T. Jordan killed; Captain C.G. Tillie died of wounds. Wounded 5. Wounded and missing 5. Other ranks killed 14. Wounded 238. Missing 247. The following officers posted as missing were later reported as killed – Captain G.R. O'Sullivan, V.C., Captain C.H. Hill, Second-Lieutenants A.K. Tarbert and E.A. Tarbert.

OCTOBER
Inspected by Lieutenant-General Sir Ian Hamilton 12.05 p.m. (1st). Embarked *River Fisher* 4.30 p.m., strength – 11 officers, 244 other ranks. Disembarked "W" Beach, Helles 7.45 p.m. Moved forward to Royal Naval Division camp between east and west Krithia roads. 87th Brigade now attached to 52nd Division. Moved to new quarters near Pink Farm (12th). Relieved 2nd South Wales Borderers in forward trenches – Horseshoe sector (23rd). War Diary notes positions as being formally held by the French. Trenches mostly very narrow and in need of repair. Sandbag parapet in danger of falling in. Many dead bodies found buried in parapet. Relieved by 1st K.O.S.B. in trench E11 (27th) and withdrew to reserve at Brown House, Eski Line.

NOVEMBER
Relieved by 1st Border and moved back to Corps Reserve (1st). Began work cutting terraces in cliff close to "X" Beach (2nd). War Diary records whole battalion began to have clothing disinfected (4th). Also, Battalion defeated 1st K.O.S.B. (after extra time) in 1st round of "Dardanelles Football Cup." Relieved 2nd South Wales Borderers in Eski Line (9th). Machine Gun Section to firing line. War Diary records (11th) – "While in the Eski Lines there has been constant complaints from each regiment in turn that they are

bombarded from the rear. The batteries always say it is the French artillery, but there is no doubt about the shells being British make." Relieved 1st K.O.S.B. in firing line – Horseshoe sector (12th). Relieved by 1st Border (16th) and to Corps Reserve. Relieved 2nd S.W.B. in firing line (24th). War Diary records British shell landing in The Horseshoe (26th) and killing two men. Relieved by 1st K.O.S.B. (28th) and to Eski Line.

DECEMBER

Moved back to rest camp (3rd). War Diary notes (6th) anniversary of Battalion leaving India on 6th December, 1914. Also calculation of casualties from commencement of campaign to 16th November – killed in action, died of wounds and disease: 267; missing: 79; wounded (approx): 1001. Strength of original battalion – 990. Drafts – 1,205. Of the original battalion there were just 2 officers – Captain M.F. Hammond-Smith (Adjutant) and Captain W.A. Morris (Quartermaster) and 118 other ranks. Relieved Hawke Battalion – Northern and Southern Barricade sector (10th). War Diary notes that transport can be taken during the day as far as Pink Farm and from there on to Church Farm by mule. At night, carts could get as far as Church Farm. Everything from there had to be man-handled. Asbestos suits issued (15th). Relieved by 1st Border (19th) and to rest camp at "X" Beach. "A" and "B" Companies to Eski Line (22nd), joined by "C" and "D" (23rd). War Diary records Christmas puddings from Lady Murray and Mrs Hylton-Foster distributed (24th). Also sardines from Mr Copeland-Smith's Fund, sweets and cigarettes. Relieved 1st Border in firing line (27th). Wires placed on north side of Northern Barricade (28th) also trestles placed in front of Birdcage Walk. Relieved (31st) and to rest camp.

JANUARY, 1916

Began preparations for evacuation. Booby traps, land mines, dummy figures and rifles that would fire with the aid of tins of sand attached to the triggers, set up in forward trenches. Received orders to evacuated Peninsular (8th). Withdrew to "W" Beach, last party embarked *Staunch* during early morning (9th). Sailed 4 a.m. An account by Sergeant Mannion of the evacuation (published in Sir Frank Fox's history) recalls parties of six men from each company remaining in the firing line, occasionally firing their rifles. Leaving the trenches at midnight (8th) automatic rifles and dummy figures were left to deceive the enemy. On the beach veterinary officers were shooting hundreds of mules.

5TH (SERVICE) BATTALION

JULY

Basingstoke, Hampshire. Part of 31st Brigade, 10th (Irish) Division. Entrained for Devonport (10th) and embarked *Novian*. Arrived Mudros, Lemnos (28th) the sailed for Port Iero, Mitylene, arriving (31st).

AUGUST

Landed Ghazi Baba, Suvla (7th), strength – 25 officers, 750 other ranks. Separated from 31st Brigade and took up positions west of Lala Baba in reserve. Rejoined Brigade at Kiretch Tepe Sirt (12th). Received orders to attack Kidney Hill (15th). Moved forward 1.15 p.m. – "A" Company on left, "D" on right, "B" and "C" in support. Soon came under heavy and constant shell and rifle fire. Commanding Officer – Lieutenant-Colonel A.S. Vanrenen mortally wounded about 3 p.m. Advance halted and ordered to fall back to start line. The War Diary of 31st Brigade notes that the Battalion attacked with great gallantry, the rifle fire coming from concealed trenches. Later took over trenches eastern side Kiretch Tepe Sirt. War Diary records difficulty in recovering wounded during retreat. There were no stretcher bearers – Captain Adams and Lieutenant Lindsay noted as doing good work with and oil sheet. Casualties – 7 officers, 28 other ranks killed; 13 officers, 230 other ranks wounded; 78 missing. Heavily shelled throughout day (17th). Relieved by 1/4th Norfolk at Jephson's Post and retired to reserve lines at Karakol Dagh 7 p.m. To Hill 10 2 p.m. (21st) then to reserve positions Chocolate Hill 8 p.m. Relieved 1st Royal Inniskilling Fusiliers in reserve trenches about 250 yards behind firing line (22nd). "B" and "C" Companies moved into No Man's Land during night (23rd) and dug new fire trench – 70 yards long and 30 yards from existing front line. "A" Company dug new fire trench 70 yards forward during night (24th) and took this position over (25th). Enemy opened heavy fire early hours (28th). Battalion reinforced 6th Royal Inniskilling Fusiliers 2.30 a.m., returning 3 a.m.

SEPTEMBER

Relieved 6th Royal Inniskilling Fusiliers in firing line (6th). War Diary records position running 600 yards from left of Maxwell's Sap. Line extended to right (10th). Relieved by 6th Royal Inniskilling Fusiliers (17th) and to reserve line. War Diary records Divisional Order (19th) officially naming "The Pimple" and that the laying of trip wires was to be discontinued. Relieved (30th) and embarked *Sarnia*.

OCTOBER
Sailed for Lemnos (1st), arriving Mudros 11.30 a.m. War Diary records casualties since landing on 7th August – 7 officers, 46 other ranks killed; 13 officers, 297 other ranks wounded; 81 men missing.

6TH (SERVICE) BATTALION

JULY
Basingstoke, Hampshire. Part of 31st Brigade, 10th (Irish) Division. Commanding Officer – Lieutenant-Colonel H.M. Cliffe. Entrained for Devonport (11th) and embarked *Andania*. Strength – 30 officers, 937 other ranks. Called Gibraltar (15th), arrived Malta (18th). Sailed 6 a.m. (20th). Arrived Alexandria 4 p.m. (22nd). Sailed for Lemnos 6.20 p.m. (24th), arrived Mudros Harbour 1.30 p.m. (26th). Sailed for Mitylene 6 p.m. (30th), arrived Port Iero 5.30 a.m. (31st).

AUGUST
Inspected by General Sir Ian Hamilton (2nd). War Diary of 31st Brigade records (3rd) epidemic of ptomaine poisoning broke out on *Andania*. Transhipped to *Osmanieh* (6th) and sailed for Gallipoli. Disembarked "C" Beach under shrapnel fire 5.30 a.m. (7th) and advanced towards Lala Baba Hill. Received orders to attack Chocolate Hill. Advanced over sand-pit west of Salt Lake then north side of lake – "A" and "C" Companies in firing line, "B" and "D" in reserve. Came under heavy shrapnel and sniper fire upon reaching north-east corner of Salt Lake. Major Bryan Cooper in his history of the 10th (Irish) Division records the men pressing on, the enemy being driven through the scrub before them. Officers had little information of the country or location and strength of the enemy. Leading waves delivered frontal attack on hill, crossing 500 yards of flat dried lake and suffering very heavy casualties. War Diary notes open ditch at foot of hill which was heavily entrenched and fortified by the enemy. "A" Company occupied ditch, "C" advanced up hill. Battalion assembled at foot of hill 4 a.m. (8th) and dug in. "A" and "B" Companies took up positions in firing line on north-west face of hill (9th), "B" and "D" moving to trenches at rear. Platoon under Lieutenant Barton carried small arms ammunition (29,000 rounds) forward to 5th Royal Irish Fusiliers in firing line. War Diary records machine guns under Lieutenant Smyth did "excellent work and made use of all targets offered." Continued to hold. Casualties – Second-Lieutenant W.S. Collen and 5 other ranks killed, 7 officers, 66 other ranks wounded, 21 men missing. Ordered back to Lala Baba 3 a.m. (10th) and entrenched positions. Relieved 5th Dorsetshire in firing line – Kiretch Tepe Sirt during night (11th).

Improved and strengthened trenches. Machine guns in support of attack on Kidney Hill (15th). Moved forward along north side of Kiretch Tepe Sirt (16th) and took over trenches down north slope near Jephson's Post. Relieved by 1/4th Norfolk 9 p.m. (18th) and to Brigade reserve bivouacs at Karakol Dagh. To positions west face of Hill 10 (21st). Heavy casualties from shell fire. Advanced on Chocolate Hill 7.30 p.m. and occupied reserve trenches on edge of west slope. Relieved 1st King's Own Scottish Borderers in front line trenches just north of Chocolate Hill (22nd).

SEPTEMBER
Second-Lieutenant I.J. Smyth killed (3rd). Relieved by 5th Royal Inniskilling Fusiliers (6th) and to reserve trenches. Returned to firing line (17th). Relieved by 6th South Lancashire (30th) and to Brigade reserve trenches. Moved to "C" Beach 9.30 p.m. and embarked *Abassieh* for Mudros.

The Gloucestershire Regiment

"Suvla" "Sari Bair" "Scimitar Hill" "Gallipoli,1915-16"

7TH (SERVICE) BATTALION

JUNE
Blackdown, Surrey. Part of 39th Brigade, 13th (Western) Division. Sailed from Avonmouth (19th).

JULY
Arrived Mudros and after a week sailed for Gallipoli. Landed "Y" Beach, Cape Helles (11th) and to bivouacs. Moved forward to Corps Reserve lines (13th), Geogheghan's Bluff in Brigade Reserve (15th). War Diary records did not arrive until 6 a.m. (16th) – guide led Battalion to Gurkha Bluff by mistake. "B" and "C" Companies to firing line – trenches H12 and J11 attached to 9th Worcestershire (17th). Worcestershires relieved (18th). Relieved by 9th Worcestershire (21st) and to Eski Line in Divisional Reserve. To Geogheghan's Bluff in Brigade Reserve (22nd), "C" and "D" Companies moving into firing line in support of 7th North Staffordshire. "C" Company moved from J11 to firing line at J11B (23rd) and assisted 7th North Staffordshire in forcing back enemy attack. Relieved 9th Worcestershire in firing line (24th). To Geogheghan's Bluff (26th), "A" and "B" companies at Trolley Ravine. Relieved (28th) and to Gully Beach. Embarked for Mudros. Landed (29th).

AUGUST
Sailed for Anzac (3rd). Landed and to Rest Gully. To Aghyl Dere (6th). Reinforced New Zealand Brigade at Rhododendron Spur and in action at Table Top (7th). Captain P.S. Vassall and 3 other ranks killed; 1 officers, 24 other ranks wounded. Took part in attack on Chunuk Bair (8th). Moved forward 4.15 a.m. on left of Wellington Battalion – "B" and "D" Companies in front, "A" and "C" in second line. War Diary records heavy enfilade machine gun fire on left – leading platoons "practically wiped out." William Ewing, a Chaplain serving on Gallipoli, noted in his book *From Gallipoli to Baghdad* . . . "In the early morning of the 8th, the crest of Chunuk Bair was captured. A unique and glorious record is that of the 7th Gloucesters, a regiment of the New Army. Every officer and senior N.C.O. was either killed or wounded. Reduced to a few small groups of men, commanded by junior

N.C.O.'s and privates, the fought dauntlessly from midday until sunset."
War Diary records survivors taking 3 days to rejoin the Battalion at Overton
Gully. Casualties – 3 officers killed, 8 wounded. Other ranks recorded as
approximately 45 killed, 115 wounded, 190 missing. Moved to ridge
between Aghyl Dere and Overton's Gully (11th) and dug in. War Diary
record 7 killed, 14 wounded from sniper fire (12th). Relieved (14th) and to
Aghyl Dere in reserve. Temporarily amalgamated with 9th Worcestershire
(15th). Relieved 5th Connaught Rangers in firing line – Lancashire Hill
(20th). Amalgamation with 9th Worcestershire cancelled (23rd). Relieved
and to Chailak Dere (30th), Salt Lake Line (31st).

SEPTEMBER
War Diary records strength (1st) as – 8 officers, 263 other ranks. To firing
line – Sulajik sector (19th) – trenches C52, C53, C54.

OCTOBER
Relieved by 7th North Staffordshire (3rd) and to Brigade Reserve trenches.
To trenches B68, B69 (24th).

NOVEMBER
War Diary notes (26th) much of Battalion's property and equipment
destroyed in flood, almost all records lost. Heavily shelled (29th) – 6 killed,
15 wounded. One man died of exposure. Two men died of exposure (30th).

DECEMBER
Relieved by 7th North Staffordshire (2nd). Effective strength (5th) – 13 officers, 368 other ranks. Began preparations for evacuation (12th). All weak
men evacuated, equipment and stores removed during night. Sandbags slit
(15th) and embarked "A" Beach for Mudros. Rearguard of 2 officers and
48 other ranks remained. Rearguard arrived Mudros (24th). Sailed for
Helles (27th). Landed "V" Beach 6.30 p.m. and to Gully Ravine. Left half
of Battalion relieved 1/4th East Lancashire at Fusilier Bluff (28th).
Headquarters to Border Bluff. Right half took over support line (29th).

JANUARY, 1916
7th North Staffordshire reinforced firing line and supports (1st). Relieved
(4th) and to "Y" Ravine in reserve. Moved forward to support line during
enemy attack (7th). Lieutenant-Colonel F.H. Walker of 7th North
Staffordshire killed. Major H.S. Bull (7th Gloucestershire) took over
command of both battalions. Withdrew (8th) and to "W" Beach. Sailed
Ermine for Mudros.

THE WORCESTERSHIRE REGIMENT

"Helles" "Landing at Helles" "Krithia" "Suvla" "Sari Bair" "Scimitar Hill" "Gallipoli,1915-16"

4TH BATTALION

MARCH
Leamington, Warwickshire. Part of 88th Brigade, 29th Division. Left for Avonmouth in 3 trains (21st and 22nd). Embarked – Headquarters and 2 companies *Southland*, 1 Company *Caledonia*, 1 company *Aragon*. Transport embarked Melville. Officers – Lieutenant-Colonel D.E. Cayley (Commanding); Majors C.H. Seton, H.A. Carr, H.A. Lang, E.W. Boyd-Moss, D.S.O.; Captains A.D.H. Ray, J.O. Nelson, W. Barker, D.W. Pollock, E.T.J. Kerans (Adjutant), E.P.C. Amphlett, G.C. Deans; Lieutenants T.H.O. Crawley, J.V. Bridges, W.D. Bush, C.A. Wythes, H. Gordon, D. Chesney, T.L.N. Mostyn, J.F.A. Mervyn, J.M.B. Entwhistle, J.D. Dickens, D.G. Jones; Second-Lieutenants H. James, A.W. Roberts, E.C.D. Malone. Lieutenant H.C. Butler (Quartermaster), Captain W.J. Maloney (R.A.M.C., Medical Officer). Arrived Malta (31st).

APRIL
Sailed for Egypt (1st). Arrived Alexandria (4th). Disembarked (6th) and to camp at Mustapha Pasha Barracks. Embarked *Aragon* (8th). Sailed for Lemnos (11th). Arrived Mudros (13th). Sailed for Gallipoli (24th). Strength – 26 officers, 931 other ranks. In his war history of the Worcestershire Regiment, Captain H. FitzM. Stacke, M.C. records how the sound of guns was heard during the voyage. Soon troops could be seen being taken ashore in crowded boats. Fierce fighting on the beaches was noted, along with boats laden with wounded returning to the ships. Part of "X" Company under Major Carr transferred to small boats early (25th) and these were noted as having been used during the morning to land men of the Royal Dublin Fusiliers. Captain Stacke records they were badly damaged from fire and "blood mixed with sea water ran over the boots of the troops." Major Carr's party reached the *River Clyde* and attempted to land at "V" Beach. Most of the party being killed or wounded. Remainder of Battalion landed at "W" Beach. Formed up – "Z" and "Y" Companies in front, "X" and part of "W" in support. Advanced up Hill 138 to attack enemy redoubt. Thick wire held up assault but paths opened up by volunteers using hand cutters. Battalion charged with 1st Essex and cleared objective. Second redoubt

attacked – Captain Ray mortally wounded while attempting to cut wire. "X"
Company moved along cliff to lighthouse and attacked second redoubt but
also held up by wire. The bravery of wire cutting parties noted by Sir Ian
Hamilton observing from aboard ship. Second redoubt charged and taken.
Line extended to right along cliffs towards "V" Beach. Positions consolidated throughout night. Advanced and captured enemy trenches above "V"
Beach (26th). Major Carr's party landed and rejoined Battalion. Advanced
towards Krithia (27th), moving forward on right of 88th Brigade. Crossed
and advanced astride Kanli Dere halting on edge of wood for night.
Continued advance along line of Krithia Road 8 a.m. (28th) – "Z" and "Y"
Companies leading, "W" and "X" in support. Heavy casualties among
leading waves forced halt. "W" Company came forward and charged enemy
position on ridge. Objective taken with the bayonet and gains held under
heavy fire from trenches 400 yards ahead. Ordered to retire during evening.
Casualties- 9 officers wounded, other ranks (since 25th) – 35 killed, 199
wounded, 74 missing.

MAY
Enemy attacked (1st) and took part of firing line. "W", "X" and "Y"
Companies went forward and regained line. Later withdrew to reserve line.
To firing line between Krithia Nullah and Gully Ravine (2nd). Moved
during evening to western side of Krithia Nullah relieving 2nd Royal
Fusiliers. Took part in attack (6th) – advanced 11 a.m. and gaining ridge
500 yards in front of firing line. Gains held throughout day. Casualties –
Captains D.W. Pollock, G.C. Deans, T.H.O. Crawley killed; 1 other officer
wounded; 10 other ranks killed, 71 wounded, 2 missing. "Z" Company
advanced on support of 1/5th Royal Scots during morning (7th). Forced to
withdraw with heavy loss after 15 minutes severe fighting. Advanced in
support of New Zealand troops (8th). Relieved by 6th Manchester (11th)
and withdrew to rest camp behind reserve line. Strength – 11 officers, 483
other ranks. Moved forward to reserve line (16th). Relieved 2nd Royal
Fusiliers in firing line between Twelve Tree Copse and Gully Ravine (23rd).
Reinforcement of 13 officers and 159 other ranks arrived (27th).

JUNE
Third Battle of Krithia (4th). Attack at 12 noon and cleared 4 lines of enemy
trenches. 14th Sikhs on left almost wiped out and defensive flank formed on
Gully Ravine. Compton Mackenzie served on the Staff during the Gallipoli
operations and in his book *Gallipoli Memories* he notes that the trenches were
taken as easily as the achievement was marked on maps with coloured
pencils. Enemy counter attacked throughout night (5th), finally retiring 9.30

a.m. (6th). Another attack repulsed during night (6th/7th). Relieved 1st Essex in trench H11 (7th). Relieved by 1/4th Royal Scots Fusiliers (10th) and to Gully Beach. Moved forward to support trenches (12th). "W" Company assisted 1/5th Royal Scots in successful counter attack (19th). Relieved and to Gully Beach same day. Relieved 1/4th Royal Scots in firing line (24th). Second-Lieutenant H. James posted to 1/5th Royal Scots as liaison officer (28th) and successfully organised and led 2 parties in counter attacks.

JULY
Action at Gully Ravine: Attacked 9 a.m. (2nd) – 2 parties each of 30 men moving forward and entering enemy's trench. Party on left led by Second-Lieutenant H. James moved up saphead, their advance being recorded as difficult due to large numbers of unburied dead. Soon all that remained of the attacking party were Lieutenant James and 1 N.C.O. The latter being sent back for help. Single-handed, Lieutenant James held back the enemy until a strong attack forced him to retire to a position further back. There he constructed a barricade out of dead bodies and sandbags and for some time held back the enemy with rifle fire and bombs. For his gallantry and leadership both on 28th June and 3rd July he was subsequently awarded the Victoria Cross – *London Gazette* . . . "For most conspicuous bravery during the operations in the southern zone of the Gallipoli Peninsular on 28 June, 1915. When a portion of a regiment had been checked, owing to all the officers being put out of action, Second Lieut. James, who belonged to a neighbouring unit, entirely on his own initiative gathered together a body of men and led them forward under heavy shell and rifle fire. He then returned, organised a second party, and again advanced. . . . On 3rd July, in the same locality, Second Lieut. James headed a party of bomb-throwers up a Turkish communication trench, and after nearly all his bomb-throwers had been killed or wounded he remained alone at the head of the trench, and kept back the enemy single-handed till a barrier had been built behind him and the trench secured. He was throughout exposed to a murderous fire." Battalion later took over trenches – Fusilier Bluff (7th). Relieved by 9th Royal Warwickshire and to Gully Beach (15th). Sailed for Lemnos (17th). *Swiftsure*, which covered the landing of 4th Worcestershire on 25th April, gave a party on board (25th) to which all survivors of the event were invited. Captain Stacke records that less that 200 men (including 7 officers) were at that time eligible to attend. Sailed for Gallipoli (28th). Landed "W" Beach and to bivouacs at Gully Beach.

9. 1/1st County of London Yeomanry (Middlesex, Duke of Cambridge's Hussars) in reserve trenches, Suvla, August, 1915.

10. Dead Man's Gully, Suvla. Photo taken by member of 1/1st County of London Yeomanry in August, 1915. Several decaying bodies can be seen.

15. Artist's impression of
    Lieutenant William
    Thomas Forshaw, 1/9th
    Manchester Regiment,
    winning the Victoria
    Cross at The Vineyard 7
    to 9 August 1915.
16. Artist's impression of
    Acting Sergeant F. Ede,
    9th (Service) Battalion,
    Sherwood Foresters,
    winning the Distinguished
    Conduct Medal at Suvla,
    28 November, 1915.

AUGUST
Moved forward to firing line (6th). Position on right of Worcester Flat. Strength 24 officers, approx. 800 other ranks. Took part in action at The Vineyard. Attacked trench H13 at 3.50 p.m. – leading waves cut down by machine gun fire from front and both flanks while crossing No Man's Land (300 yards). *The Official History of the Great War* records that very few unwounded men of the Worcestershire reached the enemy's trenches. Those that did being attacked by large numbers of Turks. At the end of 1 hours fighting the only British still holding out in this part of the line were 30 men led by a sergeant. Just 12 survivors withdrew to their original line after midnight. Relieved dawn (7th) and to Gully Beach. Casualties – 16 officers, 752 other ranks. Relieved 1st Royal Munster Fusiliers in firing line (13th). Relieved and to Gully Beach (19th). To "V" Beach during night (20th) and embarked *Queen Victoria* for Suvla Bay. Landed and to reserve positions behind Chocolate Hill. Moved north to positions southern slope of Kiretch Tepe Sirt (22nd). Relieved 1/4th Northamptonshire in firing line (23rd). Relieved by 2nd South Wales Borderers and to Suvla Point (29th). Sailed for Imbros (30th).

SEPTEMBER
To Suvla (8th). Landed and moved forward to support line. Relieved 1st Lancashire Fusiliers in firing line – Kuchuk Anafarta Ova sector (9th). Regimental history notes high casualties, including Lieutenant James V.C., from sniping.

OCTOBER
Major Winnington evacuated sick (1st). Command then passed to Second-Lieutenant H. Arnold. Regimental history notes at this time all 20 officers were Second-Lieutenants. Captain Kerans took command (26th).

NOVEMBER
Trenches Kuchuk Anafarta Ova sector. Battalion flooded out after the great storm of (26th). Regimental history records that everyone was soaked thorough and nearly all kit was lost. Norman King-Wilson, a Canadian surgeon, recalled in Michael Moynuhan's book *People at War 1914-1918* seeing 7 Worcesters just after the storm. They were up on the parapet of a flooded trench singing "A life on the ocean wave." Second-Lieutenant K. Greenaway shot by sniper (27th). High casualties after blizzard of (27th/28th). Strength reduced from 700 to 300 after 5 days. One officer in his diary noted seeing 2 men in each others embrace and frozen to death. Norman King-Wilson saw a corporal and 2 men of 4th Worcestershire who

after treatment to their frozen feet and hands returned to their post at Dublin Castle.

DECEMBER
Began evacuation (19th). Embarked *Magnificent* for Imbros (20th). Headquarters and 2 companies embarked *Redbreast* (22nd) and sailed for Helles. Landed during night and moved to trenches south of Pink Farm. Remainder of Battalion joined (26th). Took over firing line – The Vineyard sector (31st).

JANUARY, 1916
Began evacuation during night (7th/8th). Embarked *Lawford* and *Staunch* from "W" Beach.

9TH (SERVICE) BATTALION

JUNE
Blackdown, Surrey. Part of 39th Brigade, 13th (Western) Division. Entrained for Avonmouth (20th) and embarked *Cawdor Castle*. Officers: Lieutenant-Colonel M.H. Nunn (Commanding); Majors W.C. Crofton, E.W. Boyd-Moss, D.S.O., W. Barker; Captains G.W. Rolph, W.D. Gibbon, R.B. Horsfield, J.V. Godfray (Adjutant), S. Munnick, E.M. Carter, W. Austin; Lieutenants R.N. Bellairs, T. Neame, G.T. Pearson, G.T. de Blaby, C.E. Sladden, P. MacD. Sanderson, E.H. Hiscock, C.J. Tree, J. Higgs-Walker; Second-Lieutenants R.C Marshall, J.N. Lancaster, L.E. Hiscock, R. Cavanagh, C.W. Rawle, J.C. Bourne, F.G.V. Beard. Lieutenant C.H. Inwood (Quartermaster), Lieutenant I.M. Brown (R.A.M.C., Medical Officer). Other ranks: 970. Sailed (24th).

JULY
Arrived Mudros Harbour (10th). Transhipped to *Newmarket* ("C" and "D" Companies) and *Renard* ("A" and "B" Companies) and sailed for Gallipoli (13th). Landed "V" Beach and to reserve positions Gully Beach. Attached to 2nd Hampshire for instruction in firing line, Gully Ravine (14th). Took over line – trenches H12 and J11 (16th). Second-Lieutenant J.C. Bourne killed, Lieutenant C.J. Tree mortally wounded. Relieved by 7th Gloucestershire (18th). Relieved 7th Gloucestershire (21st). Four casualties during enemy attack on right (23rd). Relieved by 7th Gloucestershire (24th). Returned to front line (26th) then relieved by 1st King's Own Scottish Borderers (28th) and to Gully Beach. Later during evening moved to "V" Beach and embarked *Ermine* for Lemnos.

AUGUST

Sailed for Anzac (3rd). Landed and to bivouacs in Rest Gully. Strength – 18 officers, 727 other ranks. Moved north 11 p.m. (6th), marching east of Plugge's Plateau to mouth of Reserve Gully. Continued march early morning (7th), arriving Aghyl Dere at dawn. Moved forward for attack behind 9th Gloucestershire 7 a.m. Reached Little Table Top then ordered to reassemble at Aghyl Dere. Ordered to attack Hill "Q" 7 p.m. Moved forward behind 7th North Staffordshire and Indian Mountain Battery 9 p.m. In his war history of the Worcestershire Regiment, Captain H. FitzM. Stacke, M.C. notes the advance as being slow due to boulders, scrub and the mules of the Mountain Battery. The latter being driven by "bewildered natives." Halted for night. Advance continued at daybreak. Deployed just below crest of Hill "Q". Later relieved by 6th South Lancashire and withdrew to support line. In support of attack on Hill "Q" (9th). Took over left of Brigade front near The Farm. Enemy attacked dawn (10th). First rolling bombs down hill side which exploded in forward trenches. Regimental history notes that Battalion held its ground against rush after rush for 3 hours until finally forced to retire down to head of ravine. Casualties – Lieutenant-Colonel Nunn, Majors Crofton, Boyd-Moss, Captain Rolph, Second-Lieutenants L.E. Hiscock, Lancaster and 34 other ranks killed. Major Barker mortally wounded. Five officers, 163 other ranks wounded, 54 missing believed killed. Later withdrew to reserve positions at Aghyl Dere. Strength – 260. Draft of 100 arrived. To Damakjelik Bair 6 p.m. (12th) and deployed for attack on Kabak Kuyu. Advanced 7.30 p.m. – leading waves soon cut down by rifle and machine gun fire. About 100 unwounded men assembled under Captain Gibbon and again moved forward. Once more heavy fire drove attackers back. All officers wounded. Survivors rejoined Battalion at Aghyl Dere. Strength now approx 200 men led by Lieutenant Inwood, the only remaining officer. Temporally amalgamated with 7th Gloucestershire and began tours in firing line – Little Table Top and Bauchop's Hill. Drafts arrived and separated from Gloucestershire (23rd). Assisted Australians with long range fire from Bauchop's Hill during attack on Hill 60 (27th).

SEPTEMBER

Relieved and to reserve bivouacs near mouth of Chailak Dere (1st). To reserve positions near Lala Baba (2nd). Drafts arrived – strength by (12th) – 19 officers, 674 other ranks. Another draft arrived (18th). Moved forward across Salt Lake to trenches near Sulajik Farm (19th).

OCTOBER
Tours in trenches near Sulajik Farm and Chocolate Hill.

NOVEMBER
Tours of trenches near Sulajik Farm.

DECEMBER
Began evacuation to Imbros (19th) – 2 companies sailing with 4th Worcestershire on *Magnificent*, remainder on *Huntsgreen* (20th). Sailed *Redbreast* for Mudros (23rd). Sailed *Ermine* for Helles (27th). Landed "V" Beach and moved forward to reserve positions at Eski Line – Gully Ravine sector. To firing line west of Gully Ravine (28th).

JANUARY, 1916
Came under heavy bombardment (7th) – 16 killed, 7 wounded. Began evacuation to Mudros (8th).

THE EAST LANCASHIRE REGIMENT

"Helles" "Krithia" "Suvla" "Sari Bair" "Gallipoli,1915"

1/4TH BATTALION (T.F.)

JANUARY
Alexandria, Egypt. Part of East Lancashire Brigade, East Lancashire
Division which became 126th Brigade, 42nd (East Lancashire) Division in
May. To Heliopolis (30th).

APRIL
To Port Said and Suez Canal Defence Zone (16th).

MAY
Embarked *Galeka* (5th) and sailed 6 a.m. (6th) for Gallipoli. Landed "V"
Beach, Helles via the *River Clyde* (9th) and moved to bivouacs on top of cliffs
near "W" Beach. Arthur Behrend, a platoon commander with "C"
Company, recalls in his book *Make Me A Soldier* a number of Senegalese
soldiers being carried to the ships. It was a shocking sight, he notes, their
dark skins now ashen and many in great pain from the wounds. He also
noted, while forming up on the beach, the ruins of Sedd el Bahr village and
fort to the right, burial parties hard at work and French infantry wearing blue
coats advancing over a hill towards the firing line. Moved forward 8 p.m.
(11th) taking over trenches in Brown House sector about 2,000 yards south
of Krithia. First casualties from shelling – 1 officer and 1 man killed, 3 men
wounded. "A" and "B" Companies in attack (16th) – some ground gained.
Relieved by "C" and "D" Companies in new line (17th). "C" and "D"
Companies relieved by troops of Royal Naval Division (18th) and returned
to Brown House. Battalion relieved and to rest area. Regimental historian
notes 11 killed, 26 wounded during first week in trenches. Majority while
being relieved on last day. Employed on road works. Returned to forward
area (21st). Arthur Behrend recalls that the trench he occupied cut across
the Krithia Road. He noted that the area was littered with kit, mostly
belonging to the 4th Worcestershire. Packs were riddled with bullets, tools,
equipment and the earth were stained with blood. Relieved by 1/7th
Manchester (25th) and moved to Gully Ravine. Attached to 4th
Worcestershire and 1st Essex to replace casualties among 29th Division
(26th). Arthur Behrend recalls several interesting items regarding headgear.

It was noted in Divisional Orders that some men of the Lancashire Fusiliers wearing balaclava helmets in a forward trench had been mistaken for Turks and shelled by the Royal Navy. As a result all use of unauthorized headgear was now forbidden. It had also come to notice that some helmets had been discarded and that any man found without one would have its value deducted from his pay. On one occasion he noted a recently arrived draft, their new helmets making a bright yellow patch that could be seen for miles when they entered dark green scrub.

JUNE
Third Battle of Krithia (4th). "D" Company and 1 platoon of "C" moved forward with 1st Essex 12 noon. Led attack from right of Gurkha Bluff towards Krithia. Leading waves met with strong rifle and machine gun fire upon leaving trenches. First three lines of Turkish trenches taken within few minutes. Attack continued – 4th line carried by 3 p.m. and consolidated. Casualties – Lieutenants P. Wolf and H.W. Whalley, Second Lieutenants T.A. Heywood and C. Crewe, 32 other ranks killed; 2 officers, 159 other ranks wounded; 2 officers, 14 other ranks missing. Withdrew to trenches between Krithia Nullah and Krithia Road (5th). Casualties – 5 killed, 7 wounded. One officer, 26 other ranks wounded (6th). Message received from Colonel D.E. Cayley, Officer Commanding 4th Worcestershire – "I wish to place on record the excellent services of all ranks of the 1/4th Battalion E. Lancashire Regiment who were attached to me in the trenches and during the attack on June 4th. Their cheerfulness and willingness under all circumstances were remarkable. In the attack on June 4th they advanced with the utmost determination in face of a heavy fire and in spite of heavy casualties. I was watching the whole of the attack and did not see a single man falter or hesitate when the order to advance was given. I would specially bring to notice the services of Captains B. Polding and C. St. J. Broadbent and Lieutenant L. Green and Lieutenant A.J.D. Robinson, who handled their men with conspicuous ability and generally performed admirable work." Assisted 1/10th Manchester in attack (18th).

JULY
Carried out tours of duty in front line. Lieutenant-Colonel G.W.G. Lindsey (Argyll and Sutherland Highlanders) replaced Lieutenant-Colonel Robinson in command. Draft of 6 officers, 281 other ranks arrived (23rd).

AUGUST
In support of attack western side of Krithia Nullah (7th). Some ground

gained and held against counter attacks. Two officers and 200 men took over captured positions near The Vineyard (9th). Captain H. Bailey and 43 other ranks wounded. Enemy counter attacks beaten off (10th) – good work noted of Lieutenant N. Hargreaves who with his machine gun section held a front of 100 yards practically all day. Enemy counter attack regained part of Vineyard trench during night (12th). Relieved by 1/5th Highland Light Infantry and to bivouacs (13th). Regimental historian records that while at The Vineyard the men "suffered severely" as it was impossible to get to them either food or water. Provided working parties for remainder of month.

SEPTEMBER
Working parties.

OCTOBER
Took over firing line north-west side of Gully Ravine (1st). Relieved by 1/5th Lancashire Fusiliers (15th) and to Eski line. Commanding Officer, 7 officers and 303 other ranks to "W" Beach and embarked for Mudros (17th).

NOVEMBER
Returned to Helles (1st). Employed on fatigue duties. To front line – Western Birdcage (7th). Attached to South Eastern Mounted Brigade (26th) and took over firing line at Fusilier Bluff.

DECEMBER
Bombing attack on enemy trenches (4th). Some 368 bombs used in 2 hours. Mines exploded opposite Fusilier Bluff (19th). Bombers went forward but forced to retire as no crater had been formed. Relieved by 7th Gloucestershire (28th). Concentrated on Gully Beach during night then in early hours of (29th) embarked *Princess Alberta* and sailed for Mudros. Strength – 18 officers, 330 other ranks.

1/5TH BATTALION (T.F.)

JANUARY
Heliopolis Camp, Cairo, Egypt. Part of East Lancashire Brigade, East Lancashire Division which became 126th Brigade, 42nd (East Lancashire) Division in May. To Abbassia Camp (3rd).

APRIL
To Kantara, Suez Canal Defence Zone during 3rd week.

MAY
To Port Said and embarked *Galeka* (5th). Sailed (6th). Arrived Helles (9th) and to reserve bivouacs. Moved forward to firing line – Achi Baba Nullah sector (11th). Relieved (18th). Casualties – 4 killed, 25 wounded. To front line (21st). Advanced 150 yards into No Man's Land under heavy fire (23rd) and dug in. Captain H. Bolton killed by sniper (24th). Relieved by 1/5th Manchester (25th). Attached to units of 29th Division in trenches between Fire Tree Wood and Gully Ravine (26th).

JUNE
Took part in Third Battle of Krithia (4th). Casualties included Lieutenant J. Bolton – brother of Captain H. Bolton (killed 24th May). Took over front line Krithia Nullah sector (11th). Relieved by 1/4th Royal Scots Fusiliers (22nd) and to bivouacks.

JULY
Sailed *Grampus* to Mudros (11th). Returned to Cape Helles on *Uganda* (25th). Began tours in line Krithia Nullah sector.

AUGUST
In action at The Vineyard (7th-8th). Remained of month in support and reserve.

SEPTEMBER
In front and support line – Vineyard sector. Relieved by 1/8th Manchester and to Eski Line (10th). Moved to Gully Ravine sector and relieved 1/6th Lancashire Fusiliers in front line near Western Birdcage (17th). Mine blown in Turkish line opposite Battalion (22nd).

OCTOBER
Temporarily amalgamated with 1/9th Manchester due to high sickness rate. Continued tours of duty in firing line western side Gully Ravine.

NOVEMBER
Western side Gully Ravine.

DECEMBER
Second-Lieutenant A.V. Smith awarded Victoria Cross for act of gallantry during night (22nd/23rd) – . . . "He was in the act of throwing a grenade when it slipped from his hand and fell to the bottom of the tench, close to several of our officers and men. He immediately shouted out a warning, and

himself jumped clear and into safety, but seeing that the officers and men were unable to get into cover, and knowing well that the grenade was due to explode, he returned without any hesitation and flung himself down on it. He was instantly killed by the explosion" (*London Gazette*). Relieved by 1/1st West Kent Yeomanry (24th). To Gully Beach (28th). Sailed *Princess Alberta* for Mudros (29th).

6TH (SERVICE) BATTALION

JUNE
Blackdown, Hampshire. Part of 38th Brigade, 13th (Western) Division. "C" and "D" Companies entrained at Frimley for Avonmouth (13th) and there embarked *Nile*. Headquarters with "A" and "B" Companies left early (14th) and embarked with 38th Brigade Headquarters *Ausonia*. Officers – Colonel A.R. Cole-Hamilton (Commanding); Majors F.H. Trent (2nd in Command), H.B. McCormick, D.S.O.; Captains C.G. Lutyens, A.E. Gayer (Adjutant), G.E. Chadwick, H.S. Bull, G.R. Treadwell, C.L. Purves, A.C. Trimmer, H.E. Wood; Lieutenants H.J.C. Mackarness, E.H. Trimmer, C.G. Wood, T.P. Watson, E.F. Smith, H. Debenham, J.C. Gilbert, F.C. Cocks, J.K. Varvill, C. Davidson (Quartermaster); 2nd Lieutenants W.R. Marshall, R.N.O. Bartlett, O.A. Watt, C.N.B. Hurt, W.A. Harris, P.L. Bathurst, J.H. Watson, R.G. Grant, R.N. Galloway. Both sailed (16th June). *Nile* arrived Alexandria 6 a.m. (26th) then to Lemnos (27th). "C" and "D" Companies disembarked and marched to bivouacs about one mile from Mudros Harbour. Battalion records note that there were no tents and the men had to camp on hard rough ground. No transport was available and all stores and baggage had to be man-handled.

JULY
Ausonia arrived (2nd). Crossed to Gallipoli (6th) and landed "V" Beach dawn (7th). Marched to dug-outs in cliff side above "W" Beach. Lance-Corporal J. Howarth drowned while bathing (8th). Relieved 6th King's Own in reserve line (Eski Line) during evening. Relieved 6th Loyal North Lancashire in support and front line trenches (9th) – positions in 88th Brigade, 29th Division sector extreme left of British Line. Battalion records note "Turkish sell-fire appeared to do little harm." Flies, however, were a problem – "It was always a fight as to whether you, or they, got your food first and it wasn't always you who won." Relieved (15th) and to Eski Line. To rest area on Gully Beach (16th). Sir Ian Hamilton met the Battalion (17th) and mentions in his book *Gallipoli Diary* how impressed he was by the men's "physique and class." Moved forward to Achi Baba Nullah sector

(18th) and attached to Royal Naval Division. Positions (captured from Turks) noted as not being as good as those previously held. Much work carried out strengthening line. Large numbers of unburied dead from action fought a few days before. Enemy bombardment recorded as "severe" – "D" Company's trenches badly hit (21st). Withdrew to bivouacs. Moved forward to front line positions – western branch, Achi Baba Nullah (22nd). Relieved (29th) and to dug-outs in Krithia Nullah. Position noted as being in full view of the enemy on Achi Baba – "any activity here drew shell-fire." Ordered to withdraw 10 p.m. (31st). Moved to "V" Beach, boarded mine-sweepers and crossed to Mudros. Casualties for period on Helles – 12.

AUGUST
Embarked *Osmanieh* (4th). Landed Watson's Pier, Anzac Cove early morning (5th) and marched along beach to Victoria Gully. Heavy shelling 7 – 11 a.m. (6th). Lieutenant H.J.C. Mackarness wounded. Regimental history records how Captain Gayer had a narrow escape – a shell-case hitting the ground between his legs without touching him. Further casualties during bombardment 5.30 – 6 p.m. Moved along beach to Reserve Gully below The Sphinx (7th) and later in afternoon to bivouacs near No. 3 Post. Now in reserve to New Zealand troops. Position noted as "uncomfortable" – bullets dropping among the men throughout the night. Moved forward early (8th) to Chailak Dere then at dusk to Bauchop's Hill – Turkish positions captured by New Zealanders on 6th August. Attack on Chunuk Bair (9th). Moved forward early morning – original rought over Cheshire Ridge into Aghyl Dere found to be crowded with returning wounded and difficult. Turned around and after reconnaissance by Captain G.E. Chadwick crossed into Aghyl Dere and moved forward. Regimental history records . . . "at daybreak they were still strung out along the ravine. All could hear the British bombardment, but at 5.15 a.m., the hour of assault, General Baldwin's column (Commander, 38th Brigade) had not arrived in its place of deployment." Leading companies reached start position by 6 a.m. – under heavy fire from enemy position on crest immediately north of Chunuk Bair and machine guns in a cornfield on eastern side of The Farm advanced across open land. First casualties included Captain A.E. Gayer (wounded) and Captain C.G. Lutyens while leading "C" Company. Regimental history records that this officer apologized to his commanding officer for having been wounded. He died latter at a dressing station. Colonel Cole-Hamilton received mortal wounds while leading his battalion, Major Trent (2nd in Command) severely wounded. "A", "B" and "C" Companies checked by fire from hidden ravine between them and objective. "D" Company under Captain H.S. Bull on right made some advance but forced to halt upon

reaching an almost sheer cliff. Relieved by party of 10th Hampshire at dusk and fell back to edge of Farm Plateau. Later assembled in Aghyl Dere. Enemy attacked 4.45 a.m. (10th) – General Baldwin's line forced back to Aghyl Dere – survivors of Battalion covering withdrawal. Artillery fire checked Turkish advance and forced retreat across the Farm Plateau. Captain A.C. Trimmer is noted as putting his machine guns to good use and Captain Bull for his "skill and courage." Strength now just about 100 men. Officer casualties – Colonel A.R. Cole-Hamilton; Captain C.G. Lutyens; Lieutenants C.G. Wood, H. Debenham, E.H. Trimmer, killed or mortally wounded. Majors F.H. Trent, H.B. McCormick; Captains A.E. Gayer, A.C. Trimmer; Lieutenants R.N.O. Bartlett, E.F. Smith, J.K. Varvill; 2nd Lieutenants J.H. Watson, C.N.B. Hurt, R.N. Galloway wounded. Position entrenched. Drafts arrived from Mudros (15th). Carried out two tours of duty in front line then relieved by 1/5th Bedfordshire (29th). Marched along beach to Suvla (31st) and to bivouacked on shoreward side of Lala Baba.

SEPTEMBER
To bivouacs at Ghazi Baba (1st) – strength 7 officers, 311 other ranks. Employed on beach fatigues. To reserve positions foot of Hill 10 (21st). Employed on road-making. Moved to reserve positions behind Chocolate Hill (30th). Strength – 7 officers, 544 other ranks.

OCTOBER
Major W.J.C. Luddington arrived and relieved Captain Bell from command (2nd). To front line on Green Hill (14th). Drafts arrived (24th). Strength – 21 officers, 741 other ranks.

NOVEMBER
Continued tours of duty – front line Green Hill, reserve line Chocolate Hill.

DECEMBER
Nine men killed from shelling while at Chocolate Hill (11th). "A" Company withdrew to Lala Baba (12th) and commenced work on beach defences. Remainder of battalion to Salt Lake line (13th). Embarked for Lemnos during evening (18th).

THE DUKE OF WELLINGTON'S (WEST RIDING REGIMENT)

"Suvla" "Landing at Suvla" "Scimitar Hill" "Gallipoli,1915"

8TH (SERVICE) BATTALION

JULY
Witley Camp, Godalming, Surrey. Part of 32nd Brigade, 11th (Northern) Division. Entrained at Milford for Liverpool (2nd). Embarked *Aquitania* and sailed (3rd). Ship attacked by enemy submarine (4th), torpedo missed by about 8 feet. Arrived Mudros Harbour, Lemnos 7 a.m. (10th). Disembarked (11th) and to bivouacs. Sailed *Rowan* for Imbros (22nd). Arrived (23rd) and to bivouacs.

AUGUST
To Suvla Bay (6th). Landed "B" Beach and moved forward in attack on Lala Baba. War Diary notes Battalion as being heavily engaged during night and day with heavy losses. Withdrew to rest area on beach (8th). Later moved forward and dug in near the Sulajik huts. Took part in advance on Tekke Tepe Ridge (9th). High casualties – Commanding Officer – Lieutenant-Colonel H.J. Johnson and Second-in-Command killed. Later withdrew to reserve positions near The Cut. In action (10th) – few casualties. Relieved from reserve trenches (11th) and to beach area, Moved forward to trenches Chocolate Hill (13th). Bombed by Turkish aeroplane (17th). Relieved and to beach area (19th). Attack on Ismail Oglu Tepe (21st). Official History of the Gallipoli Campaign records that the Battalion, with 9th West Yorkshire, were hurried forward to capture first objective, but they swung left-handed. Ending up in position north of Hetman Chair. An attempt was then made to assault a communication trench, but this turned out to be a heavily defended fire trench. "The enemy's resistance could not be overcome; and the troops fell back towards the southern slopes of Green Hill." War Diary records "high casualties." Held position under heavy artillery fire until relieved (23rd). Left beach area for trenches below Jephson's Post (27th).

SEPTEMBER
War Diary records failed Turkish attack (3rd). Relieved and to beach area

(4th). To Jephson's Post (12th). Relieved and to reserve trenches – Karakol Dagh (18th). Releived by 8th Northumberland Fusiliers and moved back to beach area (29th).

OCTOBER
Moved to reserve trenches (2nd). To trenches below Jephson's Post – Green Lane (18th). War Diary records Working parties troubled by snipers" throughout month. Casualties – 7 killed (including Second-Lieutenant B.A. Franks), 34 wounded.

NOVEMBER
Second-Lieutenant J.H. Henderson killed by sniper (2nd). Second-Lieutenant E.C. Bladon killed (3rd). Sixteen other casualties from sniper fire. Relieved by 6th Yorkshire (3rd) and to dug-outs below Preston Ridge in Brigade Reserve. War Diary records sever cases of frost bite reported (28th). Casualties while in reserve – 1 killed, 12 wounded.

DECEMBER
Second-Lieutenant J.R. Lister (11th Battalion attached) killed (15th). Part of Battalion (8 officers, 600 other ranks) under Captain G.S. Edwards evacuated to Imbros (18th). Remainder left (19th) – 100 men under Second-Lieutenant W.F. Clarke holding second line defences during operation. December casualties – 2 killed, 17 wounded. War Diary records one man "heart failure" and another wounded "self inflicted."

The Border Regiment

"Helles" "Landing at Helles" "Krithia" "Suvla" "Landing at Suvla"

"Scimitar Hill" "Gallipoli,1915-16"

1st Battalion

MARCH

Rugby, Warwickshire. Part of 87th Brigade, 29th Division. To Avonmouth and 26 officers, 887 other ranks embarked *Andania* (17th). Transport – 1 officer, 115 other ranks, embarked *Duke of Edinburgh*. Sailed during evening. Officers – Lieutenant-Colonel R.O.C. Hume (Commanding Officer); Major C.D. Vaughan, DSO (Second in Command); Captains A.J. Ellis (Adjutant), J. Forbes-Robertson (Transport Officer); Lieutenants W. Ennis (Quartermaster), J.G. Heyder (Machine Gun Officer). K.G. Hearne (Medical Officer). "A" Company: Major G.C. Brooke, Captain R. Head, Lieutenant J.T.B. Dinwiddie, Second-Lieutenant W. Clague. "B" Company: Captains G.A. Morton, R.H.H. Moore; Second-Lieutenants J.H. Proctor, A. Wright, C.S. Cay. "C" Company: Captains S.H.F. Muriel, G.H. Harrison; Lieutenants G.C. May, D.A. James, F.I.L. Perry; Second-Lieutenant J.S. Kennedy. "D" Company: Captains H. Nelson, F.H.S. Le Mesurier, H.E. Festing; Lieutenant R.B. Taylor; Second-Lieutenant W.G. Bartholomew. Arrived Malta (24th). Sailed for Egypt (26th). Arrived Alexandria (28th). Disembarked (30th) and to Mex Camp.

APRIL

To Alexandria (8th) and embarked *Andania*. Strength – 26 officers, 927 other ranks. Sailed for Lemnos (10th). Arrived Mudros Bay (12th) and remained on board ship. Sailed for Gallipoli (24th). Landed "X" Beach, Helles (25th). "B" Company ordered forward to support 2nd Royal Fusiliers attack on Hill 114. Later, these troops were forced to retire and when the enemy were within 120 yards of the beach"C" Company with part of "D" went forward. Lieutenant-General Sir William Marshall, then commanding 87th Brigade, recalls . . . "I ordered the Borders to charge, and over the cliff-edge they went with ringing cheers. The enemy fired heavily, causing some 50 casualties, but not waiting for the bayonet they fled in every direction." Advance continued to the east for over 600 yards. "A" Company attacked north east of beach, gaining some 1,000 yards before digging in.

Casualties – Major Vaughan and Lieutenant James killed, Lieutenant Bartholomew mortally wounded, 3 other officers wounded, 25 other ranks killed, 78 wounded. General Marshall records one man of 1st Border Regiment reporting that he had found a land-mine in the Turkish trenches. It turned out to be a dead tortoise. Positions held under heavy sniper fire (26th-27th). Attack on Krithia (28th). Moved forward 8 a.m. – "A" Company in firing line, "B" in support, "C" and "D" in reserve. In his history of the Border Regiment, Colonel H.C. Wylly notes that Gully Ravine, 500 yards north of the Battalion, was crossed without opposition and advance continued. Enemy seen falling back over ridge north west of Krithia and Battalion opened fire at 1,000 yards. Soon, Turks holding trenches 600 yards to the front opened with rifle and machine gun fire. Colonel Wylly records "casualties at once occurred and soon became alarmingly high." Enemy moved closer and withdrawal ordered to some 200 yards south of trenches held by 1st King's Own Scottish Borderers. Fell back further 300 yards after dark. Casualties – Major Brooke, Captains Head and Muriel, Lieutenant Taylor killed; Colonel Hume mortally wounded; 5 officers wounded; 26 other ranks killed, 131 wounded. Withdrew to Gully Beach in Brigade Reserve (30th).

MAY
Moved forward via Sniper's Hut to support line Achi Baba (1st). Formed up for attack dawn (3rd). Charge led by Captain Morton met heavy fire. Regimental History records that Captain Morton, with Lieutenant Perry, were killed within 5 yards of Turkish line. Survivors, just 6 men, held out for over half an hour in a shallow trench before making their way back one at a time. Battalion later withdrew to Gully Beach. Took part in general advance over next 5 days. Regimental History notes casualties mostly in "A" Company. Withdrew from forward area (8th) and to Divisional Reserve near "X" Beach (9th). Drafts arrived – 13 officers, 130 other ranks.

JUNE
Moved forward to trenches near White House (4th), firing line south east side of Gully Ravine (5th). Party led by Second-Lieutenant Wallace raided enemy line (10th). Some 200 yards of communication trench taken with bomb and bayonet. "D" Company followed and held and consolidated gains throughout night. Enemy counter attack early hours (12th) and regained captured line. Captain R.H.H. Moore led charge and retook trench. Casualties – Captain Moore killed, 3 officers wounded, 12 other ranks killed, 33 wounded. Relieved (12th) and to Gully Beach. To support trenches near White House (17th). Detachments sent forward as reinforcements to 1st

Royal Inniskilling Fusiliers during enemy attack on Turky Trench and trench H11 (18th-19th). Relieved 1st Royal Inniskilling Fusiliers in firing line (20th). Relieved and to Gully Beach (23rd), front line – Turkey Trench (27th). Attack on Boomerang Redoubt and enemy section of Turkey Trench (28th). Charged forward 11a.m. – "B" Company entered Boomerang Redoubt with little loss. Regimental history records that the enemy were cleared "with bomb, bayonet and butt." Supports followed – Lieutenant Dyer and several men killed. "A" Company came under heavy fire from enemy trench running between Turkey Trench and H12. Regimental history records that every man of assaulting part became a casualty. Gains consolidated, 64 prisoners taken. General Sir Ian Hamilton referred to the attack . . . "At 10.45 a small Turkish advanced work in the Saghir Dere known as the Boomerang Redoubt was assaulted. This little fort, which was very strongly sited and protected by extra strong wire entanglements, had long been a source of trouble. After special bombardment by trench mortars, and while bombardment of surrounding trenches was at its height, part of The Border Regiment at the exact moment prescribed leapt from their trenches as one man, *like a pack of hounds and, pouring out of cover, raced across* and took the work most brilliantly." Battalion advanced and dug in on reverse slope of ridge. Enemy counter attacks beaten of throughout night. Casualties – 2 officers killed, 7 wounded, 153 other ranks killed, wounded or missing. Relieved and to support line – trenches J10 and J11 (29th). "C" Company to firing line (30th).

JULY
Relieved 1st Royal Inniskilling Fusiliers in firing line (2nd). Headquarters in ravine just west of trench J12 which was later named "Border Ravine." Relieved (7th) and to Gully Beach. Moved to "V" Beach (11th) and embarked *Renard* for Mudros. "D" Company embarked *Queen Victoria*, remainder *Prince Edward* (21st) and sailed for Gallipoli. Landed "V" Beach, Cape Helles (22nd) and bivouacked on "X" Beach. Moved forward to front line – Gully Ravine sector (23rd) taking over firing line – Border Barricade and part of J11B. War Diary records trenches as requiring a lot of work. Parapets in most places were not bullet proof, trenches too narrow and shallow, no proper snipers loopholes and "sanitary arrangements non existent." Relieved (30th) and to "Y" Ravine. "C" Company remained in as garrison to trench J10.

AUGUST
To forward area (1st) – firing line running from the sea through Fusilier Bluff to barricade in trench J13; reserve line – Trolley Ravine;

Headquarters – Border Ravine. War Diary records (4th) an attempt by
G.O.C. Division to contact the enemy via an interpreter. Firing ceased
along front and 2 khaki flags were waved from 1st Border line. These were
waved for some 20 minutes but the enemy ignored them and opened fire
of the position with a mountain battery. Relieved by 2nd Royal Fusiliers at
Fusilier Bluff and to "X" Beach (16th). Later to "V" Beach and embarked
for Suvla Bay. Landed early (17th) and to bivouacs near Punar. Moved
forward during evening and attached to 158th and 159th Brigades (53rd
Division) in Sulajik sector. Later withdrew to Azmak Dere. Attack on
Scimitar Hill (21st). Advanced in support of 1st Royal Inniskilling Fusiliers
3.30 p.m. – "C" and "D" Companies leading, "A" in support, "B" in
reserve. Message received from Second-Lieutenant Armstrong of "D"
Company about 5 p.m. reporting that he was within 50 yards of summit
and in need of support. Regimental history records that casualty figures
were mounting – by 6.15 p.m. only Lieutenant Clague remained
unwounded out of the 15 officers that had gone into action. By 8 p.m. survivors of scattered companies formed line below crest of hill. Battalion
later ordered to retire. Lieutenant Clague's party held on in forward position until ordered to retire during early hours (22nd). Relieved during
night (22nd) and moved back to reserve positions. Casualties – 14 officers
wounded, 38 other ranks killed, 274 wounded, 64 missing. Working party
to "A" Beach (27th) and shelled on way. No 11 Platoon, "C" Company
loosing 6 killed, 11 wounded by a single shell. Later to bivouacks just north
of "A" Beach. To forward area reserve line near One Tree Gully (29th).
One company in firing line.

SEPTEMBER
War Diary notes during first week the official naming of Jephson's Post,
Bench Mark, Kidney Hill, Chocolate Hill, Scimitar Hill, "W" Hill and Hill
60. Newfoundland Regiment attached for instruction (21st). Relieved
(22nd) and to Border Gully. Sailed *Ermine* for Imbros (24th). Landed and
to camp at Kephalos.

OCTOBER
Returned to Cape Helles (2nd), landing "W" Beach and to rest camp
attached to 52nd (Lowland) Division. Began work construction new winter
quarters. To forward area Achi Baba Nullah – Horseshoe sector (15th).
Second line – Parsons Road. War Diary records firing line being between 40
to 120 yards from enemy. Trenches narrow, parapets not bullet proof and
fire steps so low as to be impossible to fire over the parapet. Relieved (19th)
– 1 company Parsons Road, remainder in Divisional Reserve at Eski Line.

Relieved (24th) and to rest camp. War Diary notes camp unsafe due to enemy shell fire from Asia Minor. Also received new issue of clothing, the first since leaving England.

NOVEMBER
Relieved 1st Royal Inniskilling Fusiliers in reserve at Brown house, Eski Line (1st). Began work on parapets – Oxford and Central Streets. Took over firing line – right sub-section from 2nd South Wales Borderers (4th). War Diary notes action (8th) of Sergeant J. Cooper who having instructed the men on his right and left to cease firing, climbed over the parapet and ran towards the enemy. Having covered some 120 yards to the Turkish parapet, he . . . "coolly emptied his magazine into the trench below him." Sergeant Cooper returned to his line unhurt and reported that he had shot five of the enemy. Relieved and to rest camp (8th). Began work on winter quarters on cliffs between "W" and "X" Beaches. Relieved 1st Inniskilling Fusiliers in firing line (16th). Relieved by 2nd South Wales Borderers in Horseshoe sector (20th) and moved back to Eski Line. One company at Parsons Road. Relieved and to rest camp (26th).

DECEMBER
To reserve at Eski Line and Parsons Road (3rd). Relieved 2nd South Wales Borderers in firing line – trench E11 (6th). Relieved by Howe Battalion and to rest camp (9th). Relieved 1st Inniskilling Fusiliers in firing line – Northern and Southern Barricade sector (18th). Companies in Fusilier Street and Eski Line. Relieved (27th) and to Eski Line in reserve. Employed on New Fusilier Street and Mule Track. To firing line (30th) – support at Russel's Loop, Weavers Venell.

JANUARY, 1916
Relieved and to rest camp (3rd). To beach defences – "W" Beach (7th). Covered evacuation at "W" Beach during night (8th) – "A" Company around Bakery Gully, "B" near the cemetery, "C" at Hunter Western Hill, "D" in support. Ammunition dump at "W" Beach blown up – 5 men injured by falling debris. Battalion left via No. 2 Pier on *Staunch* for Mudros.

6TH (SERVICE) BATTALION

JUNE
Frensham Camp, Surrey. Part of 33rd Brigade, 11th (Northern) Division. To Farnham and entrained for Liverpool (30th). Embarked *Empress of Britain*.

JULY
Sailed (1st). Arrived Malta (8th) then to Alexandria (10th). Arrived (12th), left for Lemnos (16th), arriving Mudros Harbour (18th). Embarked *Whitley Castle* and *Partridge* for Gallipoli (20th). Landed Helles via beached *River Clyde* (21st). First party came ashore safely, remainder heavily shelled and forced to fall back until nightfall. Moved forward to positions about 3 miles from Achi Baba. Provided carrying parties to front line tenches and to and from beach area. Some 50 enemy shells records as landing within an area of approx. 100 yards by 50. Casualties – 2 killed, 1 wounded. Moved forward to Brown House – Eski Line in reserve (25th). Relieved 6th Lincolnshire on either side of Achi Baba Nullah (27th). Line held from left to right by "C", "D" and "A" Companies with "B" in reserve. "A" Company's position recorded as being The Horseshoe. War Diary records (29th) Turk shot by Sergeant Gibson at range of 200 yards. The body later being thrown out of the trench along with rifle and equipment. Relieved and to rest camp (30th). Embarked for Imbros (31st).

AUGUST
Embarked for Suvla Bay (6th). Officers present – Lieutenant-Colonel G.F. Broadrick (Commanding); Major A.M. Caulfield, D.S.O.; Captain G. Darwell (Adjutant), Lieutenant E. O'B. White (Quartermaster); Lieutenant L. Skene (R.A.M.C.); Second-Lieutenant R.P. Cowen (Signals), Lieutenant B.F. Crewdson (Machine Guns). "A" Company: Captain C.A. Cuningham. Lieutenant J.A. Dixon, Second Lieutenants H.W. Hill and H.B. de Montmorency. "B" Company: Captain A.F.C. Rutherfoord; Lieutenants R.P. Gilbanks and G.K. Leach. "C" Company: Major F.C. March, Captain H. Johnson, Lieutenant W.A. Welsh, Second-Lieutenants R.N. Carr and W.S. Ross. "D" Company: Captains B. McAuley and F.C. Clegg, Lieutenant N. Oxland, Second-Lieutenants C.R. Darwell and G.A. Collingwood. Landed "B" Beach and to Divisional Reserve positions at Lala Baba. Casualties from shelling – 1 killed, 22 wounded. Moved forward via north side of Salt Lake 5.30 p.m. (7th). In close support of 6th Lincolnshire took part in attack on Chocolate Hill. Moved from top of Chocolate Hill to reserve positions on beach behind Lala Baba (8th). Casualties – 4 killed, 53 wounded, 3 missing. Moved forward to positions under Chocolate Hill (9th). Advanced for attack on Ismail Oglu Tepe 5.15 a.m. – "C" and "D" Companies in front, "A" and "B" in reserve. Soon came under fire from Scimitar Hill. Records show that advancing troops (6th Border, 7th South Staffordshire, 6th Lincolnshire) had been informed that Scimitar Hill was held by British troops. "A" and "B" suffered heavy casualties – all officers except one being killed. Survivors moved forward to firing line. Battalion

collected along road near Torgut Cheshme and held position. Roll call at dawn (10th) – 5 officers, 120 other ranks. Casualties Major F.C. March; Captains C.A. Cuningham, A.F.C. Rutherfoord, B. McAuley; Lieutenants J.A. Dixon, R.P. Gilbanks, G.K. Leach, N. Oxland; Second-Lieutenants H.W. Hill, A.J.K. McCausland, C.R. Darwell, G.A. Collingwood and 26 other ranks killed; 5 officers, 241 other ranks wounded; 1 officer, 131 other ranks missing. Losses included almost all senior N.C.Os. Relieved and to reserve area at Lala Baba (12th). To firing line – Chocolate Hill (18th). Relieved by 1st Royal Dublin Fusiliers and to Lala Baba (20th). Went into action (21st) – strength 483 all ranks. Advanced behind 9th Sherwood Foresters – "A" Company met strong fire when about level with Chocolate Hill. "C" and "D" Companies moved to right and took enemy redoubt. Advance continued to base of Green Hill. Positions held. Relieved at night-fall (22nd) and to reserve line running from south east corner of Salt Lake to the sea. Casualties – Lieutenant-Colonel G.F. Broadrick, Captain F.C. Clegg, Second-Lieutenant F.B.D. Stalker and 12 other ranks killed; 2 officers and 56 other ranks wounded; 32 missing. Formed composite battalion with 6th Lincolnshire. To Karakol Dagh (27th), firing line – Jephson's Post (28th), support line (30th).

SEPTEMBER
To firing line (5th). Releived (12th) and to rest camp at West Beach. To forward area – support line 300 yards north of Shaftesbury Avenue (21st). Separated from 6th Lincolnshire (23rd). Began work on Green Lane (24th). Relieved 6th Lincolnshire in firing line (28th). Line extended to include Jephson's Post (30th).

OCTOBER
Engaged enemy at Green Knoll (3rd-6th). Relieved from firing line by 7th South Staffordshire (7th) and to Brigade Reserve at Shaftesbury Avenue. To Divisional Reserve at Lizard's Tail (20th), "A" Beach (31st).

NOVEMBER
Took over firing line – Jephson's Post (11th). "D" Company moved to support line – Preston Ridge (12th). Relieved by 7th South Staffordshire (24th) and to support and reserve lines. Many cases of frost-bite and exposure due to severe weather conditions during last week.

DECEMBER
Embarked *Huntsgreen* for Imbros (18th).

THE ROYAL SUSSEX REGIMENT

"Suvla" "Landing at Suvla" "Scimitar Hill" "Gallipoli,1915"

1/4TH BATTALION (T.F.)

JULY
Bedford, Bedfordshire. Part of 160th Brigade, 53rd (Welsh) Division. Entrained for Devonport (16th). Sailed *Ulysses* (17th). Arrived Alexandria, Egypt (28th) and to Port Said (30th).

AUGUST
Sailed for Lemnos (4th). Arrived Mudros Bay (7th). Sailed for Imbros (8th). Arrived 2 p.m. then to Suvla Bay 6.15 p.m., landing "C" Beach after midnight. To Divisional Reserve positions near Lala Baba (9th). Attached to 33rd Brigade and ordered forward to Chocolate Hill 11 a.m. Advanced in support of 2/4th Queen's attack on Scimitar Hill. Came under heavy shell fire and enfilade fire from right. Scrub caught fire and withdrawal ordered to former Turkish trenches running south from Sulajik 3.30 p.m. Casualties – 1 officer and 11 other ranks killed, 3 officers, 60 other ranks wounded. Withdrew to support trenches (11th). Rejoined 160th Brigade at "C" Beach (12th). Moved forward and relieved 1/5th Royal Welsh Fusiliers in trenches – Sulajik sector facing Scimitar Hill (13th). Relieved by 1/5th Welsh and to rest camp at "A" Beach (31st).

SEPTEMBER
To forward trenches Kiretch Tepe Sirt (4th), rest camp at Suvla Bay (12th). To trenches Sulajik sector (16th). Relieved (19th) and to Salt Lake line. Began fatigues Lala Baba area. To "A" Section Reserve area (24th). Heavy shelling (26th) – 2 killed, 9 wounded.

OCTOBER
To Salt Lake Line (2nd), dug outs eastern slope of Lala Baba (5th). Began fatigues under Royal Engineers. War Diary records strength (20th) as 17 officers, 197 other ranks. Temporarily amalgamated with 2/4th Queens (21st). Strength (31st) – 12 officers, 282 other ranks.

NOVEMBER

To dug outs southern slope Lala Baba (1st). Worked on communications and defence of Lala Baba throughout month.

DECEMBER

In dug outs, southern slope Lala Baba. Fatigues as for November. Received orders to evacuate Peninsular (13th). Moved to South Pier and embarked *El Kahirah*. Sailed for Mudros.

The Hampshire Regiment

"Helles" "Landing at Helles" "Krithia" "Suvla" "Sari Bair" "Landing at Suvla" "Scimitar Hill" "Gallipoli,1915-16"

2ND BATTALION

MARCH

Warwick, Warwickshire. Part of 88th Brigade, 29th Division. Entrained for Avonmouth (20th). Embarked – "W" and "X" Companies with Headquarters *Aragon* (sailed 21st), "Y" and "Z" Companies *Manitou* (sailed 20th), Transport *Tintorette* (sailed 20th). Strength: Officers – Lieutenant-Colonel H. Carrington-Smith (Commanding); Majors E. Leigh, J.H. Deane, A.T. Beckwith; Captains A.C. Addison, H.J. de C. Wymer, B.S. Parker, W. Penn-Gaskell, E.A. Corner, C.L. Boxall, O.H.L. Day (Transport Officer), R.O. Spencer-Smith, G.W. Reid (Adjutant); Lieutenants G.A. Rosser (Machine Gun Officer), C.R. Smith, G.V.T. Webb, F.A. Silk, J. White, C.J.W. Pakenham, A. Smith (Quartermaster); Second-Lieutenants C.C. Harland, R.B. Gillet, G.R.D. Moor, A. Howard, R.P. Lord, H. Parker. Lieutenant H.F. Panton (R.A.M.C., Medical Officer). Other ranks – 993.

APRIL

Arrived Alexandria (2nd) and to camp at Mustapha Pasha, Barracks. Entrained for Alexandria (9th) and embarked *Aragon* 2.30 p.m. Arrived Lemnos (13th). Remained in Mudros Harbour. Headquarters, "Y" and "Z" Companies transferred to *Alaunia* (21st) and sailed for Tenedos (23rd). Transferred to *River Clyde* (24th) and sailed for Gallipoli. *River Clyde* arrived off Cape Helles dawn (25th) and run ashore on "V" Beach between Cape Helles and Sedd el Bahr. Heavy casualties on landing – many men hit while wading ashore in shoulder-deep water, most of the wounded being drowned. "W" and "X" Companies, on *Aragon*, landed "W" Beach between Cape Helles and Tekke Burnu. Seven killed, 18 wounded, 3 missing during landing. Lieutenant-Colonel Carrington-Smith shot by sniper on bridge of *River Clyde*. "Y" and "Z" Companies attacked and cleared village and fort of Sedd el Bahr by nightfall (26th). "W" and "X" Companies took Hill 138. Captain Addison and 8 men killed, 2 officers, 33 men wounded. "Y" and "Z" Companies relieved from Sedd el Bahr (27th) and joined rest of Battalion at Hill 138. Then moved forward to positions astride Krithia Road. Captain Boxall died of wounds. Continued advance (28th) – French on right counter attacked and retired. Whole line then withdrew to start positions. Major Deane, Lieutenants Pakenham and Howard, 53 other ranks killed; 4 officers and 246 other ranks wounded, 46 missing. Second-Lieutenant Parker died of wounds (29th). Relieved by French troops (30th) and withdrew to reserve positions at Morto Bay.

MAY
Relieved 1st Essex in firing line (1st) – right on track leading to Krithia, left on Krithia Nullah. Enemy attacked during night and entered left of support line. War Diary records a "bogus message" being passed – "All officers on left." In his history of the Royal Hampshire Regiment, C.T. Atkinson recalls the affair and suggests that the cry was probably from an English-speaking German. Rushing to the left Major Leigh and Captain Reid, along with 2 Royal Artillery officers, were killed. Moved forward towards Krithia (2nd). Advanced under heavy shrapnel fire 10 a.m. and after 500 yards met by heavy fire and forced to withdraw to start positions. Casualties – 22 killed and missing, 91 wounded. To reserve near Morto Bay (4th). Advanced up Fir Tree Spur between Krithia Nullah and Gully Ravine 11 a.m. (6th). Halted west of Fir Tree Wood and consolidated gains. Casualties – 6 killed, 55 wounded. Orders received 5 p.m. (8th) for Battalion "to advance and go in with bayonet." Moved forward and soon came under fire from machine guns in hidden trenches. Held on to forward position throughout night but forced to withdraw before dawn. Casualties – 6 killed, 94 wounded, Captain Hodson and 21 men missing. Relieved by Australian troops (9th) and to reserve positions north of Sedd el Bahr. Strength – 4 officers, 204 other ranks. C.T. Atkinson records casualty figures up to and including 14th May – 11 officers killed, 12 wounded, 1 invalided; 198 other ranks killed, missing or died of wounds, 507 wounded. To firing line 200 yards north-west of Fire Tree Wood (16th). Began improvements to trenches. Draft of 1 officer and 46 men arrived (17th). Line advanced some 100 yards during night (17th/18th). War Diary records (24th) that company in front line saw "Turks engaged in a violent quarrel and hitting each other with picks." Relieved and to Pink Farm (25th). Casualties since (16th) – 18 killed and missing, 28 wounded. Draft of 5 officers and 28 other ranks arrived (26th). Party of 1/10th Manchester attached for instruction (27th). To reserve trenches about 2 miles south-west of Krithia (30th). Began work digging communication trenches. "X" and "Y" Companies to firing line south-east of Fir Tree Wood during evening (31st).

JUNE
Party of 14 officers attached (1st). Took over positions to right of 88th

Brigade – Fir Tree Wood (3rd). Attack on enemy trenches (4th) – "X" and "Y" Companies moved forward under heavy fire 11.45 a.m. First 2 trenches, H8 and H9 taken with some 30 prisoners. Supporting companies, "W" and "Z" came forward 12.15 p.m. and moving through leading companies took trench H10 and south-east end of H11. Advance continued and another trench taken during afternoon. Forward area became untenable and Battalion forced to fall back to H11. Casualties – 3 officers and 25 other ranks killed, 11 officers, 43 other ranks wounded, 1 officer, 31 other ranks missing. War Diary records (6th) that no Regular Army officers remained. Battalion now under command of Second-Lieutenant G.R.D. Moor of 3rd (Reserve) Battalion, aged 18 years. Enemy counter attacked about 3 a.m. (6th) – "Battalion held firm despite retirement on left." C.T. Atkinson records Battalion being forced to throw back its right due to loss of trenches G11 and G12 by 42nd Division. On the left the enemy had forced its way between 2nd Royal Fusiliers and 1st King's Own Scottish Borders where 1 company of 1st Essex had come forward. C.T. Atkinson records "a disorganised mass of men was being pressed back against the Royal Fusiliers' left . . . officerless men were retreating in confusion." Seeing the situation, and noting the danger to the line, Second-Lieutenant Moor left his trench and ran across the open. Confronting the men he then stemmed the retirement by use of his revolver – he was forced to shoot several men. After this he led the men back to their former line and successfully recaptured the lost trench. For his bravery and resource Second-Lieutenant George Raymond Dallas Moor was awarded the Victoria Cross. Relieved 4 p.m. (7th) and to support trenches at Twelve Tree Copse. Casualties – 2 officers, 1 man killed, 2 officers, 26 men wounded. Strength – 6 officers, 188 other ranks. Relieved and to Gully Beach (10th). Relieved 1/5th King's Own Scottish Borderers in reserve trenches during night (13th). Draft of 6 officers and 360 other ranks arrived (15th). War Diary records (17th) burial of 8 dead from K.O.S.B. and Royal Fusiliers – it being impossible to remove identity discs due to advance state of decomposition. Relieved by 1/7th Scottish Rifles and to "Y" Beach (19th). Battalion under constant shelling from Asia Minor. Moved to firing line – trench H11 (24th), reserve trenches behind Twelve Tree Copse (27th), firing line – Turkey Trench (28th). War Diary notes successful attacks by 87th, 86th and Indian Brigades on right and left. Advanced 11 p.m. to relieved 1/7th Scottish Rifles and 1/4th Royal Scots in trenches H12A and H12. War Diary notes confused relief due to trenches being crowded with dead and wounded from both sides. Enemy counter attacked during relief. Casualties – 13 killed, 27 wounded, 2 missing. Began work digging trench to link up H12 and H12A.

JULY
Attacks on Turkish sections of H12 and H12A by "X" and "W" Companies
(2nd). Some 20 yards gained in each and barricades constructed. Enemy
bombing attack during evening. Casualties – 4 killed, 2 wounded. "Y" and
"Z" Companies relieved "X" and "W" at barricades (3rd). Casualties during
day – 6 killed, 23 wounded. Relieved (4th) and to "Y" Beach. Casualties –
16 wounded. Took over firing line west end of trench H12 and East end
trench J11 (7th). Company of 1/5th Argyll and Sutherland Highlanders
attached for 48 hours instruction (7th). Company of 6th Loyal North
Lancashire attached for 24 hours instruction (9th), Company of 6th East
Lancashire attached for instruction (10th). War Diary (11th) records 40,000
rounds of enemy fire drawn by cheering and waving bayonets etc. Three
machine guns located. Relieved (16th) and marched via "X" Beach to "V"
Beach. Casualties since (7th) – 10 killed, 40 wounded. Embarked *El Kahirah*
for Lemnos 3 a.m. (17th). Arrived 10 a.m. Received draft of 4 officers and
300 other ranks. Strength now 24 officers, 732 other ranks. Embarked
Newmarket 2 p.m. (28th). Landed "W" Beach 11.30 p.m. and to Brigade
Reserve bivouacs on Gully Beach. Began work on road along beach. News
of Second-Lieutenant Moor's award of Victoria Cross received (29th).

AUGUST
Moved forward to firing line east of Gully Ravine (3rd). Attack on trenches
H12A and H13 (6th). Went forward 3.50 p.m. C.T. Atkinson records
Battalion advancing in 4 waves and reaching a low crest 50 yards to the front
with little loss. Then machine gun fire swept the lines causing heavy casualties. Guns from across the Krithia Nullah to the right are recorded as doing
particular damage. Few men reached Turkish lines, parties from "Z"
Company entering H12A and a small number H13. Unable to hold their
gains the men were overcome by large numbers of the enemy and forced to
retire. Casualties during attack – 18 officers, 224 other ranks killed and
missing, 2 officers, 210 other ranks wounded. Wounded remained out in the
open until nightfall when those able crawled back to their lines. Throughout
the night tremendous courage was shown by many in brining in the
wounded. During the morning Captain K.M. Levi (Australian Medical
Corps attached) who had worked all night was killed in the dressing station
by a shell. Relieved (7th) and to Gully Beach. Strength – 6 officers, about
400 other ranks. Draft of 250 men lost through torpedoing of *Royal Edward*
(13th). To firing line – "H" trenches (14th). Moved to front line positions
near Fusilier Bluff (16th). Relieved and to Gully Ravine (19th). Embarked
"V" Beach (20th) and sailed for Suvla Bay. Arrived early morning (21st),
disembarking under shell fire. Moved across Salt Lake to reserve positions

behind Chocolate Hill. Moved positions left to One Tree Gully (22nd). Relieved by 1st Border (29th) and to Imbros (30th).

SEPTEMBER
To Suvla Bay (7th). Disembarked and to bivouacs in ravine about 2 miles from beach. Moved forward to firing line (8th) taking over positions Sulajik sector. Patrol engaged enemy (17th) – 4 wounded. Detachments from Newfoundland Regiment and 2/1st London Regiment attached during month for instruction. Casualties for September – 5 other ranks killed, 17 wounded. 136 men to hospital sick, mostly from diarrhoea and dysentery. Drafts arrived throughout month, strength at (30th) – 12 officers, 564 other ranks.

OCTOBER
Relieved and to reserve lines (6th). Fatigue parties found daily for work on support and communication trenches. Relieved 2/1st London in firing line – lower slopes of Kiretch Tepe Sirt (16th). Position on extreme left of 29th Division and according to War Diary "by far the worst ever occupied by the Battalion." Relieved (30th) and to Brigade Reserve. Casualties for October – 8 other ranks killed, 32 wounded. 137 to hospital sick. Drafts arrived throughout month, strength at (31st) – 19 officers, 693 other ranks.

NOVEMBER
Began work on 3rd line of defence. Relieved 1st Essex in firing line – Dublin Castle (6th). Relieved by 4th Worcestershire (20th) and to reserve line. Began work on 3rd line trenches. "X" and "Y" Companies sent to firing line at Dublin Castle due to heavy casualties among 86th Brigade. Brigade had suffered severely from recent storm and freezing conditions. War Diary records (30th) that whole of 86th Brigade line (1,200 yards) was being held by 4 officers and 170 men. Casualties during November – 8 other ranks killed, 1 officer and 18 other ranks wounded. Some 207 men had been sent to hospital sick, 3 officers and over 100 men during last 3 days suffering from exposure.

DECEMBER
"Y" Company relieved (1st), "X" Company (2nd) and rejoined Battalion. Began work on communication trenches leading to beach. Moved to 2nd line trenches in front of Hill 10 (10th), Battalion's left on Sulajik Road. "X" Company moved to Hill 10 (11th). Remaining companies took over front line (13th). Packs and surplus stores sent to beach in readiness for evacuation (16th). First party of 5 officers and 309 other ranks withdrew to beach

6.45 p.m. (18th) and embarked for Mudros. During (19th) another party of 100 withdrew to Essex Ravine in reserve 5 a.m. and later embarked. Machine guns moved back to Hill 10 and embarked during evening. Headquarters left firing line and embarked about 11.15 p.m. Just 40 men remained holding firing line. Last party left trenches 1.30 a.m. (20th) and embarked 3 a.m. Battalion (less 16th detachment) sailed *Magnificient* for Imbros. Imbros detachment embarked *Redbreast* (22nd) and sailed for Cape Helles. Landed "W" Beach and moved inland to dug outs. Officers visited firing line around trench H11 (24th) and noted little had charged since the Battalion attacked in this sector on 6th August. Remainder of Battalion joined from Mudros (25th). Moved forward to Eski Line (31st) – position held between Krithia Nullah and Achi Baba Nullah. One company in Redoubt Line. Machine guns and party of 20 bombers reinforced 1st Essex in firing line between East and West Krithia Nullahs. Casualties during December – 9 killed, 25 wounded, 150 sick to hospital. Strength at (31st) – 19 officers, 571 other ranks.

JANUARY, 1916
"Y" and "W" Companies relieved 1st Essex in firing line between East and West Krithia Nullahs (3rd). Evacuated Peninsular (8th) – "Z" Company moved first to "W" Beach followed by "X". During evening 160 men left leaving just 80 holding firing line. Whole Battalion sailed and reached Mudros early morning (9th).

1/8TH (ISLE OF WIGHT RIFLES, 'PRINCESS BEATRICE'S') BATTALION (T.F.)

JULY
Watford, Hertfordshire. Part of 163rd Brigade, 54th (East Anglian) Division. Entrained for Liverpool (29th) and embarked *Aquitania*. Strength – 29 officers, 959 other ranks. Officers – Lieutenant-Colonel J.E. Rhodes (Commanding); Majors E.H. Lewis, A.C.T. Veasey (Adjutant); Captains D. W. Ratsey, C.L. Ellery, J.G. Fardell, J.H. Marsh, C. Ratsey, A. Holmes-Gore, G.C. Loader; Lieutenants C.W. Brannon, C.S. Pittis, W. Read, C.G. Seely, A.S. Weeding, G. Giddens (Quartermaster); Second-Lieutenant P. Latham, J.P.J. Murphy, L.C. Watson, F.C.M. Raymond, G.W. Fox, S. Ratsey, A.Y. Young-James, J.P. Shelton, H.W. Kingdon, A.G.A. Sutton, W.B. Bartlett. Captain G. Raymond (R.A.M.C., Medical Officer). Sailed (30th).

AUGUST

Arrived Mudros Harbour, Lemnos (6th). Transferred to *Osmanieh, Fauvette* and *Carron* (9th) and sailed for Imbros. Proceeded to Gallipoli (10th), landing Suvla Bay 9.10 p.m. and moving forward to positions around Hill 28 – west side of Anafarta Plain. Advanced in centre of Brigade across plain 4.45 p.m. (12th) – 3 companies in line, "A" Company in support. Soon came under heavy enfilading fire from left. War Diary records heavy casualties throughout the Brigade which moved forward some 2 miles. Battalions lost touch with each other. At about 6 p.m. line established in sunken ditch in front of wells at Kuchuk Anafarta Ova. During the attack most of the 1/5th Norfolk (on right of 1/8th Hampshire) disappeared. Their bodies not being found, with some 1/8th Hampshire among them, until after the armistice. Enemy counter attacked 1.15 p.m. (14th) and driven of by machine guns. War Diary notes Battalions left being "in the air" and if enemy attack had been successful would have been completely surrounded. Relieved 6.30 p.m. and withdrew to former positions at Hill 28. Casualties since (12th) – Major Lewis, Captains Holmes-Gore, C and D.W. Ratsey (brothers) and Loader, Lieutenant Young-James and Second-Lieutenants Raymond and Watson killed or missing, 150 men killed or missing, 1 officer and 140 men wounded. Commanding Officer evacuated with sunstroke. Received orders 3.10 p.m. (16th) to moved to north side of Kiretch Tepe Sirt and take over support trenches of the 10th Division. War Diary records positions . . . "certainly could not be called reserve or support trenches as there were no trenches in front of us." Heavy sniper activity also noted – Lieutenants Bartlett and Latham among those killed. Relieved and to Karakol Dagh (26th). Moved to "A" Beach 10 a.m. (27th) then at 1 a.m. to Lala Baba in reserve. Moved to trenches south-east of Lala Baba by side of Salt Lake (29th). War Diary records (30th) British aeroplane landing near Battalion, the enemy shelling it for some time without success. Returned to Lala Baba 10.30 p.m. (31st).

SEPTEMBER

Moved forward to South Wales Borderers Gully (1st) and dug in. Took over trenches Hill 60 and Cheshire Ridge (3rd). Records note the dead on Hill 60, it being impossible to clear the bodies due to closeness of enemy's lines. Flies and smell unbearable. Relieved and to South Wales Borderers Gully (5th). Casualties for week ending 5th September – 4 killed, 7 wounded. To Hill 60 (7th). War Diary records enemy's bombing attacks continuous during night . . . "although many fell in centre sector of tench no damage was done, the bombs taking a long time to explode and a coat thrown over effectively lessened damage." Relieved and to South Wales Borderers Gully

(11th). Attached to 161st Brigade (12th) and moved to new bivouacs in reserve. Casualties for week ending 12th September – 2 killed, 8 wounded. Strength – 10 officers, 440 other ranks. War Diary records much sickness – about 100 attending hospital each day. Stood by during enemy attack on trenches to the front (18th). Casualties (13th-19th) – 3 killed, 5 wounded. War Diary records (20th) receiving casualty list from Alexandria and finding that 18 men previously reported as missing on 12th August were in hospital wounded. Twelve men had died of their wounds. No men sent from Gallipoli wounded or sick had yet rejoined the Battalion. "A" and "C" Companies attached to 1/5th Essex (23rd) and to firing line – Laindon Hill. Total casualties for September – 9 killed, 3 died of wounds, 22 wounded. Strength – 9 officers, 403 other ranks.

OCTOBER
Remainder of Battalion to firing line (4th) – positions about 800 yards right of Hill 60. Major Hon. Walter Guinness of the Suffolk Yeomanry recall visiting the Hampshire's trenches in his diaries (see *Staff Officer, The Diaries of Lord Moyne 1914-1918*). He notes that on the right there were no trenches, just dug outs in the rock, and that the line run down eastwards towards Hill 100 and the end of Sandbag Ridge. "A" and "C" Companies rejoined (11th). Party from 1/1st Norfolk Yeomanry attached for instruction (14th). Relieved by 1/6th Essex in Culver Trench (28th) and to Inglenook.

NOVEMBER
Relieved 1/4th Essex in firing line (6th). Relieved and to Hatfield Park (27th), Waterfall Gully (29th).

DECEMBER
Embarked at Williams Pier, Anzac for Mudros (3rd).

10TH (SERVICE) BATTALION

JULY
Basingstoke, Hampshire. Part of 29th Brigade, 10th (Irish) Division. Entrained for Liverpool (6th) and sailed *Transylvania* (7th). Strength – 30 officers, 897 other ranks. Called at Gibraltar (11th), Malta (14th). Arrived Alexandria, Egypt (17th). Sailed for Lemnos (18th). Arrived Mudros (21st). Disembarked (22nd) and to bivouacs on south side of harbour.

AUGUST
To Gallipoli (5th). Men now wearing claret and yellow cloth patches on their

helmets for unit identification. Embarked *Abassieh* (5th) and sailed 3.15 p.m. for Gallipoli. Landed Anzac Cove (6th) and to dug outs in Bridges Road, south side Shrapnel Gully. Ten men wounded from shrapnel (6th). Moved forward north of Russell's Top (7th). Ordered back to Shrapnel Gully same day. Marched north along coast to Fisherman's Hut (8th). Advanced in evening crossing the Chailak Dere under shell fire. Moved on through narrow gully crowded with wounded to bivouacs at Rest Gully. Advance continued about 10 p.m. Records show that guides became lost and battalion had to retrace its steps in the dark. Track later found leading into the Aghyl Dere early morning (9th). Moved forward north of Rhododendron Spur 6 a.m. In action at The Farm. "A" Company with part of "D" advancing to the south-west halted by heavy machine gun and shrapnel fire. Detachment under Major Pilleau moved forward to the right in support of New Zealanders. Positions held under fierce attacks. Bryan Cooper in his history of the 10th (Irish) Division records how the commanding officer of the 10th Hampshire, Lieutenant-Colonel W.D. Bewsher, had been seriously wounded. Hearing that his battalion was loosing heavily and probably without officers, he returned to the firing line. There he learned that all officers had been either killed or wounded (save for two still with the detachment holding the New Zealand position) along with all senior N.C.Os. Relieved and withdrew to Cheshire Ridge (10th). Then to small valley in rear (11th). Casualties – Captains C.C.R. Black-Hawkins, H.W. Savage; Lieutenants G.L. Cheesman, P.C. Williams; 2nd Lieutenants S.A. Smith, O.S. Whalley killed, 13 other officers wounded or missing. Other ranks – 55 killed, 276 wounded, 97 missing, 3 wounded and missing. To position north side of Aghyl Dere (13th). Later relieved Gurkhas in trenches upper end of Damakjelik Bair. Ground recorded as hard and rocky and trenches under 3 feet deep. Position under constant machine gun fire. Relieved by 6th King's Own (20th) and marched via Hampshire Lane to Australian Gully. Strength – 5 officers, 330 other ranks. Attack on Hill 60 (21st). Moved forward in support of New Zealand Mounted Rifles – "C" Company in front followed by "D", "A" and "B". Leading waves cut down by machine gun and rifle fire. Second-Lieutenant A.T. Calderwood ("D" Company) killed. "A" Company also checked – Captain G.E. Hellyer mortally wounded. "B" Company changed direction and reached captured positions at Susak Kuyu. Survivors joined "B" Company after dark, the Battalion then retiring to South Wales Borderers Gully. Casualties – 43 killed or missing, 110 wounded. Strength now under 200 with just two officers. Withdrew to beach area near No. 3 Post and employed on fatigues.

SEPTEMBER
Employed on beach duties. Draft of 134 arrived (9th). Embarked *Partridge* for Mudros (30th).

THE SOUTH STAFFORDSHIRE REGIMENT

"Suvla" "Landing at Suvla" "Scimitar Hill" "Gallipoli,1915"

7TH (SERVICE) BATTALION

JUNE
Frensham, Surrey. Part of 33rd Brigade, 11th (Northern) Division. Entrained at Farnham for Liverpool (30th) and embarked *Empress of Britain.*

JULY
Sailed (1st). Arrived Malta (8th), sailed for Alexandra (11th). Arrived (12th) and remained in harbour. Sailed for Lemnos (16th), arriving Mudros (18th). Transhipped to *Abassieh* and sailed for Cape Helles (20th). Landed and moved to reserve bivouacs. Attached to Royal Naval Division and to reserve trenches – Brown House – Eski Line (23rd). In his history of the Battalion Major A.H. Ashcroft, D.S.O. records that the parapets were to a great extent built from dead bodies. Moved to firing line – The Horseshoe (25th). Relieved (28th) and marched to rest camp.Embarked *Osmanieh* for Imbros.

AUGUST
Embarked *Osmanieh* and sailed for Imbros (1st). Sailed for Suvla during night (6th/7th). Landed "B" Beach, moved forward and dug in on reserve line running from south-west corner of Salt Lake to the sea. Moved forward during night (7th/8th) to Chocolate Hill. Attack on Ismail Oglu Tepe (9th). Advanced and soon came under heavy fire from Scimitar Hill. Major Ashcroft records "Every single officer in "A" and "D" Companies (firing line) and in "B" Company (supporting line) was either killed or wounded in the first ten minutes. At about 1800. support arrived from the 10th Division, but even with this assistance no headway could be made." Relieved by 5th Royal Irish Fusiliers and withdrew to communication trench running from Chocolate Hill. Casualties estimated as over 400. Relieved and to rest area on beach (12th). Moved forward to trenches near Chocolate Hill (18th). Relieved and to beach bivouacs (20th). Moved forward from Lala Baba 3.30 p.m. (21st) in support of attack. Heavy casualties during advance – all officers except 2 hit. Casualties over 300. Withdrew to reserve trenches at Lala Baba (22nd) and formed composite battalion with 9th Sherwood Foresters (24th). To positions on eastern

slope of Karakol Dagh (28th). Began tours of duty in front line – Jephson's Post.

SEPTEMBER
Relieved (12th) and to rest camp at West Beach. Took over line from Jephson's Post to the sea (20th). Temporary amalgamation with 9th Sherwood Foresters cancelled (21st). Relieved by 9th Sherwood Foresters (28th) and to beach in Brigade Reserve. Provided working parties nightly to Rotten Row.

OCTOBER
Drafts arrived throughout month. Took over line – Jephson's Post to half-way to the sea from 6th Border (7th). One company holding Green Lane. Moved to Corps Reserve at "A" Beach (19th).

NOVEMBER
To reserve and support lines – Leather Lane, near Oxford Circus, Oxford Street behind Jephson's Post (12th). Employed in digging new communication trenches on right of Jephson's Post. Relieved 6th Border in firing line – Jephson's Post (24th). Heavy storm (26th) – some trenches four feet deep in water, equipment and kit swept away.

DECEMBER
Enemy attack (1st) driven of with bombs and rifle fire. Relieved by 9th Sherwood Foresters (8th) and to Lone Tree Gully in Brigade Reserve. Relieved 6th Lincolnshire in firing line – Grouse Butts (9th). Evacuation began (18th) – 10 officers, 411 other ranks leaving during night for Imbros. "B" Company remained in front line supported by "C", embarking *Derfflinger* for Imbros (19th).

THE DORSETSHIRE REGIMENT

"Suvla" "Landing at Suvla" "Scimitar Hill" "Gallipoli, 1915"

5TH (SERVICE) BATTALION

JULY

Witley Camp, Godalming, Surrey. Part of 34th Brigade, 11th (Northern) Division. Entrained in 2 trains for Liverpool (2nd) and embarked *Aquitania*. Officers: Headquarters – Lieutenant-Colonel C.C. Hannay (Commanding); Major E.S. Weldon (Second in Command); Captain A. Caruthers-Little (Adjutant); Lieutenant V.T.A. Hayden (Quartermaster); Second-Lieutenant G.W. Smith (Machine Gun Officer). "A" Company – Captain A.L. Gregory; Lieutenants E.F. Horton, C.H. Clayton; Second-Lieutenants R.B. LeCornu, F.W. George. "B" Company – Major A.G. Fitz. R. Day; Lieutenants B. Lloyd, E. Sanders, T.G. Bowler; Second-Lieutenants G.E. Montgomery, F. Smith. "C" Company – Captains H.N. Le Marchant, A.C.W. Vincent; Lieutenants L.D. Cooke, S. Eason; Second-Lieutenants C.Y. Richards, A.G.C. Grant. "D" Company – Major R.F.W.F. Leslie; Captain A. Moody; Lieutenant C.S. Higgins; Second-Lieutenants D.R. Drysdale, O.A. Derry, A.M. Bear. Lieutenant T.A. Peel (R.A.M.C., Medical Officer). Strength – 29 officers, 875 other ranks. Sailed 1.30 p.m. (3rd). Attacked by submarine (4th) – torpedo passed 100 yards astern. Arrived Lemnos 7.00 a.m. (10th). Disembarked during afternoon (11th) and to bivouacs north of Mudros Harbour. Employed in fatigues, carrying stores and ammunition, road making, digging wells. War Diary (16th) records Second-Lieutenant F. Smith going to the Aragon (Lines of Communication H.Q.) to receive pay for the Battalion. "A" Company £54, "B" £43.4, "C" £62.16, "D" £50. Men paid same day. Embarked Mosquito and Racoon (19th) and sailed for Imbros. Arrived 10.30 a.m. and to camp. Employed on Battalion or Garrison fatigues. War Diary (31st) records men suffering severely from diarrhoea.

AUGUST

Sailed for Suvla Bay about 5 p.m. (6th) – "A," "B" and "C" Companies *Beagle*, Headquarters and "D" Company *Bulldog*. Landed "A" Beach just before dawn – some casualties from shrapnel fire. Lieutenant Eason killed. Personnel from *Beagle* (120 men) came under heavy fire and landing had to be suspended. Company taken to "B" Beach and did not join Battalion until next day. Began advance on Hill 10 at 4 a.m. (7th). "A" Company providing covering fire, remainder successfully attacked enemy trenches west and north of hill. Continued advance. Lieutenant Lloyd killed. About mid-day halted at Hill 28, having advanced some mile and a half from Hill 10. Captain Caruthers-Little killed by sniper. Some 300 men under Major Leslie ordered to form left flank-guard for attack on Chocolate Hill. Party moved forward in support of 31st Brigade under shrapnel and sniper fire. Reached sunken road at foot of Chocolate Hill just before dark. Battalion concentrated at Hill 28 (8th). Casualties so far – 3 officers and 11 other ranks killed, 2 officers, 58 other ranks wounded 5 men missing. Moved forward against enemy trenches south of Karakol Dagh (9th). Battalion historian – C.T. Atkinson, records that Lieutenant-Colonel Hannay had been ordered to advance by 6 a.m. to a position half-mile north-east of Hill 28 and make ready for an attack. This point of deployment was overlooked by a ridge to the north which the Battalion charged and took. Continued advance 7.30 a.m. – "D" Company leading over difficult and broken ground. Arrived at point running south-east from Jephson'a Post in Kiretch Tepe Sirt and halted. Captain Le Marchant killed, 3 other officers wounded. Unsupported on right or left, withdrew during evening to trenches on Karakol Dagh. War Diary records exhausted condition of the men. Some having had no water for 2 days. Casualties – 1 officer, 20 other ranks killed, 3 officers and more than 60 other ranks wounded, 12 men missing. War Diary records water being brought up on mules early hours (10th) – "In spite of its muddy colour and taste of petrol it was enthusiastically welcomed." Relieved by 6th Royal Inniskilling Fusiliers (11th) and retired to reserve positions on beach behind Lala Baba. Strength – 16 officers, approx 700 other ranks. Moved forward to reserve trenches at Dead Man's House south of Salt Lake (13th). Relieved 8th Northumberland Fusiliers in firing line (15th). "C" and "D" Companies extended line forward on left flank some 300 yards in direction of Green Hill. Part of "A" Company under Lieutenant George carried out attack on house occupied by the enemy (17th) – 14 prisoners taken. Casualties – 3 killed, 5 wounded and missing. Returned to firing line (18th) and in support of failed attack by 8th Northumberland Fusiliers 4 a.m. (19th). "D" Company and half of "C" forced to retire with some 30 casualties. Medical Officer – Lieutenant Peel mortally wounded by sniper while tending wounded in No Man's Land (19th). War Diary records (20th) arrival of Turks bearing white flags and requesting a truce so as wounded and dead could be collected. Temporary armistice arranged. Moved into trenches on right of Dead Man's House during evening. Attacked 3 p.m. (21st) – "B" and "C" Companies leading with "A" and "D" following 50 yards behind. Covered 500 yards of open ground under heavy fire, first enemy trench taken and enemy retired to support line. Second line attacked but heavy fire from left flank forced withdrawal to captured first line. War Diary records (22nd) "In the morning those who had not already retired realised the hopelessness of hanging on any longer and began to fall back." Withdrawal was under heavy shrapnel fire and with high casualties. War Diary records loss of Major Leslie and Second-Lieutenant George, killed; Captains Vincent and Gregory, Lieutenants Bowler and Higgins, wounded; Captain Moody and Lieutenant Montgomery, missing (both killed). Only 2 officers were found surviving. Remnants of Battalion collected and strength recorded by evening as about 280. War Diary records strength at opening of engagement as 650. Withdrew under command of Second-Lieutenant C.J. Richards 9 p.m. and to beach behind Lala Baba. Losses to date – 8 officers and 298 other ranks killed and missing; 11 officers, 246 men wounded. Temporary amalgamated with 11th Manchester as No. 2 Battalion, 34th Brigade. Strength of 5th Dorsetshire – 5 officers, 281 men. Moved to firing line near Kazlar Chair (25th). Relieved and to reserve positions near Salt Lake (26th). Marched by night (28th) across Salt Lake to Kangaroo Bay. From there taken by guide to reserve positions at Karakol Dagh. Occupied dug outs overlooking the sea.

SEPTEMBER
To support trenches (4th). Began work improving and deepening trenches. First drafts arrived (9th) – 150 men. Snipers operating from Bench Mark successful. Second draft arrived (15th) – 100 men. War Diary records many men from drafts taken sick with diarrhoea. Enemy snipers very active (16th) – nullah on flank unsafe – "2 killed, mainly to carelessness." Relieved and to beach (20th). C.T. Atkinson in his history of the 5th Dorsetshire recalls the September period – the men being required to work very hard under difficult and depressing conditions. He notes the problems of re-constructing a battalion "in the face of the enemy." Reinforcements were, in the main, "imperfectly trained." Officers themselves were mostly new and also inexperienced. Only the Quartermaster remained from the original battalion, all other officers either being killed or invalided by the beginning of October. Further drafts arrived and Battalion separated from 11th Manchester. Position inspected (26th) and considered "too insanitary." Moved 1,500 yards east along beach. To front line – Kiretch Tepe Sirt (28th). Battalion's left on Jephson's Post.

OCTOBER
War Diary (9th) records "Enemy seen again moving their guns and hoist Red Cross flag where party halted." Relieved by 11th Manchester (18th)

and to reserve lines – 2 companies Lone Tree Gully, other 2 with Headquarters in Leather Lane. Machine gun section remaining in firing line.

NOVEMBER
Moved to beach in Divisional Reserve (8th), Corps Reserve west end of Karakol Dagh (10th). Dug outs flooded during storm (26th). War Diary records severe weather that followed and storm of (28th) – "Battalion moved to West Beach and took shelter under A.S.C. boxes covered with tarpaulins. A good many cases of frost bitten feet." Three men died of exposure during night (29th). Three officers and 138 other ranks to hospital through effects of storm (30th).

DECEMBER
War Diary records most of Battalion suffering from frostbite (1st). Moved to Anson lines on West Beach (2nd). Inspection by G.O.C. 11th Division (7th) who criticised behaviour of Battalion during recent storm. Battalion evacuated (15th). Arrived Mudros 7 a.m. (16th).

The Prince of Wales's Volunteers (South Lancashire Regiment)

"Suvla" "Sari Bair" "Gallipoli,1915"

6TH (SERVICE) BATTALION

JUNE
Blackdown, Hampshire. Part of 38th Brigade, 13th (Western) Division.
Sailed from Avonmouth to Malta then Egypt.

JULY
Moved to Mudros and from there landed at "W" Beach, Helles (7th).
Served in Gully Ravine sector with units of 29th and 42nd Divisions.
Relieved by 8th Royal Welsh Fusiliers in treches H11, H12, Worster Flat
sector (17th). Returned to Mudros (31st).

AUGUST
Landed Anzac Cove (4th) and to Victoria Gully. Heavy shell fire (6th) – 68
casualties. Moved forward in support of Australian and New Zealand troops
– Chailak Dere (7th). Ordered at 11 p.m. to join 39th Brigade near Aghyl
Dere. Attack on Chunuk Bair (8th) – formed part of No. 1 Column. Captain
H. Whalley-Kelly in his history of the Regiment mentions the Battalion
receiving orders to follow 9th Royal Warwickshire and to attack the northern
slopes of Chunuk Bair. He notes that "confused fighting followed" and the
Battalion being divided up "in attempts to exploit the success of other
units." *Official History of the Great War – Military Operations, Gallipoli Vol II*
records that Major C.J.L. Allanson with his 1/6th Gurkhas, was held up
during the attack on Hill "Q". He then went back in search of reinforcements and found in a deep ravine one company of 7th North Staffordshire
and a party of 6th South Lancashire. Moving again forward, the South
Lancashire with the Gurkhas pushed upwards to a position about 100 feet
below the crest of the hill and there dug in. Regimental history records that
operations having been suspended, the scattered units of No. 1 Column
were collected . . . "the difficulties of the march having caused the attack
timed to start at 4.15 a.m. to miscarry." In the darkness the Battalion had
lost touch with 9th Royal Warwickshire. "D" Company moved forward to
relieve 9th Worcestershire, "B" and "A" Companies linked with 10th
Gurkhas and "C" remained in support. Captain Whalley-Kelly suggests that

it was a detachment of "B" Company that joined Major Allanson for his attack on Hill "Q". He points out, however, that "details are difficult to verify, particularly as in these operations the situation was never very clear." Two companies sent to reinforce Major Allanson on Hill "Q" (9th). Reached crest of hill where fierce hand-to-hand fighting took place. Enemy driven back down the slope. "C" and "D" Companies took enemy trenches to their front with little loss. Held positions on Gurkha Hill. At Hill "Q", enemy put forward strong counter attack. Then a number of high-explosive shells landed on the crest forcing a withdrawal. Captain Whalley-Kelly records that no troops were sent up to support the units on Hill "Q" and that evidence was conflicting as to whether the shells were fired by our guns of the enemy's. Remained on lower slopes of the ridge, withdraw ordered at 10 a.m. Relieved by 9th Royal Warwickshire during evening – one company remained in support, machine guns covering left flank. Enemy counter attacked 4.45 a.m. (10th) forcing withdrawal to second line. Held trenches in Aghyl Dere sector – Farm Gully area, for remainder of August. High casualties led to formation of composite battalion with 6th Loyal North Lancashire (28th). Casualties among officers during August: Major H.J.U. Wilkins, Lieutenant G.H. Willis, 2nd Lieutenant W. Morgan killed; Lieutenants G. Shruffrey, H. Longbottom missing, believed killed; Captains E. March, J.M. Birch, G.R. Cattarns, E.C. Jarvis; Lieutenants T.R. Faulkner, G. Hughes, T.H. Naylor, W.F. Powner; 2nd Lieutenant H.E. Voelcker wounded.

SEPTEMBER
Received draft of 151 other ranks (10th). Moved to Suvla (21st) and took over Rest Camp "B" near "A" Beach from 1/1st Herefordshire (21st). Releived 7th Royal Dublin Fusiliers in reserve dug outs (29th). To firing line just north of Chocolate Hill (30th).

NOVEMBER
War Diary refers to the great storm during night (26th/27th) and the subsequent flooding of the trenches. Also the blizzard that followed and freezing conditions – "The situation, however, was taken in hand by the officers and a serious state of affairs prevented by the immediate construction of braziers from old biscuit tins, and fires and hot meals were soon got going. No death from exposure occurred in this Battalion. The temperature remained below freezing-point until the 30th. The cheerfulness of all ranks during this extremely trying period was most notable and prevented the morale of the Battalion suffering in any way." Captain H. Whalley-Kelly records that during the three-day blizzard other units at Suvla suffered over 5,000 cases

of frostbite and more than 200 men were drowned or frozen to death. He also mentions the enemy being affected and the establishment of an unofficial truce.

DECEMBER

"D" Company and other details left for Mudros during night (18th). Remainder in four detachments left during night (19th). "B" Company with parts of "A" and "C" Companies and 206 bombers held covering position at Lala Baba. Finally sailing on *Princess Irene* 3.30 a.m. (20th).

THE WELSH REGIMENT

"Suvla" "Sari Bair" "Landing at Suvla" "Scimitar Hill" "Gallipoli,1915"

1/4TH BATTALION (T.F.)

JULY
Bedford, Bedfordshire. Part of 159th Brigade, 53rd (Welsh) Division. To Devonport (18th) and sailed (19th). Arrived Alexandria, Egypt (30th) then to Port Said.

AUGUST
Sailed (4th). Arrived Lemnos (7th) then to Gallipoli. Landed "C" Beach, Suvla (9th). Advanced and took part in fighting at Scimitar Hill. Relieved in front line by 1/6th Royal Welsh Fusiliers (27th) and to bivouacs near "A" Beach.

SEPTEMBER
To front line (1st), "A" Beach (8th), front line (11th). Relieved and to rest camp at Lala Baba (20th).

OCTOBER
Temporarily amalgamated with 1/5th Welsh (8th).

NOVEMBER
To front line south west of Chocolate Hill (29th).

DECEMBER
Relieved by Scottish Horse Yeomanry (9th) and to Lala Baba. To "C" Beach (12th) and evacuated to Mudros.

1/5TH BATTALION (T.F.)

JULY
Bedford, Bedfordshire. Part of 159th Brigade, 53rd (Welsh) Division. To Devonport (18th) and embarked *Huntsgreen*. Sailed (19th). Called Malta (26th) then to Egypt (27th). Arrived Alexandria (30th).

AUGUST

Sailed for Port Said (3rd), Lemnos (7th). Landed "C" Beach, Suvla (9th) and moved forward for attack on Scimitar Hill. War Diary (10th) records "pushed forward into Turkish trenches." Dug in at night. Casualties – 1 officer killed, 5 wounded; 17 other ranks killed, 107 wounded. Moved position to right (13th) and took over part of line held by 160th Brigade. Pushed first line of defence forward 250 yards (18th). Relieved by 1/1st Herefordshire (27th) and to bivouacs near "A" Beach. Relieved 1/4th Royal Sussex in front line Sulajik sector facing Scimitar Hill (31st).

SEPTEMBER

Relieved and to "A" Beach (8th). To front line trenches F1, F2, F3, F4 (11th). Relieved (20th) and to rest camp at Lala Baba.

OCTOBER

Temporally amalgamated with 1/4th Welsh (8th). War Diary records the issue of "short rifles" (Short Lee Enfield) to replace long pattern (19th).

NOVEMBER

To front line south west of Chocolate Hill (29th).

DECEMBER

War Diary records (7th) the surrender of a Turkish soldier. He was fired on from his own side white crossing No Man's Land. Relieved (9th) and to rest camp. To "C" Beach (12th) and evacuated to Mudros. War Diary records strength as 17 officers, 273 other ranks and also notes that just 1 officer (Captain T.C.L. Phillips) remained out of the originals that had landed in the previous August.

8TH (SERVICE) BATTALION (PIONEERS)

JUNE

Aldershot, Hampshire. Pioneer Battalion, 13th (Western) Division. To Avonmouth and sailed (15th).

JULY

Arrived Mudros, Lemnos (2nd). Disembarked (3rd) and began work making roads and sinking a well. Moved to West Mudros (5th) and began work on North Jetty. Worked on roads, wells and making a causeway at Turk's Island (11th-31st).

AUGUST
To Gallipoli (3rd). Disembarked Anzac (4th) and to bivouacs in Shrapnel Gully. Strength – 26 officers, 749 other ranks. Moved 10 p.m. (6th) via Anzac and Beach Road to Chailak Dere to support attack on Chunuk Bair. To bivouacs on Rhododendron Ridge (7th). Moved forward in support of attack (8th) – "A" and "B" Companies in first line, "C" and "D" second. First wave came under fire from enemy on both flanks. War Diary notes that Battalion deployed ... "but were gradually shot down and dispersed by machine gun fire." Party under Major Yates continued forward and took up positions on slopes of Chunuk Bair. War Diary records heavy casualties from fire from the rear. Enemy made repeated counter attacks throughout day. Major Yates's party (25 men) retired after 9 p.m. to Rhododendron Ridge. Casualties – 4 officers killed, 9 wounded, 4 missing; 4 other ranks killed, 154 wounded, 266 missing. Took over No. 1 Post (24th).

SEPTEMBER
Relieved by 1st Australian Light Horse (5th) and to Suvla Bay. Began work constructing winter quarters. Came under orders of 53rd (Welsh) Division (21st) and began work at South Pier. War Diary records effective strength (28th) – 6 officers, 263 other ranks.

OCTOBER
War Diary records (8th) "A" Company ordered to trenches "for skilled work only." "B" Company relieved "A" at Chocolate Hill (27th).

NOVEMBER
"C" relieved "B" (17th).

DECEMBER
Evacuated (16th) sailing *Abassieh* for Mudros. Arrived (17th) and to Portianos Camp.

THE ESSEX REGIMENT

"Helles" "Landing at Helles" "Krithia" "Suvla" "Landing at Suvla"

"Scimitar Hill" "Gallipoli,1915-16"

1ST BATTALION

MARCH
Warwick, Warwickshire. Part of 88th Brigade, 29th Division. To Avonmouth (21st) and embarked *Caledonia*.

APRIL
Arrived Alexandria (2nd). Disembarked (6th) and to Mustapha Camp. Embarked *Dongola* and sailed for Lemnos (11th). Arrived Mudros Harbour (13th). To Cape Helles (24th). Landed "W" Beach during morning. Moved forward and with 4th Worcestershire took part in attack on Hill 138. Major H.M. Farmer, DSO (86th Brigade-Major) recalls – "The Worcestershire and Essex battalions of the 88th Brigade began operations about 2 p.m., and by 5.20 p.m. they had the Turkish positions on Hill 138 in their hands. The troops then entrenched themselves." Enemy counter attacks during night repulsed. Casualties since landing – 3 officers killed, 3 wounded; 15 other ranks killed, 87 wounded. Consolidated gains (26th). Advanced on Krithia (27th). Entrenched astride Kirte Dere. Continued attack (28th) – strong opposition from enemy positions about 1 mile outside Krithia forced withdrawal. Casualties – 123 killed, 76 wounded, 33 missing. Took up position with left on Krithia Nullah.

MAY
Relieved by 2nd Hampshire and to reserve at Morto Bay (1st). Ruched forward during night and in action on right of 86th Brigade where enemy had entered part of line held by 1st Royal Munster Fusiliers and 1st Royal Dublin Fusiliers. "X" Company under Captain A.G.L. Pepys charged with the bayonet and cleared enemy from lost position. Further gains made. It was noted by one witness that many of the Irishmen had been killed while they slept. The trenches in many places were ankle-deep in blood. Casualties – 14 killed, 31 wounded, 5 missing. The dead included Commanding Officer Lieutenant-Colonel O.G. Godfrey-Faussett, D.S.O. and Major H.J. Sammut. Lieutenant H.J. Dixon was mortally wounded. According to one

officer (Lieutenant R.S.M. Hare) , the Colonel had been called by name by one of the enemy and shot as he got up from his dug out. To reserve (5th). Moved forward to firing line (6th) and took part in fighting at Fir Tree Wood. Cleared enemy from Wood (7th) and advanced 300-400 yards. Gains held and consolidated. Covered advance of New Zealand troops (8th). Relieved and to rest area (10th). Casualties – 5 officers wounded, 15 other ranks killed, 137 wounded. Relieved 1/8th Manchester in firing line between Fir Tree Wood and Gully Ravine (16th). In action (18th) – some 200 yards gained. Casualties – 6 killed, 20 wounded, 3 missing. "Z" Company in action (31st) – 22 casualties. Relieved by 2nd Royal Fusiliers and to rest area half mile beyond Pink Farm.

JUNE
Moved forward to Twelve Tree Copse sector (2nd) and in Brigade Reserve trenches at start of attack (4th). Sent forward 3.05 p.m. to reinforce 2nd Royal Fusiliers and 1st King's Own Scottish Borderers in captured line H12. Arthur Behrend was a young officer attached to the Essex from 1/4th East Lancashire and in his book *Make Me A Soldier* he recalls the advance as confused – companies and platoons soon losing touch with each other. He heard the call for "stretcher bearers" all around, one RAMC man moving out to assist a wounded man and instantly having his head blown clean of by a shell case. Casualties – 2 officers, 9 other ranks killed, 2 officers, 36 other ranks wounded, 9 missing. Enemy counter attacked (6th). Battalion historian, John Burrows records "stiff and confused fighting. "Y" Company, 90 strong under Captain Shepheard hung on to the last and only 25 of them returned." Fell back to trench H11. Casualties – Captain Shepheard mortally wounded, 2 attached officers killed, 6 wounded, 3 missing; 16 other ranks killed, 31 wounded, 59 missing. John Burrows notes that out of the 25 officers that left England, just 4 remained still serving. Relieved by 4th Worcestershire (7th) and to reserve at Gully Beach. Relieved 1/4th Royal Scots Fusiliers in firing line opposite trench H12 (13th). Enemy attack beaten off (15th). Attempt under Red Cross flag to bring in Turkish wounded fired upon. Lieutenant N.A. de Vera Beauclerk (attached) killed by sniper (17th). Relieved by 1/8th Scottish Rifles during night (18th/19th) and to Gully Beach. To forward area reserve trenches (24th), support area east of Fir Tree Wood (27th). Moved forward (28th) and with 1/5th Royal Scots took part in unsuccessful attack on trench H12. Operation recorded as difficult due to communication trenches being congested with large numbers of dead and wounded from previous attack by 156th Brigade. Casualties – 3 officers, 11 other ranks killed; 49 wounded, 11 missing believed killed.

JULY
Relieved from forward area (3rd) and to Gully Ravine. Embarked "V" Beach (11th) and to Mudros. Returned to Cape Helles (28th) and to reserve at Gully Beach.

AUGUST
Moved forward to firing line and in attack on trenches H12, H12A and enemy positions further north-east (5th). Moved forward 3.50 p.m. – "Y" and "Z" Companies on H12A, "W" Company on H12. John Burrows records that the initial rush on H12 was successful and with little loss. H12A was taken under heavy shrapnel fire, and with "great Gallantry." Moving on, the now weak companies came under heavy fire and were forced to retire to corner of Southern Barricade. By nightfall, corner of H12 and communication trench to H12A secured. Position exposed on 3 sides to enemy fire. Orders received to hold at all costs. Relieved at daybreak (7th) and to Gully Beach. Casualties – 13 officers, 37 other ranks killed, 202 wounded, 180 missing. Relieved 1st Lancashire Fusiliers in Hampshire Cut (14th). Moved to western side Gully Ravine (16th) and relieved 1st Royal Inniskilling Fusiliers in front line – trench J12. Relieved by 1/7th Manchester (19th). To "V" Beach (20th) and embarked for Suvla Bay. Landed "C" Beach 2 a.m. and moved forward to Chocolate Hill. In reserve during attack on Scimitar Hill. Casualties – 3 killed, 15 wounded. Relieved 1/10th London in firing line Kiretch Tepe Sirt sector (22nd). Relieved and embarked "A" Beach for Imbros (30th).

SEPTEMBER
Embarked *Osmanieh* for Suvla Bay (7th). Landed and to bivouacs De Lisle's Gully. To reserve trenches behind Hill 28 (8th). Began tours of duty in forward trenches – Kuchuk Anafarta Ova. Newfoundland Regiment attached for instruction (21st). Relieved 2nd Royal Fusiliers in front line – Kiretch Tepe Sirt (30th).

OCTOBER
Detachments from 2/1st London attached for instruction (2nd). Releived by 2/1st London and to reserve line (12th). To front line (23rd). Major A.G.N. Wood, D.S.O. killed by sniper (30th).

NOVEMBER
Tours in front line – Dublin Castle sector.

DECEMBER

Began evacuation (18th). Arrived Imbros (20th). Landed "W" Beach, Cape
Helles (22nd) and to reserve at Pink Farm. Captain G.P. Cox killed by aerial
bomb (24th). John Burrows records that this officer was the last of those that
landed in April. Relieved 1/4th Royal Scots Fusiliers in firing line between
East and West Krithia Nullahs (31st).

JANUARY, 1916

Relieved by 2nd Hampshire (3rd) and to Eski Line. "X" Company left for
Mudros (7th), remainder from "W" Beach on *Prince Abbas* (8th).

1/4TH BATTALION (T.F.)

JULY

St. Albans, Hertfordshire. Part of 161st Brigade, 54th (East Anglian)
Division. Entrained (2 trains) for Devonport (21st). Sailed *Marquette* 6 p.m.
Strength – 29 officers, 753 other ranks. Officers – Lieutenant-Colonel F.
Hankins (Commanding); Major C.H. Rimington-Taylor; Captains B.C.
Wells, M.M. Morgan-Owen, J.G. Gowan, H.R. Tyler, P.H. Manbey, C.L.
Awbrey, K. de S. Calthrop, W.C. Church, A.H. Cooper (Adjutant), A.J.
Gibson (R.A.M.C., Medical Officer); Lieutenants G.M. Emery, C.S.
Attwood, J. Macadam, J.M. Marshall, F.C. Donner, C.F. Batsford, W.H.
Butcher (Machine Gun Officer), W.H. Todd (Quartermaster); Second-
Lieutenants D.D.R. Dale, A.W. New, H.C. Naldrett, E.J. Hickman, W.S.
Thomas, J.C. Lockwood, E. Austin-Miller, H.B. New, J.W. Chitty (Signals
Officer); Rev. Dolan (Chaplain). Called at Malta (29th).

AUGUST

Arrived Alexandria 7 a.m. (1st). Sailed for Lemnos same day. Arrived
Mudros (3rd). Disembarked (8th) and began work on board *Minnetonka*.
Battalion's first casualty – Private W. Pearce died of heart failure.
Headquarters, "B" and "C" Companies sailed *Barry* 2.15 p.m. (12th).
Landed "C" Beach, Suvla Bay during evening and moved to Lala Baba area
(13th). "A" and "D" Companies sailed *Queen Victoria* 2.15 p.m. (13th).
Landed 10.30 p.m. and to reserve trenches (14th) then to Norfolk Hill in
support (15th). "B" and "C" Companies arrived 4 p.m. Casualties from
shell fire and sniping (16th) – Captain Gowan, Second-Lieutenant Hickman
killed, Lieutenant Macadam fatally wounded, 3 other ranks killed, 1 officer,
14 other ranks wounded. To southern slope Kiretch Tepe Sirt (17th).
Advanced to straighten line 5.30 p.m. (18th) – "A" and "D" Companies in
front, "B" and "C" Companies in support. Captain Tyler and 9 other ranks

killed, Colonel Hankins wounded. Some ground gained and consolidated. Headquarters set up at Lone Tree Gully. Heavy bombardment (19th) – 9 other ranks killed, 3 officers, 32 other ranks wounded. Part of line handed over to 1st Essex (22nd). Headquarters now at The Razorback. Relieved and to rest camp (27th). Lieutenant Todd died of heart attack (28th). To Lala Baba (29th), Anzac sector (31st). Attached to Australian and New Zealand Army Corps. Casualties to end August – 157 all ranks, killed, wounded, 217 sick.

SEPTEMBER
Relieved 15th Battalion, A.I.F. in trenches Hill 60 area – Laindon Hill (1st). Relieved by 1/5th Essex and 2 companies of 1/8th Hampshire (23rd) and to Hatfield Park. Casualties since landing and until end September – 20 officers, 354 other ranks, killed, wounded or sick. Strength – 9 officers, 337 other ranks.

OCTOBER
Drafts received – 7 officers (7th), 2 officers, 83 other ranks (8th). Relieved 1/5th Essex in front line (11th). 1/1st Norfolk Yeomanry attached for instruction (14th). Yeomanry left (21st) and part of line taken over by 1/5th Essex. Lieutenant Marshall died of wounds (23rd). Second-Lieutenant B.J.B. Walch mortally wounded while leading patrol (26th).

NOVEMBER
John Burrows in his history of the Essex Territorial Infantry Brigade records arrival of mail from England. Journey time 18 days – the shortest so far. Large black and white dogs noted being used by enemy patrols. Relieved by 1/8th Hampshire (6th). Battalion strength now under 300 and formed into 2 companies. Relieved 1/5th Essex in front line (15th). Strength – 17 officers, 285 other ranks. Line extended to left to include Carisbrooke Post and New Cut (23rd). Relieved by New Zealand Mounted Rifles and to Romford Road Gully (28th). To Taylor's Gully (29th).

DECEMBER
To Waterfall Gully (1st). Embarked 11 p.m. for Lemnos (3rd). Arrived Mudros 9 a.m. (4th).

1/5TH BATTALION (T.F.)

JULY
St. Albans, Hertfordshire. Part of 161st Brigade, 54th (East Anglian) Division. Entrained for Plymouth midnight (21st). Arrived noon (22nd) and

embarked *Grampian*. Strength – 29 officers, 649 other ranks. Officers – Lieutenant-Colonel J.M. Welch, T.D. (Commanding); Majors T. Gibbons, J.M. Heron; Captains H.C. Bridges (Adjutant), W.E. Wilson, H.T. Argent, F.W. Bacon, A. Denton, C.A. Gould, K.S. Storrs (R.A.M.C., Medical Officer); Lieutenants E.B. Deakin, T.G.N. Frankilin, W.H. Brooks, G.W.F. Bellward, E. Mackenzie Taylor, H.L. Yonge, B. Carlyon-Hughes, H. Mavor, G.M. Nobbs (Quartermaster); Second-Lieutenants H.K. Chester, L.D. Womersley, C. Portway, J.L. French, R.S. Horton, A. Colvin, J.F. Finn, .E. Sheldon, R.Turner. Rev. A.J. Sacr, (Chaplain). In his history of the Essex Territorial Infantry Brigade, John Burrows records that many members of the Battalion were not more than 20 years old. In one platoon, the average age was well under 20 – a few men having enlisted under age and between 16 and 17. Sailed (23rd). Called at Malta (30th).

AUGUST
Arrived Alexandria (2nd). Sailed for Lemnos (6th). Arrived Mudros Harbour (7th). Transferred to *Hazel* (9th) and sailed after dark for Imbros. Arrived 5 a.m. (10th). In his history of the Battalion, Major T. Gibbons recalls arriving at Imbros and hearing heavy firing from the Peninsular. Puffs of smoke could also be seen from shells bursting inland. Sailed 12.30 p.m. Landed "A" Beach, Suvla without casualties and concentrated a short distance inland. Moved forward to reserve positions 10 p.m. Ordered forward to second line trenches during night (12th). Advanced in single file, halting at daybreak and forming 2 lines. Advanced to relieved 163rd Brigade firing line 4 p.m. (14th). Major Gibbons records distance covered as being just over a mile. He also notes heavy shrapnel fire and snipers operating to the left. Relieved 1/5th Norfolk and 1/8th Hampshire in "C" Sector. Line held being a fenched ditch facing Kuchuk Anafarta Ova. Casualties during advance – 14 other ranks killed, some 60 wounded. Second-Lieutenant Turner killed while out with patrol after dark. Captain Denton killed by sniper (16th). Battalion records note fighting of 10th (Irish) Division on left at Kiretch Tepe Sirt and the cheering and waving helmets in the air by the Irishmen. Relieved 3 a.m. (17th) and withdrew to reserve positions. Later relieved Royal Munster Fusiliers at Jephson's Post, Kiretch Tepe Sirt. Major Gibbons records position giving little cover and movement by day being on hands and knees. Enemy's line (lit by searchlight from a destroyer) was 300 yards to the front and ground between thick with dead. John Burrows recalls and incident concerning a patrol led by Lieutenant Carlyon-Hughes (19th). Wearing a Balaclava helmet and unshaved for 10 days, the officer was almost arrested by sentries thinking he was a Turk. Lieutenant Sheldon mortally wounded by sniper (22nd). Relieved (23rd) and to dug-outs northern side

of ridge. Bathing in the sea was enjoyed by all, records Major Gibbons, and "well worth the 600 feet climb back to the bivouacs." To western slope Lala Baba (28th) and dug in on beach. Attached to Australian and New Zealand Army Corps (30th) and moved forward to South Wales Borderers Gully in rear of 4th Australian Brigade.

SEPTEMBER
Relieved 13th Battalion, A.I.F. in front line – Norfolk Street (1st). Position held – 600 yards of line on right of Hill 60 and in parts just 60 yards from enemy. Began work on communication trench forward to Hill 60. Relieved by 1/4th Norfolk (5th) and to gully off Australia Valley – 400 yards behind front line. Began work on digging saps and communication trenches. To rest area – Hatfield Park (12th). Strength (18th) – 11 officers, 281 other ranks. Relieved 1/4th Essex in front line – Laindon Hill (23rd). Two companies of 1/8th Hampshire attached.

OCTOBER
Draft of 8 officers arrived (7th). Relieved by 1/4th Essex dawn (11th) and to reserve line at Hatfield Park. Draft of 4 officers arrived (18th). Relieved part of 1/4th Essex in front line (21st). Strength at end of month – 21 officers, 191 other ranks.

NOVEMBER
Relieved by 1/4th Essex (15th) and to Brigade Reserve at Inglenook Gully. To front line (23rd). Sever flooding in trenches noted during storm (26th). Relieved by New Zealand Mounted Rifles (27th) and to West Ham Gully. Received orders to go to Mudros and moved to beach 4 p.m. Piers found washed away and ordered to return to bivouacs. Spent night in open throughout snow storm. Major Gibbons notes . . . "Battalion was literally buried in snow." To Taylor's Gully (28th).

DECEMBER
To Waterfall Gully (1st). Embarked *Ermine* midnight (3rd) and sailed for Lemnos. Strength – 13 officers, 141 other ranks. Arrived Mudros noon (4th) and to Portianos Camp. Total casualties while on Peninsular – 27 killed, 10 died of disease, 133 wounded.

1/6TH BATTALION (T.F.)

JULY
St. Albans, Hertfordshire. Part of 161st Brigade, 54th (East Anglian)

Division. Entrained for Devonport (23rd). Embarked *Southland* and sailed (24th). Officers – Lieutenant-Colonel R.F. Wall (Commanding); Majors H.P.Alexander, B.J. Ward; Captains P.D. Castle, G.L. Evans, H.W. Bunch, J.M. Sly, E.A. Loftus, J.L. Sheldon, H.F. Silverwood, G. Disney (Adjutant); Lieutenants K.D. Taylor, L.B. Rayner, L.J. Stenning, R.A. Hyrons, R.J. Newman, B.C. Westall, A.C. Beeton, R.D.F. Wall, A.F.E. Maclachlan (R.A.M.C., Medical Officer), G.H. Pitt (Quartermaster); Second-Lieutenants E.W. Tee, H.P. Tavener, J.R. Adams, A.H. Asker, L.E. Smith, F.F. Langridge, C.W. Silverwood, C.W. Randall, W.L. Tavener. Rev. E.A. Gardner (Chaplain).

AUGUST
Called at Malta (1st). Arrived Alexandria (4th). To Lemnos (8th), Imbros (9th). Landed Suvla Bay (11th). Moved forward to reserve positions (12th). Advanced on Kiretch Tepe Sirt (13th) – "C" Company leading. Later forced to retire due to heavy shrapnel and sniper fire. Casualties – 2 other ranks killed, 3 officers, 54 other ranks wounded. Advanced and relieved 1/8th Hampshire in firing line (14th). Moved to support line behind Jephson's Post (15th). Took over Jephson's Post (16th) – 7 other ranks killed, 2 officers, 19 other ranks wounded, 2 men missing during move. Lieutenant Beeton and 5 other ranks killed by shrapnel (22nd). To support line – Razorback (23rd), reserve line (27th), Lala Baba (29th). Moved along coast to Anzac (30th) and relieved 13th Battalion, A.I.F. in forward trenches – Hill 60 sector (31st).

SEPTEMBER
Casualties for month – 5 killed, 12 wounded, 140 sick.

OCTOBER
Relieved (4th). Received draft of 95 other ranks (7th). To front line – Norfolk Street (11th). Relieve by 1/1st Norfolk Yeomanry (21st) and to Inglenook. Relieved 1/8th Hampshire in Culver Trench (28th). Reserve for firing line at West Ham Gully and Upton Park. Drafts of 19 officers arrived during October. Casualties for month – 4 killed, 16 wounded, 1 missing, 263 sick.

NOVEMBER
Line extended to include Carisbrooke Post (6th). Second-Lieutenant C.A. Rayner mortally wounded by sniper (7th) and Captain G.A.P. Douglas (1/10th London attached) (19th). Right half of Battalion to Inglenook (22nd). Detachment of 2 officers and 30 other ranks to Jameson's Jaunt

(23rd). Received orders to move to Mudros (27th). Left for beach 5 a.m. but returned to Inglenook same day. Recent storms had destroyed piers. Battalion remained in open under severe weather conditions. To dug outs at Waterfall Gully (29th). Casualties for month – 1 killed, 7 wounded, 1 missing, 123 sick.

DECEMBER
Embarked *Ermine* (3rd). Arrived Mudros (4th) and to Portianos Camp.

1/7TH BATTALION (T.F.)

JULY
St. Albans, Hertfordshire. Part of 161st Brigade, 54th (East Anglian) Division. "A" and "B" Companies to Devonport and sailed *Southland* (24th). "C" and "D" Companies entrained 4.50 a.m. (26th). Arrived Devonport 2.30 p.m. and embarked *Braemar Castle*. Sailed 5.30 p.m. Officers – Major H.F. Kemball (Commanding); Captains W.R. Johnson, G.G. Ewer, G. Johnson, G. Shenstone, F.R. Waller, R. Jenner Clarke, D.H. Pearson, A. Graham (R.A.M.C., Medical Officer); Lieutenants R.A. Stubbings (Adjutant), E. Whur, R. Warner (Quartermaster), E.W. Broadberry, J.R. Eve, S.C.W. Hearn, L.F.H. Bailey (Machine Gun Officer), J. Schofield, S.A. Mackie, G. Jones; Second-Lieutenants G. Hetherington, E. Lewis, H. Pelly, J.G. Kemball, A.H.F. Harwood, A.G. Johnson, D.M. Penrose, C. Needell, F.L. Thomas, A.R. Carpenter.

AUGUST
Braemar Castle called at Malta (3rd). Arrived Alexandria 2.30 p.m. (6th), sailed during afternoon (7th) for Imbros. Arrived Mudros (10th) and from there on to Imbros where *Southland* was in harbour. Landed "A" Beach, Suvla (11th). Moved forward to positions on Tekke Tepe Ridge and Kavak Tepe ready for attack (12th). Attack cancelled and withdrew to reserve line. Casualties – 17 wounded. Moved forward to relieve 163rd Brigade (14th). Came under shrapnel fire and snipers operating from rear. Halted in line on right of 1/5th Essex after dark. Casualties during advance – 25. Line extended to link up with 159th Brigade (16th). Casualties from shell and sniper fire (17th) – 21. Relieved (18th) and to Karakol Dagh. Later relieved troops of 10th (Irish) Division in forward trenches – Jephson's Post, Kiretch Tepe Sirt. Relieved and to reserve line (22nd). To Brigade Reserve at Karakol Dagh (27th), Lala Baba (29th). Eight men killed and some 35 wounded from shell (30th). To Anzac (31st).

SEPTEMBER
Arrived at bivouacs Australia Valley 1 a.m. (1st). "A" Company attached to Australian troops at Table Top, "B" Company – Rhododendron Spur (3rd). Remainder of Battalion began work on communication trench. "A" and "B" rejoined (10th). Attached to 163rd Brigade (13th) and to Hill 60 sector. John Burrows in his history of the Essex Territorial Infantry Brigade notes conditions on Hill 60 as being the worse on the Peninsular. The Hill was held both by British and Turk, trenches being divided by barricades. The dead from both sides "lay thick all around." Bombing activity is also noted. In each fire bay one man was placed as a look-out and observing that a bomb had been thrown would shout either "Bomb Right" or "Bomb Left." If a bomb landed in the trench he was required to cover the device with a blanket and take cover. Turkish bombs are noted as being unreliable, their fuses often going out. These were promptly re lit and thrown back. Realising this, the enemy began throwing bombs unlit and with instantaneous fuses. Orders were later issued in the British line instructing troops not to throw back any Turkish bomb. Tours in Hill 60 trenches were usually about 3 days. The reserve area being in South Wales Borderers Gully. Casualties for September – 50.

OCTOBER
Relieved 1/4th Northamptonshire in front line – Hill 60 (5th). Lieutenant Pelly killed (9th). Relieved by 1/4th Northamptonshire (10th). Captain Graham mortally wounded same day. Relieved 1/5th Suffolk in front line (20th). Relieved by 1/4th Northamptonshire (25th). Casualties for October – 51.

NOVEMBER
Relieved 1/5th Suffolk in front line (5th). Relieved by 1/4th Northamptonshire (9th). Relieved 1/5th Suffolk in front line (16th).Relieved by 1/5th Suffolk (17th). Relieved 1/5th Suffolk in front line (20th). Mine exploded under Essex Barricade in Beech Lane – 8 killed, 10 wounded. Relieved by 1/4th Northamptonshire (24th). One officer of the Battalion records Gurkhas taking over trenches at Hill 60. He notes their suffering during fierce winter conditions . . . "but they managed to appear as well groomed as if they were living in barracks."

DECEMBER
Embarked for Mudros (6th).

1st Garrison Battalion

AUGUST
Denham, Buckinghamshire. Sailed *Empress of Britain* from Devonport (24th). Strength – 27 officers, 984 other ranks.

SEPTEMBER
Arrived Mudros, Lemnos (3rd). Historian of the Essex Regiment, J.W. Burrows, records that "D" Company spent some time at Anzac and Cape Helles and also, during the evacuation, companies were employed at Anzac on police duties and loading ammunition. Some 15 casualties are recorded, including 2 killed.

THE SHERWOOD FORESTERS (NOTTINGHAMSHIRE AND DERBYSHIRE REGIMENT)

"Suvla" "Landing at Suvla" "Scimitar Hill" "Gallipoli,1915"

9TH (SERVICE) BATTALION

JUNE
Frensham, Surrey. Part of 33rd Brigade, 11th (Northern) Division. Entrained at Farnham for Liverpool (30th).

JULY
Sailed *Empress of Britain* (1st). Arrived Malta (8th). Sailed for Egypt (11th), Arrived Alexandria (12th) then to Lemnos (16th). Arrived Mudros (18th). Sailed *El Kahirah* for Gallipoli (20th). Landed "V" Beach, Cape Helles during early hours (21st) and moved to bivouacs at Royal Naval Division camp. Moved forward during afternoon to reserve trenches – Eski Line. Relieved Drake and Hawke Battalions in firing line (23rd). Major G.R. Fielding killed by sniper (24th). Battalion records note time in trenches given over to improving positions, opening new communication trenches and burying "masses of dead bodies."

AUGUST
Relieved by French troops and to rest camp (1st). Sailed *Osmanieh* for Imbros same night. Landed "B" Beach, Suvla Bay (6th). Moved forward and dug in on line running from south-west corner of Salt Lake to the sea. Moved forward during night (7th/8th) to Hill 50. Attack on Ismail Oglu Tepe (9th). Advanced – "B" and "C" Companies in front, "A" in support, "D" in reserve. Battalion records note that by 8 a.m. a satisfactory line of defence had been taken up at a cost of 8 officers, 150 other ranks. Enemy counter attacked about 3 p.m. forcing gap between "A and "B" Companies. By this time just 2 officers remained fit for duty. Commanding Officer, Lieutenant-Colonel L.A. Bosanquet, led support attack and succeed in driving enemy back. Battalion then withdrew. Casualties among officers – 7 killed, 11 wounded, 1 missing. Strength of other ranks reduced to about 300. Reinforced by 1/1st Herefordshire about 5 p.m. Relieved (12th) and to rest area on beach. Relieved 6th York and Lancaster in forward trenches near Chocolate Hill (18th). Relieved and to beach bivouacs (20th). Moved

forward from Lala Baba (21st) and in attack on Hetman Chair. Heavy casualties during advance. Withdrew to reserve trenches (22nd) and formed composite battalion with 7th South Staffordshire. To positions on eastern slope of Karakol Dagh (27th). Began tours in front line – Jephson's Post area.

SEPTEMBER
Relieved (12th) and to rest camp at West Beach. Took over line from Jephson's Post to the sea (20th). Temporary amalgamation with 7th South Staffordshire cancelled (21st). Continued with tours of duty in this area throughout month. During periods in reserve provided working parties nightly to Rotten Row.

OCTOBER
Tours of duty in front line – Jephson's Post. Relieved (18th) and to Divisional Reserve at West Beach. To "A" Beach (31st).

NOVEMBER
To forward area (11th) – Leather Lane, near Oxford Circus, Oxford Street behind Jephson's Post. Employed in digging new communication trenches on right of Jephson's Post. Later took over firing line at Jepson's Post. Relieved by 6th Lincolnshire (24th) and to line on slopes leading from Karakol Dagh to Salt Lake. Heavy storm (26th) – some trenches four feet deep in water, equipment and kit swept away.

DECEMBER
To Lone Tree Gully in reserve (1st). Relieved 7th South Staffordshire in firing line (8th). To Grouse Butts (9th). Evacuation to Imbros began (18th).

1ST GARRISON BATTALION

JULY
Formed at Lichfield.

OCTOBER
To Malta then Egypt.

NOVEMBER
War Diary of 2/10th Middlesex Regiment records (9th) 4 officers, 200 other ranks attached for fatigues at Lala Baba defences, Suvla.

The Loyal North Lancashire Regiment

"Suvla" "Sari Bair" "Gallipoli,1915"

6TH (SERVICE) BATTALION

JUNE

Blackdown, Surrey. Part of 38th Brigade, 13th (Western) Division. Left Blackdown for Avonmouth (14th) and embarked *Braemar Castle*. Officers present – Lieutenant-Colonel H.G. Levinge (Commanding); Majors J.G. Fairlie, G.S. Rowley-Conway; Captains B.W.O. Thompson, J.W. Mather, A.S.Walter, G.C. Wilson, H. Wright, N.S. Mann (Adjutant), H.G. Mann, C.C. de Fallot, H.W. Binks (R.A.M.C., Medical Officer); Lieutenants J.B. Pennefather, G.E. Cash, G.M. Smyth, R.M. Wilson, J.D. Crichton, H.F.A. Turner, G.B. Lockhart, N.L. Wells, W.A. Broadwood, J.W. Atherley (Quartermaster); 2nd Lieutenants C.N. Hathorn, J.T. Kewley, G.H. Grimshaw, L.C. Rice, G.P. Guilleband, T.D. Penrice, H.W. Mann, C.W. Creasey. Other ranks – 946. Left Avonmouth (17th) and anchored in Walton Bay. Sailed (18th). Passed Gibraltar (23rd). Arrived Malta (26th). Sailed for Egypt (27th). Arrived Alexandria (30th).

JULY

Sailed for Lemnos (2nd). Arrived Mudros (5th). Landed Cape Helles via *River Clyde* (6th) and to camp in Gully Ravine. Moved forward to reserve in Eski Line (7th). Moved forward to support and front line (8th) and attached to troops of 29th Division. Sector rested on the Aegean Sea – the extreme left of the British line. Relieved by 6th East Lancashire (9th). Casualties – Captain C.C. de Fallot (died of wounds 15th) Captain H. Wright, Lieutenants G.M. Smyth, J.D. Crichton and 24 other ranks wounded, one man missing. To bivouacs at Geogheghan's Bluff (11th), front line trenches (11th). Took part in unsuccessful attack during early morning (12th). Casualties – 1 killed, 11 wounded. Relieved and to Eski Line (14th). Moved forward to reserve trenches (15th). To bivouacs at Gully Beach (16th). Took over trenches – right sub-sector (18th). Relieved and to bivouacs (28th). Casualties since 18th – 3 killed, 6 wounded, 1 missing. To Mudros (31st).

AUGUST

Sailed *Osmanieh* (4th). Landed Anzac Cove (5th) and to bivouacs in Victoria Gully. Heavily shelled (6th) – two men killed, 2nd Lieutenant L.C. Rice and

31 other ranks wounded. Marched along beach to Reserve Gully below The Sphinx (7th) then to No. 3 Post. Took up positions at foot of Chailak Dere (8th). Advanced to The Apex. With 5th Wiltshire relieved New Zealand troops after attack on Chunuk Bair (9th) – "A", "B", "C" Companies in front, "D" in support. 5th Wiltshire in reserve. Enemy shelled positions and attacked in large numbers (10th). From official despatch – "The two battalions of the New Army chosen to hold Chunuk Bair were the 6th Loyal North Lancashire and the 5th Wiltshire. The first of these arrived in good time and occupied the trenches. Even in the darkness their commanding officer, Lieutenant-Colonel H.G. Levinge, recognised how dangerously these trenches were sited, and he began at once to dig observation posts on the actual crest and to strengthen the defences where he could; but he had not time given him to do much. At daybreak on Tuesday, 10th August, the Turks delivered a grand attack from Chunuk Bair – Hill "Q" against these two battalions, already weakened in numbers, though not in spirit, by previous fighting. First our men were shelled by every enemy gun, and then, at 5.30 a.m., were assaulted by a large column, consisting of no less than a full division, plus a regiment of three battalions. The North Lancashire men were simply overwhelmed in their shallow trenches by sheer weight of numbers, whilst the Wiltshire, who were caught in the open, were literally almost annihilated." General Hamilton's despatch: "Generals fought in the ranks (Brigadier-General A.H. Baldwin, commanding 38th Brigade killed) and men dropped their scientific weapons and caught one another by the throat. So desperate a fight cannot be described. The Turks came on again and again, fighting magnificently, calling upon the name of God. Our men stood to it and maintained, by many a deed of daring, the old traditions of their race. There was no flinching. They died in the ranks where they stood." War Diary records that the Turks came on in 4 lines, the first 2 being "mown down by our fire." Third line reached trenches . . . "where hand to hand fighting took place." After heavy casualties survivors fell back to support line . . . "another stubborn resistance was made, but the enemy were too strong." Captain Mather's Company inflicted heavy casualties on enemy, charging three times with the bayonet. Casualties – Lieutenant-Colonel H.G. Levinge; Major G.S. Rowley-Conway; Captains J.W. Mather, H.G. Mann, B.W.O. Thompson; Lieutenants G.P. Guilleband, G.B. Lockhart, N.L. Wells, R.M. Wilson; 2nd Lieutenants C.N. Hathorn, H.W. Mann killed. Other ranks – eight killed, thirty wounded, 445 missing believed killed. Captain H.G. Mann is buried in No. 2 Outpost Cemetery. The other officers have no known grave and are commemorated on the Helles Memorial. Withdrew and half way down Chailak Dere (12th) and temporary attached to 40th Brigade. Provided working party in trenches at

Rhododendron Spur (14th). Withdrew to bivouacs near 13th Division Headquarters (15th). War Diary records 9 wounded from stray bullets (16th). Rejoined 38th Brigade in Aghyl Dere (18th August). Company sent to support troops in firing line (19th). Detachments sent to assist troops in positions on right of No 4 Section Defences (20th). Detachment sent to support 16th Australian Battalion in firing line (21st). Formed into composite battalion with 6th South Lancashire (28th). Took over support trenches at Kazlar Chair (29th). Provided working parties digging communication trenches between 30th Brigade Headquarters and firing line.

SEPTEMBER
Relieved by Scottish Horse Yeomanry (3rd) and moved to Lala Baba. Draft of four officers and 265 other ranks received during first week of month. To reserve trenches No3 Section (21st). Attached to 31st Brigade headquarters just west of Chocolate Hill (29th) relieving 6th Royal Irish Fusiliers in support trenches. Took over fire trenches from 5th Royal Irish Fusiliers on Green Hill (30th).

OCTOBER
Relieved by 6th East Lancashire (14th) and to reserve line at Chocolate Hill. To firing line at Green Hill (28th) – trenches B50, B51, B52, B53. Shell landed in B52 (31st) – 3 killed, 4 wounded.

NOVEMBER
Relieved and to reserve line at Chocolate Hill (13th). War Diary records (27th) heavy explosive shells and shrapnel hit lines – 11 killed, 21 wounded. Further drafts arrived. Strength by end of month – 15 officers, 619 other ranks.

DECEMBER
To firing line – Green Hill (1st). During evacuation (13th-16th) three officers and 100 other ranks employed digging defensive positions at Lala Baba. Captain Crag with six other officers and 343 other ranks left for Mudros (18th). Remainder of battalion left from South Pier, Lala Baba (20th). Arrived Imbros then embarked 2 p.m. *Huntsgreen*. Sailed for Mudros (21st).

THE NORTHAMPTONSHIRE REGIMENT

"Suvla" "Landing at Suvla" "Scimitar Hill" "Gallipoli, 1915"

1/4TH BATTALION (T.F.)

JULY

St. Albans, Hertfordshire. Part of 162nd Brigade, 54th (East Anglian) Division. Entrained for Devonport (29th). Embarked and sailed *Royal George* (30th). Officers – Lieutenant-Colonel E.G. Curtis (Commanding); Majors G. Fuller, A.C. Henson; Captains J. Brown (Adjutant), L.P. Dorman, H.M. Wilson, H.L. Wright, R.D. Pendered, F.A Wright, W.S. Fisher, C.G. Guy; Lieutenants A.J. Wright, G.P. Crampton, G.P. Lancester, F.H. Preston, P.L. Murray, A.G.A. Hodges, S.J. Marlow, C.J. Crockett, J.G.C. Heywood; Second-Lieutenant M.E. Hancock, St. J. Rands (Transport), H. Burditt, G.C. Leadbitter, F.H. Cronshay, A. Howard, J.R. Dawbarn, J. White, R.W. Fay. Lieutenant C.F. Searle (R.A.M.C., Medical Officer). Major R. Coacher (Quartermaster).

AUGUST

Arrived Malta (5th). Sailed for Alexandria (7th), arrived (9th). To Lemnos (11th), arrived Mudros Harbour (13th). Embarked *Scourge* and *Foxhound* 7 a.m. (15th) for Gallipoli. Landed "A" Beach, Suvla Bay 12 noon. Strength – 28 officers, 913 other ranks. Concentrated behind Ghazi Baba then moved forward to support trenches 8.00 p.m. Captain H.L. Wright wounded. Reinforced 1/4th Essex 9.30 p.m. Attached to 163rd Brigade. Rejoined 162nd Brigade (16th). Relieved 1/11th London in forward area around Lone Tree Gully (19th). Major A.C. Henson and R.S.M. A.W. Hatton killed by shrapnel (22nd). Relieved by 4th Worcestershire (23rd) and to "A" Beach. To Lala Baba (26th), reserve trenches (27th). Battalion's left on Salt Lake. Relieved (29th) and to Brigade Reserve at Farm Gully. Lieutenant J.G.C. Heywood killed by shrapnel (30th). Casualties for August – 2 officers killed, 4 wounded; 8 other ranks killed, 53 wounded, 1 missing.

SEPTEMBER

To South Wales Borderers Gully (3rd) and attached to 163rd Brigade. Relieved 1/5th Suffolk in firing line – Hill 60 (5th). Distance from enemy's line recorded as between 15-50 yards. Relieved by 1/5th Suffolk (7th) and to South Wales Borderers Gully. To Hill 60 (9th), South Wales Borderers

Gully (10th). Relieved 1/8th Hampshire at Hill 60 (11th). Relieved by 1/7th Essex (15th) and to South Wales Borderers Gully. Camp heavily shelled (16th-19th). Relieved 1/7th Essex at Hill 60 (20th). Relieved and to South Wales Borderers Gully (25th). War Diary records Sir Ian Hamilton passing through camp same day. Enemy aeroplane fired on camp (28th). Relieved 1/7th Essex at Hill 60 (30th).

OCTOBER

Party of 24 men took over mining operations from Australians (1st). War Diary records visit of Lieutenant-General Sir W. Birdwood to trenches (4th). Relieved by 1/7th Essex and to South Wales Borderers Gully (5th). To Hill 60 (10th). Enemy exploded mine in front of position 3.30 p.m. No damage. Lieutenant-General Sir W. Birdwood visited trenches (11th). War Diary records "Artillery Duel" 2.30-3.30 p.m. (14th) – 6 men killed. Relieved by 1/5th Suffolk and to South Wales Borderers Gully (15th). Mining party sent to Hill 60 (19th) and commenced tunnelling forward from trenches on right sector of 163rd Brigade. Relieved 1/7th Essex at Hill 60 (25th). Enemy mine exploded without damage 5.00 p.m. Heavy bombing duels during night (27th/28th), very fierce artillery bombardment (11.00-12.00 a.m. (28th) – "much damage done in and near communication trenches." Bombing activity during night (28th/29th) – "enemy using catapults." Relieved by 1/5th Suffolk (30th) and to South Wales Borderers Gully.

NOVEMBER

One company in local reserve to 1/4th Norfolk at right section trenches (6th-7th). One platoon in special reserve at Kaiajik Dere (8th). Relieved 1/7th Essex at Hill 60 (9th). Relieved by 1/5th Suffolk (14th) and to South Wales Borderers Gully. One company to Norfolk Street, another to Kaiajik Dere (15th). One platoon in special reserve at Connaught Road (21st). Relieved 1/7th Essex at Hill 60 (24th). Relieved by 1/5th Gurkha Rifles (27th) and to South Wales Borderers Gully. War Diary records casualties since first week of September – 2 officers wounded, 35 other ranks killed, 129 wounded. Regarding sickness; Diary records that since 1st October the health of the men had been "considerably impaired." By end of November only 4 officers and 200 other ranks remained of the original battalion that was mobilized in August 1914.

DECEMBER

To Anzac Beach (7th). Embarked *Princess Ena* and sailed for Mudros 6.30 a.m. (8th).

THE QUEEN'S OWN (ROYAL WEST KENT REGIMENT)

"Suvla" "Landing at Suvla" "Scimitar Hill" "Gallipoli,1915"

2/4TH BATTALION (T.F.)

JULY
Bedford, Bedfordshire. Part of 160th Brigade, 53rd (Welsh) Division. Entrained for Devonport (18th) and embarked *Northland.* Sailed (20th). Officers – Lieutenant-Colonel A.T. F. Simpson (Commanding), Major H. Smithers, Captain F. Johnson (Adjutant), Second-Lieutenant Bailey (Machine Gun Officer), Lieutenant C.T. Ruse (Quartermaster); "A" Company – Captains Jude, Taunton, Lieutenants Dixon, Filmer, Second-Lieutenants Larking, Morgan; "B" Company – Captains Greatorex, Lamarque, Lieutenants Keble, Wood, Second-Lieutenants Willows, Griffin; "C" Company – Captains Dillon, Dowling, Second-Lieutenants H. J. Wilson, L.E. Wilson, Woollett, Le Fleming; "D" Company – Captains Palmer, Savage, Lieutenants Stern, Tharp, Second-Lieutenants J.C. Cobb, R.S. Cobb. Arrived Alexandria (31st).

AUGUST
To Lemnos, arriving Mudros Harbour (8th). Sailed for Gallipoli (10th), landing West Beach, Suvla. Dug in and began beach fatigues. Relieved 2/10th Middlesex in firing line – Chocolate Hill (13th). In his war history of the Queen's Own Royal West Kent Regiment, C.T. Atkinson records that the Battalion was responsible for 700 yards of front line. He also notes the intensity of sniping – Colonel Simpson being hit (15th). With 2nd South Wales Borderers extended line forward by 250 yards during night (17th/18th).

SEPTEMBER
Relieved and to Divisional Reserve at West Beach (1st). Carried out tours in firing line – Sulajik sector throughout month.

OCTOBER
Occupied reserve positions – Salt Lake Line and carried out tours in firing line throughout month.

NOVEMBER
Occupied reserve positions – Salt Lake Line and carried out tours in firing line throughout month.

DECEMBER
To Mudros (13th). C.T. Atkinson records strength at this time 12 officers and just over 200 other ranks. There had been only 4 officers and 100 other ranks wounded while at Gallipoli. The losses had been largely due to sickness.

THE DUKE OF CAMBRIDGE'S OWN (MIDDLESEX REGIMENT)

"Suvla" "Landing at Suvla" "Scimitar Hill" "Gallipoli, 1915"

2/10TH BATTALION (T.F.)

JULY
Bedford, Bedfordshire. Part of 160th Brigade, 53rd (Welsh) Division. Entrained for Devonport (17th) and embarked *Huntsgreen.*

AUGUST
Arrived Alexandria (1st). To Port Said (3rd), Lemnos (4th). Arrived (7th) and to Imbros (8th). Landed "C" Beach, Suvla (9th) and began beach fatigues. To western slopes Lala Baba at nightfall. Attached to 158th Brigade for attack (10th). Advanced across Salt Lake at dawn joining firing line at Chocolate Hill. Major C. Jarrett in the Regimental Journal *Die Hards* (August and November, 1922) records the advance towards Chocolate Hill as being with no cover and under heavy shelling, machine gun and rifle fire. He also notes that companies lost touch on the hill, the terrific heat and lack of water. "The firing line was quite unable to push on. Isolated attempts were bravely made by officers to lead on parties of their men, but all were doomed to failure." Brush caught fire during the action, wounded unable to move. Courageous work of Medical Officer – Major Paul and his staff noted. Captains E.W. Britten, M.J.A. Foley, Lieutenants H.A. Pope, J.G. Hollingsworth killed. Companies collected during night and position moved several hundred yards to left (11th). In his war history of the Middlesex Regiment, Everard Wyrall records that the Battalion dug in throughout the night (13th/14th) with many casualties. Figures not recorded. Relieved by 2/4th Royal West Kent 11 p.m. (13th) and to "A" Beach. Began beach fatigues. War Diary records (14th-31st) – "continually shelled during day."

SEPTEMBER
Moved bivouacs to gully about ½ mile east of "A" Beach (1st). To trenches at Hill 10 (4th). Carried out work clearing area of equipment, ammunition and rations during day, digging new trenches at night. "B" and "D" Companies with Headquarters joined 2/4th Queen's in trenches No.3 Section – Sulajik sector (16th). "A" and "C" Companies to reserve line. "B"

and "D" companies to reserve line west of Salt Lake (19th). "A" and "C" Companies joined Battalion (20th). To bivouacs about ½ mile east of "A" Beach (26th). Strength at end of September – 581 all ranks.

OCTOBER
To reserve trenches – No. 3 Sub Section, "B" Section (2nd). Began work on trenches at Lala Baba. To firing line (5th), rest camp at Lala Baba (8th). Began work on Lala Baba defences. Strength at end of October – 35 officers, 474 other ranks.

NOVEMBER
Four officers, 200 other ranks from 1st Garrison Battalion, Sherwood Foresters attached (9th).

DECEMBER
Evacuated (13th), sailing *El Kahira* for Lemnos.

THE DUKE OF EDINBURGH'S (WILTSHIRE REGIMENT)

"Suvla" "Sari Bair" "Gallipoli, 1915-16"

5TH (SERVICE) BATTALION

JUNE
Cowshot, Surrey. Part of 40th Brigade, 13th (Western) Division. Entrained (2 trains) at Brookwood (30th). Arrived Avonmoth and embarked *Franconia*. Strength – 30 officers, 970 other ranks.

JULY
Sailed 8.50 p.m. (1st). Arrived Malta 7.30 a.m. (8th). Sailed 6 a.m. (9th), Arrived Alexandra 2.30 p.m. (11th). Sailed for Lemnos (13th), arriving Mudros 6.45 a.m. (15th). Headquarters, "A" and "B" Companies transferred to *Osmanieh* (16th) and sailed for Cape Helles. Landed "V" Beach 1.25 a.m. and marched to bivouacs at Gully Beach. "C" and "D" Companies followed on *El Kahirah*. War Diary records (17th) – "Lieutenant J.C. Bush, Lieutenant A.W. Huckett and 50 N.C.O's and men with 3 machine guns ordered to move to fire trenches permanently." Two men killed by fall of rock during night (18th/19th). Relieved 4th South Wales Bordered in trenches – H12, H12A, H12B, Hampshire Cut, Essex Knoll, Southern Barricade (19th). Relieved by 4th South Wales Borderers 7 a.m. (21st) and to reserve line – The Strand and Foot Street. Began work on new communication trench behind Twelve Tree Copse. War Diary records (22nd) British aeroplane dropped bomb in our lines. Three men killed by shell (23rd). Lieutenant D.O. Lumley and 7 men wounded. Another man killed later same day. Relieved 4th South Wales Borderers in fire trenches (25th). One man killed (26th), another (27th). Relieved (28th) and to Gully Beach. War Diary notes bivouacs as comfortable and just north-east of end of Gully. To "V" Beach (30th) and embarked for Mudros.

AUGUST
To Anzac (4th). Occupied reserve line – Walker's Ridge and trenches – Russell's Top. In action with 4th South Wales Borderers at Damakjelik Bair (6th-7th). Withdrawn from Damakjelik Bair and moved to foot of Chunuk Bair (8th). Advanced up hill in reserve (10th). Enemy attacked over crest of Chunuk Bair – Lieutenant-Colonel F.E. Whitton in his history of the

Leinster Regiment (6th Leinster holding The Apex) recalls that 3 companies of the Wiltshire were caught in the open and "annihilated." Withdrawn and to positions on Rhododendron Spur. Casualties included Commanding Officer – Lieutenant-Colonel J. Carden killed. One regimental record notes . . . "more than half the officers and men were never seen again."

SEPTEMBER
In rest area 400 yards below The Apex, Rhododendron Spur (1st). Moved to end of Chailak Dere during evening (4th), Lala Baba (5th). Began fatigues at "C" Beach. Took over firing line – Kuchuk Anafarta Ova to Sulajik (20th). Relieved by 1st Royal Munster Fusileers during night (30th) and to firing line opposite Scimitar Hill just south of Sulajik Farm.

OCTOBER
To Brigade Reserve trenches about 600 yards in rear of support line (14th). Began work on communication trenches. War Diary records (25th) that numbers of cranes flew over the Battalion's line in a southerly direction – "Turks and our own men fire at them in the hope of having fowl for dinner." Took over front line trenches – B58 and B59 between Brecon Road and Bangor Road from 8th Royal Welsh Fusiliers and 8th Cheshire (28th). War Diary notes position as being on right of that held between 30th September and 14th October. Casualties for October – 1 officer, 4 other ranks killed, 11 other ranks wounded, 6 officers, 105 other ranks sick.

NOVEMBER
Began work on communication trench – Beaufort Road.

DECEMBER
Relieved by 4th South Wales Borderers in firing line opposite Scimitar Hill just south of Sulajik Farm (15th) and to reserve lines. To Lala Baba (18th) and embarked for Mudros. Arrived and to Portianos Camp, West Mudros (19th). Embarked for Cape Helles (30th). Landed "V" Beach and to bivouacs at Gully Beach.

JANUARY, 1916
To "V" Beach (6th) and embarked for Mudros.

THE MANCHESTER REGIMENT

"Helles" "Krithia" "Suvla" "Landing at Suvla" "Scimitar Hill" "Gallipoli,1915"

1/5TH BATTALION (T.F.)

JANUARY
Egypt. Part of Lancashire Fusiliers Brigade, East Lancashire Division which became 125th Brigade, 42nd (East Lancashire) Division in May.

MAY
Sailed *Derfflinger* 9.30 p.m. (3rd). Commenced disembarkation at Helles 4 p.m. (6th). Moved to bivouacs on cliff above "W" Beach. War Diary for 127th Brigade records that each man carried 200 rounds of ammunition, 2 days supplies and iron rations, picks and shovels. No baggage, blankets or stores were allowed. Moved forward 7 p.m. (7th) to position west of Krithia Bridge. In support of attack by Royal Naval Division (8th). Relieved New Zealand troops in forward area -- Krithia Nullah sector (11th). Relieved and to reserve bivouacs (21st). To firing and support lines (25th). With 1/6th Manchester commenced operations to get within 200 yards of enemy's line. Brigade War Diary records that men were spaced at intervals of 5 paces, each with 2 sandbags and 1 man as look-out. The sandbags were placed on the ground and men dug in behind. The line was then linked up and communication trenches dug. Ground gained between 50 to 200 yards.

JUNE
Third Battle of Krithia (4th). First objective taken with little opposition. Second reached but could not be held owing to enfilade fire. Brigade War Diary records (5th) that communication trench to front line was completely blocked by Benbow and Nelson Battalions, Royal Naval Division. Evacuation of wounded and bringing forward of supplies and ammunition impossible for 2 hours. First objective consolidated. Enemy counter attack beaten off (6th). Began withdrawal to Army Corps Reserve (7th). Embarked "V" Beach for Imbros (12th). To Helles (21st).Moved to forward area (23rd). Relieved 1/6th Manchester in firing line – Krithia Nullah sector (29th).

JULY
Relieved by 1/6th Manchester (2nd). Relieved 1/6th Manchester (5th).

Relieved by 1/6th Manchester (8th). To Divisional Reserve lines (12th). General Sir Ian Hamilton visited Battalion in Eski Lines (22nd). To firing line (29th).

AUGUST
Relieved by 1/7th Manchester (1st). Relieved 1/7th Manchester (4th). Took part in attack on trenches H11A and H11B (6th). Reported part of objective taken 4.10 p.m., H11B captured 4.40 p.m. but attack on H11A failed. Attacked H11A and south east portion of H11B (7th). Reported 11 a.m. that objectives had been taken. After strong enemy counter attacks fell back to original firing line west of Krithia Nullah. Relieved by 1/7th Manchester (10th) and to reserve line. Withdrew to rest camp (13th). To firing line (19th). Relieved by 1/8th Manchester (22nd). Relieved 1/8th Manchester (25th). Relieved by 1/8th Manchester (28th). Relieved 1/8th Manchester (31st).

SEPTEMBER
Relieved and to Gully Beach (2nd). Began fatigues at "W" Beach. To Geogheghan's Bluff in Brigade Reserve (10th). Relieved 1/6th Manchester in firing line (14th). Took over extra line extending to Southern Barricade on right. Relieved and to Gully Beach (24th).

OCTOBER
Relieved 1/10th Manchester in firing line – Fusilier Bluff (1st). Relieved by 1/6th Manchester (8th) and to Brigade Reserve. To Gully Beach (15th), front line (29th).

NOVEMBER
Brigade War Diary (8th) gives casualties figures for period 6th May – 4th November as officers:- 10 killed, 23 wounded, 6 missing; other ranks:- 144 killed, 463 wounded, 57 missing. Relieved and to Gully Beach (12th). To front line (26th).

DECEMBER
Relieved and to Divisional Reserve at Geogheghan's Bluff (10th). To forward area (24th), Geogheghan's Bluff (28th). Embarked "V" Beach for Mudros (29th).

1/6TH BATTALION (T.F.)

JANUARY
Egypt. Part of Lancashire Fusiliers Brigade, East Lancashire Division which became 125th Brigade, 42nd (East Lancashire) Division in May.

MAY
Sailed *Derfflinger* 9.30 p.m. (3rd). Commenced disembarkation at Helles 4 p.m. (6th). Moved to bivouacs on cliff above "W" Beach. War Diary for 127th Brigade records that each man carried 200 rounds of ammunition, 2 days supplies and iron rations, picks and shovels. No baggage, blankets or stores were allowed. Moved forward 7 p.m. (7th) to position west of Krithia Bridge. Moved up Krithia road to support positions 8.30 p.m. (8th). Relieved 4th Worcestershire in firing line – Krithia Nullah sector (11th). Relieved and to reserve lines (21st). Relieved 1/5th East Lancashire in firing line (25th). With 1/5th Manchester advanced line between 50 to 200 yards.

JUNE
Took part in Third Battle of Krithia (4th) – first objective taken and consolidated. Enemy counter attack beaten off (6th). Began withdrawal to Army Corps Reserve (7th). Embarked "V" Beach for Imbros (12th). Landed Cape Helles (22nd) and to firing line – Krithia Nullah sector (24th). Relieved by 1/5th Manchester (29th).

JULY
Relieved 1/5th Manchester in firing line (2nd). Relieved by 1/5th Manchester (5th). Relieved 1/5th Manchester (8th). Relieved and to Eski Line in Divisional Reserve (12th). Moved forward to reserve line (29th).

AUGUST
Relieved 1/8th Manchester in firing line east of Krithia Nullah (1st). Relieved by 1/8th Manchester (4th). Took part in attack on trenches G12A, G13, G11A, G12D (7th). Reported 10.50 a.m. first and second assaults successful, tench G10A strongly held. Fell back after heavy counter attack 7.15 p.m. Lieutenant-General Sir William Marshall in his book *Memories of Four Fronts* referred to the 1/6th Manchester as "that fine battalion" and records how it seized the Turkish redoubt in the nullah. The Battalion then held its gains . . . "until they were practically annihilated." Relieved 1/8th Manchester in firing line east of Krithia Nullah (12th). Relieved by 1/5th King's Own Scottish Borderers in Wigan Road and Redoubt Line (13th) then to rest camp. To firing line (19th). Relieved by 1/8th Manchester

(22nd). Relieved 1/8th Manchester (25th). Relieved by 1/8th Manchester (28th). Relieved 1/8th Manchester (31st).

SEPTEMBER
Relieved and to Gully Beach (2nd). Began fatigues at "W" Beach. To firing line (10th). Relieved by 1/5th Manchester and to Geogheghan's Bluff (14th). To Gully Beach (24th). Began fatigues at "W" Beach.

OCTOBER
To forward area in Brigade Reserve (1st). Relieved 1/5th Manchester in firing line – Fusilier Bluff (8th). To Gully Beach (15th), front line (29th).

NOVEMBER
Brigade War Diary (8th) gives casualties figures for period 6th May – 4th November as officers:- 20 killed, 20 wounded, 4 missing; other ranks:- 120 killed, 408 wounded, 94 missing. Relieved and to Gully Beach (12th). To front line (26th).

DECEMBER
Relieved and to Divisional Reserve at Geogheghan's Bluff (10th). To forward area (24th), Geogheghan's Bluff (28th). Embarked "V" Beach for Mudros (29th).

1/7TH BATTALION (T.F.)

JANUARY
Sudan. Part of Lancashire Fusiliers Brigade, East Lancashire Division which became 125th Brigade, 42nd (East Lancashire) Division in May.

APRIL
To Cairo.

MAY
Sailed *Ionian* 9 p.m. (3rd). Commenced landing at "V" Beach, Helles 1 p.m. (7th). War Diary of 127th Brigade records that *Ionian* was delayed at 1 day at sea due to "trouble with stokers." Moved to bivouacs on cliff near "W" Beach the at 7 p.m. forward to positions west of Krithia Bridge. Took over firing and support lines – Krithia Nullah sector during night (11th). Two platoons advanced 100 yards on left of Brigade line (13th). Unable to hold gains and forced to withdraw during night. Moved back to Brigade Reserve (16th) general reserve (21st). Relieved 1/4th East Lancashire in forward area

(25th). With 1/8th Manchester took part in operations to move line forward (28th) – "B" and "D" Companies dug in during night. Captains T.W. Savatard and R.V. Rylands killed. Some 120 to 200 yards gained. Lieutenant T.F. Brown killed (30th).

JUNE
First objective taken by "A" and "C" Companies during attack (4th). Later, "B" and "D" Companies passed through and engaged enemy in second line. Right flank came under enfilade fire but line held. Gains held and consolidated. Enemy attack driven off (6th). Began withdrawal to Army Corps Reserve (7th). Embarked "V" Beach for Imbros (12th). Landed Cape Helles (22nd) and to firing line – Krithia Nullah (23rd). Relieved by 1/8th Manchester (29th).

JULY
Relieved 1/8th Manchester in firing line (2nd). Relieved by 1/8th Manchester (5th). Relieved 1/8th Manchester (8th). Relieved and to Divisional Reserve (12th). General Sir Ian Hamilton visited Battalion (22nd) in Eski Lines. Moved forward to reserve trenches (29th).

AUGUST
Relieved 1/5th Manchester in firing line (1st). Relieved by 1/5th Manchester (4th). Reinforcements sent forward to assist 1/5th Manchester in captured trench H11B during afternoon (6th). Later "A" and "D" companies took part in attack on trench H13. Fell back just after midnight with some 40 casualties. Attack on trenches G12A, G13, G11a, G12D (7th). Reported 10.35 a.m. that first assaulting party unable to get further forward than 50 yards due to heavy fire from G10A. Fell back to original firing line west of Krithia Nullah 7.15 p.m. then to reserve line. Relieved 1/5th Manchester in firing line west of Krithia Nullah (10th). Relieved in trenches east of Krithia Nullah to The Vineyard (15th) then to rest camp. Moved forward up Gully Ravine to firing line (19th).

SEPTEMBER
To Gully Beach (2nd). Began fatigues at "W" Beach. Took over trenches at Border Barricade (8th). Major G.B. Hurst in his book *With the Manchesters In The East* recalls the naming of trenches in the area. He claims personal responsibility for Burlington Street and Greenheys Lane – both locations of Headquarters in Manchester. Enemy mine exploded (15th). Major Hurst records that this went of at "Stand To" with many men being buried alive. Enemy line at this point was just 10 yards away. Three men killed, 4

wounded from British trench mortar falling short. Relieved by 1/10th Manchester in Trolley Ravine (18th). To Geogheghan's Bluff and Eski Line (24th).

OCTOBER

To firing line (1st), Gully Beach (15th), forward area (29th). Major Hurst recalls conditions in the trenches. There were many dead buried into the parados and men worked stripped to the waist and wore simply sun helmets and shorts. Men often passed the time gathering up battlefield souvenirs. Many Turkish bandoliers stamped with the English manufacturer's name "Warner's" were found. He also reminds his readers that the Plains of Troy lay just seven miles away across the Dardanells.

NOVEMBER

Relieved 1/8th Manchester in firing line – Fusilier Bluff (2nd). Relieved and to Brigade Reserve (7th). Brigade War Diary (8th) gives total casualty figures for period 6th May – 4th November as officers:- 7 killed, 13 wounded, 2 missing; other ranks:- 156 killed, 389 wounded, 91 missing. Relieved 1/8th Manchester in firing line (10th). Relieved and to Gully Beach (12th). To Brigade Reserve (26th). Relieved 1/8th Manchester in firing line (30th).

DECEMBER

Enemy mine exploded at Cawley's Crater (4th). Some 30 yards of Battalion's trench filled with debris – 1 killed, 7 wounded. Later relieved by 1/8th Manchester. Relieved 1/8th Manchester (7th). To Divisional Reserve at "Y" Ravine (10th), forward area (24th), "Y" Ravine (28th). Embarked "V" Beach for Mudros (29th).

1/8TH BATTALION (T.F.)

JANUARY

Egypt. Part of Lancashire Fusiliers Brigade, East Lancashire Division which became 125th Brigade, 42nd (East Lancashire) Division in May.

MAY

Sailed *Ionian* 9.p.m. (3rd). Commenced landing at Helles 1 p.m. (7th) and moved to bivouacs on cliff near "W" Beach. Later moved to positions west of Krithia Bridge. Moved up Krithia Road to support positions (8th). To forward area – Krithia Nullah sector (11th). Relieved by 1st Essex in firing line between Fir Tree Wood and Gully Ravine (16th). To reserve lines (21st) forward area reserve trenches (25th). Took part in operations to advance line forward (28th). Some 120 to 200 yards gained. Two platoons became isolated in Turkish trench. Enemy attacked and regained position during afternoon (29th).

JUNE
Took part in Third Battle of Krithia (4th). First objective gained and held. Relieved during evening (5th). Embarked "V" Beach for Imbros (12th). Landed Cape Helles (22nd). Relieved 1/7th Manchester in firing line – Krithia Nullah (29th).

JULY
Relieved by 1/7th Manchester (2nd). Relieved 1/7th Manchester (5th). Relieved by 1/7th Manchester (8th). Withdrew to Eski Line in Divisional Reserve (12th). To firing line (29th).

AUGUST
Relieved by 1/6th Manchester (1st). Relieved 1/6th Manchester (4th). In reserve during attack on trenches G12A, G13, G11A, G12D (7th). Later took over firing line east of Krithia Nullah. Relieved by 1/6th and 1/9th Manchester (12th). Moved back to rest camp (13th). To forward area in reserve (19th). Relieved 1/5th and 1/6th Manchester in firing line (22nd). Relieved by 1/5th and 1/6th Manchester (25th). Relieved 1/5th and 1/6th Manchester (28th). Relieved by 1/5th and 1/6th Manchester (31st).

SEPTEMBER
To Gully Beach (2nd), Eski Line north west side of Gully Ravine (3rd). Relieved 1/5th East Lancashire in firing line – The Vineyard sector (10th). To bivouacs at Gully Beach (24th). Began fatigues at "W" Beach.

OCTOBER
To firing line – Fusilier Bluff (1st). Relieved by 1/8th Lancashire Fusiliers in Border Trench (8th). To reserve line (15th), firing line – Fusilier Bluff (29th).

NOVEMBER
Relieved by 1/7th Manchester (2nd). To firing line (7th). Brigade War Diary (8th) gives total casualty figures for period 6th May – 4th November as officers:- 16 killed, 13 wounded, 4 missing; other ranks:- 168 killed, 464 wounded, 70 missing. Relieved by 1/7th Manchester (10th). To Gully Beach (12th), firing line (26th). War Diary records Turkish deserter surren-

dering (29th). He reported that the Turks had no blankets and little food and wanted to surrender. They had been told by their officers that if they did the English would kill them. Relieved by 1/7th Manchester (30th).

DECEMBER
Relieved 1/7th Manchester in firing line (4th). British mine exploded at Fusilier Bluff then commenced to occupy and consolidate crater. Relieved by 1/7th Manchester (7th). To Divisional Reserve at Eski Line (10th). To "Y" Ravine and Douglas Street as reinforcement to firing line (16th). Took over front line – Brennan's Post (24th). Engaged enemy working party (25th) – 3 killed, 9 wounded. Relieved and to Divisional Reserve at "Y" Ravine (28th). Embarked "V" Beach for Mudros (29th).

1/9TH BATTALION (T.F.)

JANUARY
Egypt. Part of East Lancashire Brigade, East Lancashire Division which became 126th Brigade, 42nd (East Lancashire) Division (25th May).

APRIL
To Suez Canal defences during 3rd week.

MAY
Left Kantara for Port Said (4th). Sailed for Gallipoli (5th). Arrived off Cape Helles (8th), landing "V" Beach (9th) and moved inland to bivouacs. To Redoubt Line (21st). Line of rifle pits dug 100 yards in front of fire trench (23rd). "C" Company moved forward and consolidated advanced position (24th). Second-Lieutenant F. Jones killed. Relieved and to bivouacs (25th).

JUNE
Moved forward to Eski Line (3rd). "C" Company to firing line (7th) and in successful attack between The Vineyard and Krithia Nullah – Captain F. Hamer, Second-Lieutenant A.E. Stringer killed, 3 other ranks killed, 25 wounded, 13 missing. Moved forward to new firing line (9th). Withdrew to Redoubt Line (12th). Second-Lieutenant A.H. Hudson killed (13th). To fire trenches (15th). "B" Company and part of "C" in unsuccessful attack on enemy trenches in Krithia Nullah (18th). Captain H. Sugden mortally wounded, Lieutenant J.M. Wade wounded and missing, 9 other ranks killed, 33 wounded, 17 missing. Relieved by 1/4th Royal Scots Fusiliers and to bivouacs (22nd).

JULY
To trenches in No. 1 Australian Line (2nd), Eski Line (7th), firing line (10th), Redoubt Line (14th). Relieved and to bivouacs (18th). Received draft of 5 officers, 222 other ranks (23rd).

AUGUST
To Redoubt Line in reserve (7th). Half of Battalion attached to 125th Brigade on right, half attached to 127th Brigade on left. One party reenforced line on left of Achi Baba Nullah. Part of "C" Company also sent forward as reinforcement to firing line. Lieutenant Porter mortally wounded. Later took part in unsuccessful attack on trench H 11. Machine guns under Lieutenant Knowles in action at The Horseshoe. A" Company under Lieutenant W.T. Forshaw to firing line and in action at The Vineyard. Lieutenant Forshaw holding northern corner was repeatedly attacked and is noted in the Official Report – "He held his own, not only directing his men and encouraging them by exposing himself with the utmost disregard of danger, but personally throwing bombs continuously for forty-one hours. When his detachment was relieved after twenty-four hours, he volunteered to continue the direction of operations. Three times during the night of August 8-9 he was again heavily attacked, and once the Turks got over the barricade; but after shooting three with his revolver he led his men forward and recaptured it." "C" and "D" companies took over firing line (8th), remainder to Redoubt Line. War Diary records Lieutenant Forshaw arriving at Headquarters 9 a.m. (9th) . . . "Lt. Forshaw was quite done up and covered with bomb fumes. He had been hit with a shrapnel case and had been fighting for practically two night and days without ceasing. He had shown extraordinary bravery and by his personal example had been the cause of the Vineyard trenches G 12 being retained by us." Moved from Redoubt Line to firing line east of Krithia Nullah (12th). Relieved by 1/4th Royal Scots Fusiliers and to bivouacs (13th). Casualties (7th-13th) – 17 killed, 86 wounded, 1 missing. To Gully Beach (19th). Moved to forward trenches – left sub-section, Gully Ravine (25th).

SEPTEMBER
Turkish mine exploded in front of line (3rd) causing little dammage. Relieved and to Gully Beach (10th). Telegram received from Major-General W. Douglas (G.O.C. 42nd Division) informing Battalion of award of Victoria Cross to Lieutenant Forshaw. To forward trenches (18th).

OCTOBER
To Divisional Reserve at Geogheghan's Bluff (1st), bivouacs Gully Beach

(8th). Battalion now heavily reduced in strength due to sickness. To forward trenches (14th) – "A" and "C" Companies attached to 1/5th East Lancashire, "B" and "D" to 1/10th Manchester. Major W.J. Anderson killed by bomb (19th). Draft of 3 officers, 134 other ranks arrived from England (22nd). Draft of 11 officers arrived from England (26th). Relieved and to Gully Beach (29th). Casualties for month – 1 officer killed, 2 sick, 3 other ranks killed, 10 wounded, 114 sick.

NOVEMBER
To forward trenches (12th). Second-Lieutenant J. Dearnaley killed (23rd). Relieved and to Gully Ravine (26th). Casualties for month – 1 officer killed, 1 wounded, 2 sick, 4 other ranks killed, 18 wounded, 117 sick.

DECEMBER
To forward trenches (10th). Began work on 2 saps forward from north east corner of Fusilier Bluff (17th). Mine exploded in enemy line 300 yards from north east corner of Fusilier Bluff – 2.15 (19th). Party of 16 bombers and 26 men of "B" company under Second-Lieutenant Gray charged forward but due to mine failing to form a crater were forced to retire. Relieved and to Divisional Reserve at Geogheghan's Bluff (24th). To "Y" Beach (28th) and embarked *Redbreast* for Mudros.

1/10TH BATTALION (T.F.)

JANUARY
Egypt. Part of East Lancashire Brigade, East Lancashire Division which became 126th Brigade, 42nd (East Lancashire) Division in May.

MAY
Sailed for Gallipoli (5th). Arrived Helles (9th) and to reserve bivouacs. Later moved forward to reserve positions and began instruction in firing line – Achi Baba Nullah sector attached to units of 29th Division. In his history of the 42nd Lancashire Division, Frederick P. Gibbon notes that 2 companies of 1/10th Manchester and 1 of 1/5th East Lancashire, . . . "when about to follow their comrades ashore, were carried off by the naval authorities for some unexplained reason, and were not landed until the 14th."

JUNE
In action at Gully Ravine attached to 88th Brigade (4th). Took part in operations around The Vineyard (7th-12th) and attack on enemy trenches between The Vineyard and Krithia Nullah (18th). Frederick P. Gibbon

notes that the Battalion "suffered severely" in the latter action. Relieved and to Imbros (24th).

JULY
Returned to Helles (10th) and in firing line, support and reserve at No. 1 Australian Line and Eski Line.

AUGUST
Very little of the 1/10th Manchester War Diary has survived and the first entry (18th) records that the Battalion was in dug-outs (Corps Reserve) recently occupied by the 52nd (Lowland) Division . . . "having previously been continuously engaged for 3 months in firing line and adjacent trenches." To dug-outs on Gully Beach (22nd). Relieved 1/7th Lancashire Fusiliers in firing line – Gully Ravine sector (25th). Reserve line held at Geogheghan's Bluff.

SEPTEMBER
Relieved (10th) and to Gully Beach. Took over firing line at Fusilier Bluff and reserve line at Trolley Ravine (18th). War Diary records visit of General Sir Ian Hamilton to trenches (18th). Took over part of line near Western Birdcage (27th). War Diary notes that Turkish trenches were between 20-30 yards away. Also 5 rounds rapid fire at 7 p.m. *"Feu de Joie"* to celebrate recent good news from France.

OCTOBER
Relieved by 1/5th Manchester (1st) and to Gully Beach. To reserve trenches – Geogheghan's Bluff (8th). War Diary records (14th) 3 men buried alive by mine explosion while on fatigue duty in forward area. To firing line – Fusilier Bluff (15th). Relieved (29th) and to Eski line in reserve. War Diary records that drafts received from England were insufficiently trained. Musketry and fire control courses were set up, a range being made in Gully Ravine.

NOVEMBER
Relieved 1/1st Royal East Kent and 1/1st West Kent Yeomanries in firing line – Fusilier bluff (12th). Reserve line held at Trolley and Border Ravines. War Diary records (25th) a Turkish dog passing through barrier at 7 a.m. Relieved by 1/4th East Lancashire and 1/1st West Kent Yeomanry (26th) and to bivouacs on left bank of Gully Ravine near Gully Beach.

DECEMBER

To Fusilier bluff (10th). War Diary records demonstration (19th) to cover evacuation of Suvla Bay by Anzac Division. Moved back to reserve - Geogheghan's Bluff and Frith Walk (24th). To "Y" Beach (28th) and sailed *Redbreast* for Mudros.

11TH (SERVICE) BATTALION

JULY

Witley Camp, Godalming, Surrey. Part of 34th Brigade, 11th (Northern) Division. "R" Company to Devonport and embarked *Empress of Britain* (1st). Officers – Major H.C. Bates, Lieutenants E.H. Hartley, A.L. Allen, H.S. Painter; Second-Lieutenants E.H.K. Smithers, R.S. Innes. Other ranks – 220. Remainder to Devonport (5th) and embarked *Ascania*. Officers – Lieutenant-Colonel B.A. Wright, D.S.O. (Commanding); Major J.J.D. Sillery; Captains J.M. Ferguson, J.E. Muegens, J.F. Oliver, J.M. Rymer, J.M. Stevens, H.Ellershaw (Adjutant); Lieutenants H. Campbell, W.H. Hoffert, J.S. Lithiby, S.H. Marsland, E.M. Reidy, C.H. Frazier (Quartermaster), J.W. Parker (R.A.M.C., Medical Officer); Second-Lieutenants V.C. Stafford-Badger, E.V. Bell, T.A.E. Evanson-Jones, K. Lees, A.L. Norbury, C.F. Osborn, R.H. Royle, G. Sproat. Rev. R.S. Hipwell (Chaplain). Other ranks – 686. Sailed (7th). Arrived Alexandria (18th), sailed for Lemnos (20th). Arrived Mudros (23rd), sailed for Imbros (24th) where "R" Company re-joined Battalion.

AUGUST

Sailed for Gallipoli (6th). Landed Suvla Bay under heavy fire from Lala Baba. Part of Battalion under Major Bates moved forward in attack on Lala Baba then returned to beach after landing of remainder of 34th Brigade. Advanced north driving enemy along ridge of Karakol Dagh towards Kiretch Tepe Sirt. At daybreak (7th) held positions astride ridge. Later advanced on enemy, halting about 3 miles inland during morning due to strong opposition in front and fire from right and left. General Sir Ian Hamilton's Despatch of 6th January, 1916 refers to the Battalion's advance as being in "very fine style." The same report also mentions how the 9th Lancashire Fusiliers and 11th Manchester engaged the enemy with the bayonet, driving him back in disorder over Hill 10. Relieved early morning (8th) and retired to reserve line on "A" Beach. Moved forward (9th) and held throughout day in readiness for attack. Withdrew to trenches near beach at night. Casualties since landing – Majors Bates, Sillery; Captain Rymer, Lieutenants Marsland; Second-Lieutenants Evanson-Jones, Innes killed. Casualties among other ranks estimated at between 200-250. "P" and "R" Companies took part in attack on Kuchuk Anafarta Ova (10th). In support of 32nd Brigade (11th). Later relieved from firing line and to reserve trenches behind Hetman Chair. To firing line (13th). Lieutenant Bell mortally wounded. Relieved by 9th Lancashire Fusiliers (15th) and to Salt Lake Line. Part of "P" Company in support of attack by 8th Northumberland Fusiliers (19th). Enemy counter attacked and withdraw forced. Casualties 5 killed, 22 wounded. Advanced under heavy shell fire to trenches – Chocolate Hill (21st). Later, "P" and "S" Companies moved forward near Kazlar Chair and established new line 500 yards in front. "R" Company supported 9th Lancashire Fusiliers in attack on trenches between Hetman Chair and Aire Kavak (21st). Relieved by 6th Royal Dublin Fusiliers and to Lala Baba (22nd). Began work constructing dug outs on side of cliff. Due to casualties, formed composite battalion (No. 2 Battalion, 34th Brigade) with 5th Dorsetshire (25th). Moved forward at 7.30 p.m. to trenches Kazlar Chair – Susak Kuyu. Relieved and to reserve near Lala Baba (26th). Marched across Salt Lake to reserve positions – Karakol Dagh (28th).

SEPTEMBER
To firing line – Jephson's Post (4th). Relieved and to Karakol Dagh (7th). Later returned to firing line. Relieved and to reserve on beach (20th). Became separate battalion (23rd). Releived 9th West Yorkshire in firing line – right of Jephson's Post (28th).

OCTOBER
Relieved by 8th Northumberland Fusiliers (7th). Relieved 5th Dorsetshire in firing line below Jephson's Post (18th). Reserve line – Oxford Street.

NOVEMBER
Second-Lieutenant J.S. Brocklehurst killed by shell (1st). To reserve dug-outs – Holborn-Leather Lane (3rd), dug-outs below Karakol Gap (7th), Corps Reserve – West Beach (11th). Began beach fatigues. Dug-outs flooded during storm (26th). Moved to A.S.C. dump and took shelter behind packing cases due to severe weather (29th).

DECEMBER
Returned to dug-outs (2nd). Casualties from exposure and frost bite – 2 officers, 231 other ranks to hospital, 23 men missing. Draft of 3 officers, 250 other ranks arrived (5th). To Suvla Point (15th) and embarked *Carron*. Sailed for Mudros (16th).

THE PRINCE OF WALES'S (NORTH STAFFORDSHIRE REGIMENT)

"Suvla" "Sari Bair" "Gallipoli,1915-16"

7TH (SERVICE) BATTALION

JUNE
Blackdown, Surrey. Part of 39th Brigade, 13th (Western) Division. To Avonmouth and sailed (19th).

JULY
Arrived Mudros and after a week sailed for Gallipoli. Landed Cape Helles (11th). Moved to forward area – reserve and support lines (13th). Relieved 9th Royal Warwickshire in front line – trenches H12 and J11 (18th). Took part in attack (19th) – Captain C.G. Grail and 19 other ranks killed; 3 officers and 39 other ranks wounded. Relieved by 9th Royal Warwickshire (20th). Relieved 9th Royal Warwickshire in front line (22nd). Repulsed enemy attack on J11B (23rd). Relieved by 9th Royal Warwickshire (25th). Embarked from "V" Beach for Lemnos (28th).

AUGUST
To Anzac (3rd). Strength – 25 officers, 750 other ranks. C.T. Atkinson in his war history of the South Wales Borders records the trip being made in a small vessel that had previously been used on the ferry service between Ardrossan and Belfast. The steamer also carried 7th North Staffordshire and was overcrowded, the men being told to keep still in case they capsized. Landed Gaba Tepe around 10 p.m. and to White Gully. Began advance forward. Battalion historian, Captain L.R. Missen, MC, notes that the Battalion's memories of the first day at Anzac "are anything but pleasant. The advance forward was over open ground and under "an intense and accurate barrage." Later ordered to dig in on ground completely overlooked from enemy position on the heights of Sari Bair. Captain Missen records that all movement brought casualties, communication was difficult and ammunition, food and water could not be brought forward. He also notes high casualties and the death (6th) of Captain and Adjutant H.P.L. Heyworth. Assembled at entrance to Aghyl Dere (7th). Took part in attack on Hill "Q" – Captain Missen notes the advance being checked (9th), the enemy counter attacking and driving back the Battalion's left. There then

followed, he notes "one of the fiercest fights of Gallipoli. Every inch of ground was disputed with bayonet and bomb." Enemy finally driven off and line readjusted. Casualties (5th-11th) – Lieutenant-Colonel T.A. Andrus; Captain W.C. Ratcliffe; Lieutenants J.Y. Robinson, H.M. Robinson, A. Menzies; Second-Lieutenants T.H. Averill, R.A. Hope, R. Jesson, C.G. Arbuthnot, G.C.D. Cotes and 266 other ranks killed, wounded or missing. Relieved from forward area (30th) and moved back to Lala Baba.

SEPTEMBER
Moved forward to Sulajik sector (7th). Captain Missen records that the Battalion now commenced a long period of trench warfare. Principle occupation being digging forward, wiring and patrol work. Heat, sand and flies, he notes, "accounted for nearly as many lives as did the bullets and shells of the enemy."

OCTOBER
Relieved 7th Gloucestershire in firing line – trenches C52, C53, C54 (3rd) and 9th Royal Warwickshire in fire trenches – Sulajik sector, left of Chocolate Hill (10th). Relieved by 7th Gloucestershire in trenches – B68, B69 (24th).

NOVEMBER
Relieved 9th Lancashire Fusiliers in reserve positions north of Karakol Dagh – Leather Lane (7th). Captain Missen recalls the great storm and blizzard of late November. Trenches and dug-outs were flooded, icy water sweeping all before it. Men were caught without any chance of escape. Many drowned, others killed by collapsing trench walls and dug-out roofs or battered to death against rocks. Trenches remained waist-deep in water for some time.

DECEMBER
War Diary notes (1st-17th) Battalion occupied in clearing out and rebuilding damaged trenches. Oil was issued to the men and orders issued for them to treat their feet every day. Whale oil was found to be most suitable. Also noted are the preparations for evacuation – firing discourage unless necessary, a silence was observed during night. Anything that could be of value to the enemy that could not be taken away was either buried or destroyed. Ammunition was retained – 220 rounds per man, with 12,000 in reserve. Relieved 7th Gloucestershire in firing line (2nd). Enemy shell fire from The Pimple, on left of Battalion, caused 9 casualties (6th). More casualties among working party at The Broadway (11th). First party – 2 officer,

150 other ranks, evacuated (17th). Remainder left for Imbros (19th). To Mudros (23rd). To Cape Helles (28th). Landed "V" Beach and moved forward to Eski Line.

JANUARY

Reinforced 7th Gloucestershire in firing line and supports – Fusilier Bluff (1st). Relieved 7th Gloucestershire during night (3rd-4th). Trenches heavily bombarded (7th). Later, during afternoon, enemy attacked, but, Captain Missen notes . . . "seemed disinclined to face our rifle fire, notwithstanding the urgent efforts of their officers." Lieutenant-Colonel F.H. Walker (Commanding Officer) and 44 other ranks killed; 3 officers, 106 other ranks wounded. Began evacuation during night (7th). Last party left for Mudros (9th).

THE YORK AND LANCASTER REGIMENT

"Suvla" "Landing at Suvla" "Scimitar Hill" "Gallipoli,1915"

6TH (SERVICE) BATTALION

JULY
Witley Camp, Godalming, Surrey. Part of 32nd Division, 11th (Northern) Division. Entrained at Milford for Liverpool (1st). Arrived (2nd) and embarked *Aquitania* Sailed (3rd). Passed Gibraltar (6th), Malta (8th). Arrived Mudros Bay, Lemnos 7 a.m. (10th). Embarked *Uganda* for Imbros (22nd). Arrived (23rd).

AUGUST
Embarked *Racoon* (6th) and sailed for Suvla Bay. Landed (7th) and assembled on slope of Lala Baba. Moved forward 5.30 a.m. in support of 9th West Yorkshire's attack on Hill 10. "A" and "B" Companies in firing line, "C" and "D" in support. Major F.T.C. Hill and Captain J.F. Mott killed. Top of Charak Cheshme Ridge cleared of enemy. "C" and "D" Companies dug in east side of Hill 10 to cover advance of 10th (Irish) Division. During evening advanced towards Chocolate Hill in support of 33rd Brigade. Returned to Hill 10 by 8.30 p.m. Advanced 9.45 a.m. towards Sulajik and in support of Brigade attack on Scimitar Hill. War Diary records position held against numerous counter attacks. Enemy reinforcements noted coming over the Tekke Tepe Ridge. Strong attack on left (11 a.m.) repulsed. Ground repeatedly lost and gained throughout day. Received orders to dig in 8.40 p.m. Further attempts to advance unsuccessful (10th). Withdrew to Lala Baba 7 p.m. (11th). Casualties since (7th) – 8 officers killed, 11 wounded, 1 missing; 78 other ranks killed, 167 wounded, 12 missing. Relieved 2/4th Queen's at Chocolate Hill (12th). Came under heavy shrapnel fire during move – 32 casualties. Relieved by 9th Sherwood Foresters (18th) and to beach behind Lala Baba. Took over trenches east of Chocolate Hill from 5th Dorset (20th). Strength – 12 officers, 634 other ranks. Took part in attack (21st). "A" and "B" Companies led followed by "C" and "D" in support and reserve. War Diary records heavy shrapnel at almost point-blank range caused high casualties. First objective taken and quickly advanced to second line. War Diary notes that fighting had become confused mainly due to loss of officers. Came under heavy machine gun fire and forced to dig in. Retired to positions behind Chocolate Hill (22nd) then

to reserve area on "C" Beach. Strength now – 5 officers, 287 other ranks. Formed composite battalion with 9th West Yorkshire (23rd). Began work digging defence line at Lala Baba. Took over trenches left section, Jephson's Post (26th).

SEPTEMBER
Relieved by 8th Northumberland Fusiliers and to rest camp (4th). Began fatigues at "A" Beach (5th). To right section, Jephson's Post (11th). Relieved by 9th West Yorkshire (23rd) and to support dug outs at Karakol Dagh. Moved to reserve area, Karakol Dagh (30th).

OCTOBER
Began work constructing winter quarters (1st). To Preston Ridge reserve area (9th). Relieved 6th Lincolnshire in left section, Jephson's Post (20th). War Diary notes that between 22nd-31st October, 1,400 sand bags had been used by working parties in strengthening positions and construction of new trenches and posts. Rocky ground made digging very had work.

NOVEMBER
New post established (18th) about 100 yards north east of Grouse Butts. Position held for some 2 hours then forced to withdraw after strong enemy bombing attack. Casualties – 9 killed, 21 wounded, 5 missing. War Diary records 55,000 sand bags used during November.

DECEMBER
War Diary notes working parties at Grouse Butts, Priestman's Road, Cartridge Road, Lombard Street and Green Knoll. Land mines laid in front of lines (10th). Evacuation – first party of 9 officers, 557 other ranks left for Imbros (18th), remainder followed (19th).

THE HIGHLAND LIGHT INFANTRY

"Gallipoli, 1915-16"

1/5TH (CITY OF GLASGOW) BATTALION (T.F.)

MAY
Dunfermline, Fifeshire. Part of 157th Brigade, 52nd (Lowland) Division. To Plymouth (24th). Embarked *Transylvania* (25th) and sailed (26th). Strength – 31 officers, 967 other ranks. Called Gibraltar (31st).

JUNE
Arrived Malta (2nd). Sailed for Egypt (3rd). Arrived (5th) and to camp at Abukir. To Alexandria (13th). Embarked *Transylvania* and sailed for Lemnos. Ordered back to Alexandria (14th). Arrived (15th) and to Abukir. To Alexandria (28th) and sailed *Menominee* for Lemnos.

JULY
Arrived Mudros (1st). Transhipped to *Racoon* and *Whitby Abbey* and to Cape Helles. Landed via *River Clyde*. Attached to 86th Brigade, 29th Division. "D" Company moved forward to trenches near Pink Farm. Battalion moved forward to front line trenches – Twelve Tree Copse (5th). Relieved during night (8th) and to rest trenches. Relieved 1/7th Highland Light Infantry in forward area (9th) – Parsons Road, Trotman Road, Mercer Street, Backhouse Road. Relieved by 1/7th H.L.I. (11th). In Brigade Reserve during attack (12th). War Diary records – party sent forward to assist 1/7th H.L.I. in trench E10. "C" Company ordered forward 7.05 p.m. . . . "no room for them in captured trenches." Second-Lieutenants J.W. Malcoln and R.E. May killed. Party escorted Turkish prisoners back to Backhouse Road. Positions (13th) – "A" Company in firing line with 1/6th H.L.I., "B" Company in Nelson Avenue and Parsons Road. "D" sent forward to reinforce 1/5th King's Own Scottish Borderers on right. War Diary records 7.30 p.m. – due to misunderstanding men from firing line began to retreat. Captain J. Macdonald with "B" Company rallied the troops and moving forward reoccupied abandoned trenches. Captain Macdonald was subsequently killed. Battalion relieved – War Diary records (14th) "on general fatigues south of Backhouse Road." Relieved Plymouth Battalion, R.M.L.I. in trenches west of Achi Baba Nullah (15th). Relieved and to rest trenches west of Pink Farm Road (18th). "B" Company remained in front line – Horseshoe Trench. War Diary records casualties (11th-17th), officers

– 3 killed, 3 wounded, 1 missing. Other ranks – 16 killed, 70 wounded, 16 missing. "B" Company relieved (19th). Began digging new communication trench along Pink Farm Road (20th). Also provided working parties at "X" Beach. Strength (31st) – 18 officers, 686 other ranks.

AUGUST
Moved forward up Krithia Nullah (8th) and relieved Chatham and Deal Battalions, R.M.L.I. at Clapham Common, Eski Lines. "A" and "B" Companies sent forward to Nos 1 and 2 Australian Lines (12th) and attached to 125th Brigade. Returned next day. Moved forward (13th) via Mule Track and Plymouth Avenue and took over trenches right sub-sector – The Horseshoe to Small Nullah. Began work on new trench (later named Argyle Street). Provided covering fire during attack by 1/6th H.L.I. on The Vineyard (16th). Relieved 4 p.m. – Headquarters to Plymouth Avenue and companies in Wigan Road, Redoubt and 1st Australian Line. Relieved 1/7th H.L.I. in right sub-sector – The Horseshoe – Small Nullah (20th). Took over part of Argyle Street (21st). Relieved by 1/7th H.L.I. and to Plymouth Avenue (24th). War Diary records that a "pre arranged" cheer went up in the front line trenches after news of Italy's declaration of war against Turkey. This drew heavy fire from the enemy. Relieved 1/5th Argyll and Sutherland Highlanders in firing line – Sap 6 – Krithia Road (30th). Third line in Wigan Road.

SEPTEMBER
Relieved by 1/5th Argyll and Sutherland Highlanders (3rd) and to Divisional Reserve at Oblique Trench – Eski Line to Backhouse Post. War Diary (4th) records Private A. Holland, with Machine Gun Section in Redoubt Line, accidently discharged his rifle during cleaning, killing Private R.M. Wilson and mortally wounding Private T. Stark. Relieved 1/5th Argyll and Sutherland Highlanders in firing line (8th). Relieved and to Plymouth Avenue (13th). To firing line (18th). War Diary records (19th) – "enemy apparently using a rifle with silencer in G12 to right of Sap 7." Relieved by 1/5th Argyll and Sutherland Highlanders and to rest camp (23rd). "C" and "D" Companies to Eski Lines (26th). Took over firing line (27th). Order received to cheer at 7 p.m. recent success in Flanders. Worked during night on loopholes in Argyle Street and parados of St. Vincent Street. War Diary records "state" of Battalion on Peninsular at (30th) – 16 officers, 492 other ranks. Casualties – 5 officers and 37 other ranks, killed or died of wounds; wounded – 2 officers, 68 other ranks; missing – 1 officer, 5 other ranks; sick in hospital – 12 officers, 287 other ranks; died of sickness – 6.

OCTOBER

Relieved (1st) and to Redoubt Line and Eski Line. Headquarters in Plymouth Avenue. Relieved and to Torres Lines (3rd). War Diary (7th) records lecture on "The Past History of Gallipoli" given. Moved forward via Princes Street to reserve at Redoubt Line and Wigan Road (10th). "C" Company sent forward from Wigan Road to Renfiled Street in support of 1/7th H.L.I. Relieved 1/5th Argyll and Sutherland Highlanders in firing line (14th). Relieved and to Redoubt Line (18th). Headquarters east of Krithia Nullah. Relieved 1/5th Argyll and Sutherland Highlanders in firing line – Hope Street, Argyle Street, St. Vincent Street, Queen Street, Renfield Street (22nd). Relieved by 1/4th Royal Scots Fusiliers (24th) and to Eski Lines east of Krithia Nullah. One company in Oblique Trench. Working parties to Port Arthur and Redoubt Line. Relieved 1/4th Royal Scots in firing line – Main Street, Argyle Street, St. Vincent Street (31st).

NOVEMBER

War Diary (2nd) records death of Private N. Lewis of "D" Company, killed by Private D. Aitkenhead who had mistook him for the enemy. Relieved by 1/5th Argyll and Sutherland Highlanders (4th) and to reserve at Wigan Rad and Redoubt Line. To firing line (9th). Relieved by 1/5th Royal Scots Fusiliers (14th) and to Torres Lines. Moved forward via Princess Street (21st) and took over firing line – Argyle Street, Hope Street, St. Vincent Street. Relieved by 1/5th Argyll and Sutherland Highlanders (25th) and to support – Wigan Road, Queen Street; reserve – Redoubt Line. Headquarters moved from Wigan Road to behind St. Vincent Street between "B" and "C" Avenues (28th). War Diary notes "men suffering severely from exposure." To firing line (29th). "D" Company relieved 1/6th H.L.I. in firing line between G10 and East Krithia Nullah (30th).

DECEMBER

Relieved and to Torres Lines (5th). To Eski Line west of Krithia Nullah (11th). Moved forward to Rosebery Street (19th) and took part in successful attack on Trenches G11A and G12. Casualties – Second-Lieutenants S.H. Kirby (10th Border, attached), A. Macfarlane Turner killed; Captain E.F.M. Frost mortally wounded; 5 officers wounded; 17 other ranks killed, 67 wounded. Consolidated gains (20th). Relieved by 1/5th Argyll and Sutherland Highlanders (21st) and to Great Western Road, Wigan Road, Dalmeny Street, Clunes Vennel. Relieved by 1/5th Royal Scots Fusiliers (26th) and to Torres Lines.

JANUARY, 1916
Evacuated to Mudros (8th).

1/6TH (CITY OF GLASGOW) BATTALION (T.F.)

MAY
Dunfermline, Fifeshire. Part of 157th Brigade, 52nd (Lowland) Division. To Plymouth (24th). Embarked *Transylvania* (25th) and sailed (26th). Called Gibraltar (31st).

JUNE
Arrived Malta (2nd). Sailed for Egypt (3rd). Arrived (5th) and to camp at Abukir. To Alexandria (13th). Embarked *Transylvania* and sailed for Lemnos. Ordered back to Alexandria (14th). Arrived (15th) and to Abukir. To Alexandria (28th) and sailed *Annaberg* for Lemnos.

JULY
Arrived Mudros (1st). "C" and "D" Companies transhipped to *Mosquito*, "A" and "B" Companies *Newmarket* then to Cape Helles. Landed "W" Beach (2nd) and to rest camp at Torres Lines. Heavily shelled (5th), first casualties – 1 killed, 9 wounded. Relieved Nelson Battalion in firing line (6th) – Lunette, Nelson Avenue, Trotman Road, Plymouth Avenue. Relieved by 1/5th Argyll and Sutherland Highlanders (9th) and to rest camp. To firing line (11th). Took part in successful attack on Trenchs F12 and E10 (12th). Official History of the Gallipoli campaign records that first troops to enter enemy trenches were driven out by counter attack, but after being reinforced by 1/5th Highland Light Infantry held gains. Took 90 prisoners. Casualties – 5 officers killed, 6 wounded, 1 missing; 31 other ranks killed, 161 wounded, 71 missing. Consolidated gains (13th). Withdrew to support – Nelson Avenue, Parsons Road, Trotman Road during evening. Took over trenches E11 and E10A (14th). "C" Company relieved Drake Battalion in E12A and E12B. Relieved by 1/7th H.L.I. and to Torres Lines (17th). War Diary notes gas helmets issued (23rd) and lecture regarding their use by Lieutenant-General Hunter-Wilson given (24th).

AUGUST
Began tours of duty in firing line, support and reserve (12th).

SEPTEMBER
Relieved by 1/7th Highland Light Infantry (1st). To firing line (4th), reserve (10th) and to Torres Lines (17th). To firing line (23rd).

OCTOBER
Relieved by 1/5th Royal Scots Fusiliers and to Torres Lines (3rd). Relieved 1/7th Highland Light Infantry in firing line (13th). Relieved (18th). Relieved 1/7th Highland Light Infantry in firing line (22nd). Later to support in Wigan Road and Redoubt Line. To forward area (31st). Front line – Main Street.

NOVEMBER
Relieved by 1/7th Highland Light Infantry (4th). Held support positions – Redoubt Line and No. 1 Australian Line. Relieved (14th). To Eski Line (18th). Later to firing line. Relieved by 1/7th Highland Light Infantry (30th).

DECEMBER
To Torres Lines (5th), front line – Rosebury Street to Rue de Paris (11th). Relieved by 1/4th Royal Scots (14th). Relieved 1/5th Royal Scots Fusiliers in front line (20th). Relieved and to Torres Lines (26th). To Eski Line (29th).

JANUARY
Began evacuation (8th). *Prince George* hit by torpedo (failed to explode). Arrived Mudros (9th).

1/7TH (BLYTHSWOOD) BATTALION (T.F.)

MAY
Dunfermline, Fifeshire. Part of 157th Brigade, 52nd (Lowland) Division. To Plymouth (24th). Embarked *Transylvania* (25th) and sailed (26th). Called Gibraltar (31st).

JUNE
Arrived Malta (2nd). Sailed for Egypt (3rd). Arrived (5th) and to camp at Abukir. To Alexandria (13th). Embarked *Transylvania* and sailed for Lemnos. Ordered back to Alexandria (14th). Arrived (15th) and to Abukir. To Alexandria (28th) and sailed *Mauitour* for Lemnos. Strength – 30 officers, 941 other ranks.

JULY
Arrived Mudros (1st). To Imbros (2nd) and to camp at Kephalos. To Cape Helles (3rd) and to Torres Lines. Moved forward to firing line and support trenches (5th) – Parsons Road, Trotman Road, Mercer Street, Backhouse

Road. Relieved by 1/5th Highland Light Infantry (9th) and to rest camp. Relieved 1/5th Highland Light Infantry in firing line (11th). Took part in attack on Trenches F12 and E10 (12th). Advanced under heavy shrapnel, machine gun and rifle fire. Objectives taken and gains consolidated. War Diary notes that consolidation was difficult due to the number of dead and wounded in trenches. Came under heavy enfilade fire during morning (13th) and retreated to Parsons Road. Men rallied, charged and re-took their positions. Relieved (15th) and to rest camp at Pink Farm. Casualties (12th-13th) – Officers: Captain W.H. Gandy, Lieutenants W.B. Galbraith, G. Dickson, G.H. Weller, Second-Lieutenants A.J. McKersie, H.G. Russell killed or died of wounds; 2 wounded. Other ranks: 40 killed, 149 wounded, 53 missing. Moved back to rest camp at Torres Lines (16th). To Eski Line at rear of Brown House Farm (17th). Relieved by 6th King's Own (19th) and to Torres Lines.

AUGUST
To Redoubt Line and No. 1 Australian Line (13th). Took over firing line from 1/6th Highland Light Infantry – The Horseshoe, Argyle Street (17th). Second-Lieutenant D.B. Galbraith (brother of W.B. Galbraith) killed (20th). Later withdrew to supports – Redoubt Line, Wigan Road, No. 1 Australian Line. Relieved 1/5th Highland Light Infantry in firing line – The Horseshoe – Small Nullah (24th). Relieved and to reserve trenches (27th).

SEPTEMBER
Relieved 1/6th Highland Light Infantry in firing line (1st). To reserve trenches (4th). Relieved 1/6th Highland Light Infantry in firing line (10th). Relieved and to rest camp (13th). Relieved 1/6th Highland Light Infantry in firing line (17th). War Diary records (23rd) that an enemy deserter, a medical sergeant major, came over to Battalion's lines. Relieved (23rd) and to Eski Line. Relieved 1/6th Highland Light Infantry in firing Line (27th). Relieved and to Eski Line (30th).

OCTOBER
Relieved 1/4th Royal Scots in firing line (10th). Relieved by 1/6th Highland Light Infantry (13th) and to Wigan Road and Redoubt Line. Relieved 1/6th Highland Light Infantry in firing line (18th). In action during night (20th). Attacked Trench H11A and established bomb sap. Enemy counter attack repulsed during night (21st). Casualties – 2 killed, 8 wounded. Relieved by 1/6th Highland Light Infantry (22nd) and to Wigan Road and Redoubt Line. To Torres Lines (24th). Moved forward to Nos 1 and 3 Australian Lines (31st).

NOVEMBER
Relieved 1/6th Highland Light Infantry in firing line (4th). Relieved (9th) and to Redoubt and No.1 Australian Lines. To rest camp (13th), firing line (21st). War Diary records heavy shelling on way up. Enemy attacked during take over, but soon driven back. Enemy shelling 3p.m. – 5.30 p.m. – "Turks made several attacks but were easily repulsed." Casualties – 1 killed, 6 wounded. Withdrew to support lines (24th). Relieved 1/6th Highland Light Infantry in firing line (30th).

DECEMBER
War Diary records "A bomb accident occurred" (1st) – Second-Lieutenant N.H.P. Salusbury (10th Border, attached) killed and several men wounded. Relieved (4th) and to Torres Lines. To Eski Line (10th). Took over support lines (20th) – 1 company to recently gained trenches – G11A and G12. War Diary records (24th) heavy bombardment . . . "coal boxes very plentiful." Enemy aeroplane dropped bombs. Relieved and to rest camp (26th).

JANUARY, 1916
Relieved Anson Battalion in firing line – Hyde Park Corner (1st). Headquarters and 150 men held Eglington Tunnel during evacuation (8th). War Diary notes last party set up "trip bombs" and automatic rifles and very pistols . . . "of which all worked well." All clear of beach by about 2.45 a.m. (9th). Sailed *Prince George* for Mudros. War Diary provides the following figures: strength upon landing – 30 officers, 941 other ranks. Officers – 7 killed, 5 wounded, 26 to hospital sick. Other ranks – 79 killed, 279 wounded, 450 to hospital sick. Missing – 30. Reinforcements received – 19 officers, 104 other ranks.

THE ROYAL IRISH RIFLES

"Suvla" "Sari Bair" "Gallipoli,1915"

6TH (SERVICE) BATTALION

JULY
Basingstoke, Hampshire. Part of 29th Brigade, 10th (Irish) Division. Entrained for Liverpool (6th). Arrived (7th) and embarked *Transylvania*. Called Gibraltar (11th). Arrived Malta (14th). Sailed for Egypt (15th). Arrived Alexandria (17th). Sailed for Lemnos (18th). Arrived Mudros (21st). Disembarked (22nd).

AUGUST
Landed Anzac Cove (5th) and to bivouacs at Shrapnel Gully. Strength – 23 officers, 743 other ranks. Marched (8th) via Walker's Ridge, Fisherman's Hut. Advanced up Chailak Dere. Came under heavy shell fire – 3 killed and approx. 20 wounded. Moved forward about 440 yards and took up defensive position on right. Resumed advance 9 p.m. War Diary records marching for about 2 hours then ordered to return "as rought taken was found to be unpractical." Later turned off to right and reached Aghyl Dere. Continued advance (9th). Deployed in support of firing line near The Farm. Enemy attacked 4.30 a.m. (10th). Position held for about 1« hours then ordered to withdraw. 5th Connaught Rangers took over line and Battalion held support. War Diary records strength now about 270. Casualties "as far as can be ascertained" – 3 officers, 42 other ranks killed; 15 officers, 274 other ranks wounded, 38 missing. Took over trenches on left of No. 8 Section – Gurkha Post (13th). Attached to Australians and to No. 3 Post (17th). Later to Reserve Gully and began tours on duty in Russell's Top area.

SEPTEMBER
To Mudros (29th).

PRINCESS VICTORIA'S (ROYAL IRISH FUSILIERS)

"Suvla" "Landing at Suvla" "Scimitar Hill" "Gallipoli,1915"

5TH (SERVICE) BATTALION

JULY

Basingstoke, Hampshire. Part of 31st Brigade, 10th (Irish) Division. Entrained for Devonport (11th) and embarked *Andania*. Sailed (12th). Called Gibraltar (15th), arrived Malta (18th). Sailed for Egypt (20th), arriving Alexandria (22nd). Sailed (24th). Arrived Mudros Harbour, Lemnos (26th). Sailed to Mitylene (30th). Arrived Port Iero (31st) and remained in harbour.

AUGUST

Transhipped to *Osmanieh* (6th) and sailed for Gallipoli. In *A Short Record of the Services and Experiences of the 5th Battalion, Royal Irish Fusiliers in the Great War* (published 1919) the author recalls "On board the "Osmanieh" the final preparations for the struggle were put in train: machine guns were stripped and cleaned, rifle bolts were given their final oiling, and many a man ran his finger along his bayonet." Anchored in Suvla Bay 4.30 a.m. (7th). War Diary records action in progress on shore and 2 bombs dropped near ship from aeroplane. Disembarked "C" Beach and advanced under shrapnel fire over ridge to Lala Baba. Later took part in successful attack on Chocolate Hill – advanced towards Hill 10, crossed Salt Lake with many sinking above the knees. Enemy concentrated their shell fire – many casualties. Changed direction and commenced attack across the Anafarta Plain. Further casualties from snipers hiding in scrub. Objective stormed and taken by 8 p.m. War Diary (8th) notes that Chocolate Hill was "honey combed" with enemy trenches. Relieved 7th South Staffordshire in firing line at Green Hill (9th). War Diary notes – trenches very shallow and difficult to walk about due to sniping – wounded had to remain where they fell. Also difficulty in getting supplies of ammunition forward. Two strong enemy counter attacks on right repulsed. Heavy sniping throughout night. Party of volunteers under Second-Lieutenant Crossley sent out (10th) to clear snipers from dense bushes to the front. War Diary records "This precaution temporally put a stop to the nuisance." Relieved by 6th Royal Dublin Fusiliers

(12th) and moved back to Chocolate Hill. Later marched via east side of Salt Lake to trenches south of Lala Baba Hill, then to "C" Beach. Moved 3 p.m. via west side of Lala Baba to "A" Beach. Came under heavy shell fire while passing north side of Salt Lake. Continued march and took up positions south side of slopes between Karakol Dagh and Kiretch Tepe Sirt. Moved forward along Kiretch Tepe Sirt (16th), past through Jephson's Post and relieved 6th Royal Irish Fusiliers in firing line. In action at The Pimple. *A Short Record* recalls . . . "enfiladed from the left by eight machine guns, and from the right by artillery fire. All day long the hill was held, in spite of repeated counter attacks, and the men were often in hand-to-hand conflict with the enemy." Later ordered to retire, falling back to positions held at beginning of day. Strength now – 4 officers, 537 other ranks. Moved via Hill 10 to "A" Beach (21st). Later moved forward to Chocolate Hill. Relieved 1st Royal Dublin Fusiliers at Green Hill (22nd).

SEPTEMBER
Relieved by 6th Royal Irish Fusiliers (6th) and to western slopes Chocolate Hill. Efficient strength (16th) – 4 officers, 160 other ranks. Relieved 6th Royal Irish Fusiliers at Green Hill (17th). Relieved by 6th Loyal North Lancashire (30th) and to Chocolate Hill. Later to "C" Beach and embarked *Osmanieth* for Mudros.

6TH (SERVICE) BATTALION

JULY
Basingstoke, Hampshire. Part of 31st Brigade, 10th (Irish) Division. Entrained for Keyham (12th). Arrived and to camp at Pullpoint. Embarked *Canada* at Devonport (13th). Sailed (14th). Passed Gibraltar (18th), arrived Malta (21st). Sailed for Egypt (22nd). Arrived Alexandria (24th). Sailed for Lemnos (25th). Arrived Mudros (27th) and remained in harbour. To Mitylene (31st). Strength – 27 officers, 756 other ranks.

AUGUST
Arrived 6.30 a.m. (1st) and remained in harbour. War Diary of 31st Brigade records (3rd) epidemic of ptomaine poising broke out on *Canada*. Headquarter, "C" and "D" Companies transhipped to *Snaefell*, "A" and "B" Companies to *Honeysuckle* (6th) and sailed for Gallipoli. Landed Suvla (7th) under heavy shell fire. Moved forward and in support of attack on Chocolate Hill by 5th Royal Irish Fusiliers. War Diary records on arrival at enemy's trenches, left flank only met with opposition. The centre and right flanks found that the Turks had evacuated their line leaving only dead and

wounded. Gains consolidated at top of hill. Casualties – 12 killed, 77 wounded or missing. Took part in attack on Scimitar Hill (9th). Casualties – 5 officers killed, 12 wounded or missing; 12 other ranks killed, 220 wounded or missing. War Diary notes that no rations had been received since landing. Entrenched during night about 1,000 yards north east of Chocolate Hill. Relieved (10th) and to reserve at Lala Baba. Moved forward to support trenches Karakol Dagh (13th). Moved forward to 1 p.m. (15th) and in action at The Pimple throughout night. Enemy attacked with bombs 4 a.m. (16th) and forced withdrawal of 50 yards. Later relieved by 5th Royal Irish Fusiliers and returned to support trenches. War Diary estimates casualties as – 10 officers, 210 other ranks killed, wounded, missing. Relieved (17th) and to rest camp near beach. To Chocolate Hill (21st). Took over support trenches (22nd). Strength – 5 officers, 388 other ranks.

SEPTEMBER
Relieved 5th Royal Irish Fusiliers in fire trenches Green Hill (6th). Relieved by 5th Royal Irish Fusiliers (17th) and to support trenches Chocolate Hill. Relieved by 6th Loyal North Lancashire (29th) and to South Pier, "C" Beach. Embarked *Abassieh* and sailed for Lemnos (30th).

THE CONNAUGHT RANGERS

"Suvla" "Sari Bair" "Scimitar Hill" "Gallipoli, 1915"

5TH (SERVICE) BATTALION

JULY

Basingstoke, Hampshire. Part of 29th Brigade, 10th (Irish) Division. Majority of battalion moved in two trains for Devonport (8th). Arrived early morning (9th) and embarked *Bornu*. Strength – Officers: Lieutenant-Colonel H.F.N. Jourdain (Commanding); Majors N.C.K. Money, H.J. Nolan-Ferrall; Captains A.S. Hog, A. Webber, B.W. Bond, R.J.H. Shaw, H.B.W. Maling (Adjutant); Lieutenants S.H. Lewis, R.R. Martin, J.W. Cartmel-Robinson, P. Farrell (Quartermaster), J.I. O'Sullivan (Medical Officer); 2nd Lieutenants H.T. Godber, E.J.G. Kelly, G.R. Bennett, J. Wallace and 786 other ranks. Remainder of battalion (mostly "A" Company) – Captains B.R. Cooper, F.C. Burke, G.J.B.E. Massy; Lieutenants A.J.W. Blake, F.J. Charlton, T.S.P. Martin, O.M. Tweedy; 2nd Lieutenants A. St. J. Mahony, J.E. Burke, A.D. Mulligan, T.W.G. Johnson, C.F.B. Harvey and 159 other ranks entrained for Liverpool 11 p.m. (8th) and sailed *Mauretania* 5.45 p.m. (9th). Arrived Lemnos (16th). Landed (20th) and to bivouacs about half mile from pier. *Bornu* arrived Alexandra, Egypt (23rd) then sailed for Lemnos (26th). Arrived Mudros 6 a.m. (28th). Disembarked 8.15 a.m. (29th) and joined *Mauretania* detachment in bivouac.

AUGUST

Sailed *Clacton* 4 p.m. (5th) for Gallipoli. Strength – 25 officers, 749 other ranks. Landed Anzac Cove 3 a.m. (6th) and to dug outs north side Shrapnel Gully. Bryan Cooper in his history of the 10th (Irish) Division records how for identification purposes the battalion ordered shamrock badges with the device "5 C.R." He points out that these took so long to make that most of those who were to wear them were either killed or wounded before stocks arrived. Came under heavy shell fire. Casualties – 1 killed, 9 wounded. Moved forward to gully at bottom of Shrapnel Gully 12.40 a.m. (7th) then turned northward towards Russell's Top. Later moved on to Monash Gully and Quinn's Post then returned to upper part of Bridges Road. Attack on Lone Pine: "B" Company moved forward to Brown's Dip and The Pimple 7 p.m. Trenches had to be cleared of dead before positions could be taken up. Remainder of battalion attached to 3rd Australian Brigade and to Victoria Gully behind The Pimple (8th). "B" Company rejoined battalion (9th) and "C" Company to front line. "D" later relieved "C". Battalion ordered to proceed at once to Anzac Cove 7 a.m. (10th). Arrived 9 a.m. and then to No. 2 Post. Received orders to proceed up the Aghyl Dere and report to 39th Brigade. "A" and "B" Companies advanced under heavy fire towards The Farm 2.10 p.m. and engaged enemy. "C" and "D" Companies advanced to position in front of and north-east of Green Hill. Came under heavy rifle and machine gun fire and ordered to withdraw to Cheshire Ridge. "A" and "B" Companies withdrew after dark. Lieutenant-Colonel H.F.N. Jourdain and Edward Fraser in their history of the Connaught Rangers record the battalion's work in assisting the wounded during the Aghyl Dere fighting. Some 320 being collected in a small space and helped to the dressing station. The devoted work of Lieutenant J.I. O'Sullivan (Medical Officer) is specially noted by Bryan Cooper. Working throughout the night without rest he was responsible for saving many lives. "C" and "D" Companies ordered forward to hold line between foot of Rhododendron Ridge and the north-eastern extremity of the Damakjelik Bair (11th). Heavily snipped and shelled throughout day. "A" and "B" Companies advanced to foot of the Chunuk Bair 9 p.m and dug in. Enemy positions taken with just two men wounded. New line consolidated and held. Captain A.S. Hog mortally wounded (12th). Relieved by 6th King's Own during night and withdrew to bivouacs at Olive Grove. Casualties since 6th August recorded as over 118 all ranks. To forward trenches on Lancashire Hill (17th) relieving 6th East Lancashire and 6th South Lancashire. Relieved by 7th Gloucestershire 2.40p.m. (20th) and to Olive Grove. Moved down the Aghyl Dere to forward positions at Damakjelik Bair during evening. Attack on Hill 60 (21st). "C" Company in front followed by "D". "A" Company in support, "B" in reserve. "C" and "D" Companies under heavy fire took enemy positions by the wells at Kabak Kuyu and in creek in bed of the Kaiajik Dere with the bayonet. Gallantry of 2nd Lieutenant T.W.G. Johnson, an international amateur footballer, noted . . . "before his platoon caught him up he had bayoneted six Turks and shot two more." Advance continued joined by "A" Company. Hill 60 stormed – enemy's first trench taken on north-western side but further advance halted by shell fire. Leading waves cut down by strong machine gun and rifle fire. Lieutenant-Colonel Jourdain records that not a single man returned down the slopes of Hill 60 and that later lines of dead could be seen – "each man with his rifle beside him, as if on parade, but all were still and dead." He also notes the bravery and devotion to duty of several individuals – one being Private Michael Judge who as orderly to the

Lieutenant-Colonel Jourdain was shot in the face from a distance of just three yards. Upon being carried away he apologized to his commander for having become a casualty and remarked how glad he was that he was hit and not the Colonel. Positions consolidated and held throughout night against counter attacks. Further enemy attacks beaten of (22nd). Relieved by 18th Australian Infantry during evening and to bivouacs at Damakjelik Bair. Casualties during operations (21st-22nd): Strength at beginning of attack – 670 and after relief – 409. Of the 30 men that held the captured Turkish trench on Hill 60 only two returned alive. Three officers killed – Lieutenant A.J.W. Blake, 2nd Lieutenants J.E. Burke and G.R. Bennett, 9 wounded. Other ranks – 43 killed, 159 wounded, 47 missing presumed killed. August 25th noted as first day that battalion had not sustained a casualty since the 5th. Attack on Hill 60 (27th). Leading wave under Lieutenant S.H. Lewis advanced on left, attacking along Turkish trench at 5 p.m. Heavy casualties from shell, machine gun and rifle fire. Attack moved forward along north-western side of hill. Northern trench taken. Enemy dead later noted as being six deep in places. Lieutenant Lewis (twice wounded) killed during enemy counter attack. Close quarter fighting throughout night. Edmund Dane in his book *British Campaigns in the Nearer East* noted how the Connaught Rangers swept the enemy from their trenches within five minutes. He records the subsequent counter attack on the 250 strong Rangers as being by "six times their number." The fighting went of until midnight when "the heroic remnant of the Rangers was at length out-bombed." Relieved 7.47 a.m., (28th) and to bivouacs at Damakjelik Bair. Casualties – two officers and 152 other ranks killed, wounded or missing. Lieutenant-Colonel Jourdain again records the bravery of several individuals during the fighting for Hill 60. Private Glavey, he points out, was past the military age when he enlisted and had three sons fighting in France. He was killed by a shell upon leaving his trench. Lance-Corporal MacNeely, who was also killed, was seen after bayoneting six Turks standing in a hail of machine gun fire enquiring as to if there were any more of the enemy about.

SEPTEMBER
Major N.C.K. Money fatally wounded by shrapnel (2nd). Moved to Bauchop's Hill 7.30 p.m. (3rd). Strength – 134 all ranks. Draft of 2 officers and 202 arrived (7th). Began road-making work in the Chailak Dere (8th). Records show that work in the area became dangerous and after (14th) could only be carried out at night. Draft of 6 officers and 350 other ranks joined (25th). Lieutenant-Colonel Jourdain notes at this point that only himself

and Lieutenant P. Farrell remained out of the original officers that had landed at Mudros in July. Moved to Walker's Pier, Anzac 8.45 p.m. (29th). Sailed *Abbas* for Mudros early hours (30th). Casualties during service on Gallipoli – 6 officers killed, 16 wounded. 214 other ranks killed, 355 wounded.

PRINCESS LOUISE'S (ARGYLL AND SUTHERLAND HIGHLANDERS)

"Gallipoli, 1915-16"

1/5TH (RENFREWSHIRE) BATTALION (T.F.)

MAY
Dunfermline, Fifeshire. Part of 157th Brigade, 52nd (Lowland) Division. Commanding Officer Lieutenant-Colonel D. Darroch, Second in Command Major R.A. Clapperton-Stewart. Entrained for Keyham, Devonport (31st). Arrived and embarked *Andania*.

JUNE
Sailed 4 a.m. (2nd). Called at Gibraltar (5th) leaving same day. Arrived Malta (8th) leaving for Alexandria (9th). Arrived (12th). Sailed for Lemnos (14th) but ship returned to Alexandria same day. Disembarked (16th) and by train to Abukir. War Diary notes Regimental transport was met at Abukir, it having arrived previous day. Also that 5 officers who went out in advance of battalion arrived from Lemnos (18th). Carried out war training (19th-27th). Embarked *Alnwick Castle* (28th).

JULY
Arrived Mudros Bay, Lemnos (1st). Transhipped (2nd) to *Bulldog* and *Fauvette* and sailed for Cape Helles. Landed via beached *River Clyde* (3rd). Landing held up by shelling then moved into dug-outs near Pink Farm. Attached to 29th Division at Gurkha Gully (5th). Companies began instruction in firing and support lines (6th). Lieutenant W. Rodger killed (8th). Later relieved and to Pink Farm bivouacs. Relieved 1/6th H.L.I. in trenches – Lunette, Nelson Avenue, Trotman Road and Plymouth Avenue (9th). Took part in atack on trenches east of Achi Baba Nullah (12th). Battalion advanced in four waves: 1st – "C" Company (Captain W.B. Lang, Lieutenants W. Millar and R.H.M. Carmichael), 2nd – "B" Company (Captain J. Nesmith, Lieutenant J.L. Rowan, Second-Lieutenant A. Nicol), 3rd – "D" Company (Captain R.F. McKirdy, Lieutenants R. Brown and J.E. McGlashan), 4th – "A" Company (Captain J. Agnew, Second-Lieutenants R. Wilson and R. Orkney). Lieutenant M.J.H. Fleming with 36 bombers went forward on left of 1st wave in Achi Baba Nullah and Lieutenant A.P.H. Stride with consolidation party of some 60 to 80 men accompanied 2nd Wave. War Diary records enemy trenches taken by a

simultaneous charge of the various waves. Rifle fire was not severe, losses mostly due to machine guns and shrapnel. *Official History of the Great War – Gallipoli Operations* records that all objectives were taken along with two small trenches, E12A and E12B, in advance of E12. Casualties: Captains Nesmith, Lang and McKirdy, Lieutenants Carmichael, McGlashan, Rowan and Nicol killed; Lieutenant-Colonel Darroch, Captain (Adjutant) Hewison, Lieutenants Stride, Wilson and Fleming wounded. Captured trenches consolidated. Lieutenant Stewart mortally wounded (13th). Relieved by 1/5th H.L.I. (14th) and to Parsons Road. Lieutenant Fleming died of his wounds. Took over reserve trenches on extreme right joining French sector during night (15th). Relieved and to rest camp near beach 7 p.m. (17th). War Diary records position as being dug-outs which were quite open to view from enemy on Achi Baba Hill.

AUGUST
To support trenches – Plymouth Avenue (12th). Draft of officers – Second-Lieutenants J.C. Adam, R. Wilson, W. Guy, W.E. Shearer, J.S. Gibb, A.Carmichael and C.W. Stewart arrived (13th). To reserve trenches – Eski Line (17th). Moved to front line trenches east of The Vineyard (26th) – Argyle Street, St. Vincent Street, Wigan Road. Relieved by 1/5th Highland Light Infantry and to support line (30th).

SEPTEMBER
Relieved 1/5th H.L.I. in front line (3rd). To support (8th), front line (13th), Eski Line (18th). Draft of officers – Second-Lieutenants D.M. Macbrayne and D.R. Lapthorne arrived (22nd). To front line – Sap 8 to Small Nullah (23rd), support trenches (26th).

OCTOBER
To rest camp (2nd), firing line – Hope Street, Argyle Street, St. Vincent Street, Queen Street, Renfield Street (10th), Eski Line (14th), front line (18th). 1/1st Glasgow Yeomanry attached for instruction. Lieutenant Orkney killed by shell fire (20th). Relieved by 1/5th Highland Light Infantry and to support trenches (22nd), rest camp (24th). One killed and 8 wounded from shell fire during afternoon. To support trenches (31st).

NOVEMBER
Relieved 1/5th Highland Light Infantry in firing line (4th). Draft of 1 officer – Second-Lieutenant R. Kerr, and 55 other ranks arrived (6th). To support trenches (8th), front line (12th), rest camp (14th). One machine gun in support of attack by 156th Brigade east of Krithia Nullah (15th). To support

trenches west of Krithia Nullah to Krithia Gully (21st). Came under heavy bombardment 4.30 p.m. Casualties – 4 killed, 7 wounded. Relieved 1/5th H.L.I. in front line – Argyle Street (25th). Worked on consolidation of recently captured positions and digging of new firing line in front. Relieved and to support line at St. Vincent Street (29th).

DECEMBER
Moved down from east side of Krithia Nullah to rest camp (5th). Captain P.Mc. L. Thomson (1/5th H.L.I.) attached and took over command (8th). To west side Krithia Nullah in support (10th), rest camp (14th). Second-Lieutenants Deas and A. McLardie with party of 43 bombers took part in successful attack on enemy trenches (19th). Casualties – 1 killed, 9 wounded. To support trenches – Wigan Road, Great Western Road, Clunes Vennel and Dalmeny Street (20th). Releived 1/5th Highland Light Infantry in firing line (21st) – two companies on east side of Krithia Nullah in Argyle Street and St. Vincent Street with support in Renfield Street; two companies on west side of Nullah, one in Rosebery Street. Positions heavily shelled daily. Captain Thomson killed by shrapnel (24th). Later moved to support trenches. War Diary notes that during burial of Captain Thomson a Taube dropped bomb on funeral party and wounded Second-Lieutenant R. Wilson. Position heavily shelled – Second-Lieutenant A. McLardie and 5 men killed, 5 wounded. Three companies to Eski Line, one to Redoubt Line (26th). Redoubt Line company to front line – Main Street as reinforcement to Lowland Mounted Brigade (28th). Replaced by company from Eski Line. Relieved and to rest camp (29th). Captain Brown, Second-Lieutenants Deas and McGilvray, Lieutenant Whetter (R.A.M.C.) and 204 other ranks evacuated to Mudros (31st). Captain Thompson (1/4th Royal Scots Fusiliers) took over command.

JANUARY, 1916
Commanding officer, Captain Thompson, Lieutenant Watson, Second-Lieutenants D. Carmichael, A. Carmichael, Tait, Leask, MacBrayne and 200 other ranks left for Mudros 10 p.m. (9th).

THE PRINCE OF WALES'S LEINSTER REGIMENT (ROYAL CANADIANS)

"Suvla" "Sari Bair" "Gallipoli,1915"

6TH (SERVICE) BATTALION

JULY

Basingstoke, Hampshire. Part of 29th Brigade, 10th (Irish) Division. Entrained for Liverpool (8th). Arrived 3 a.m. (9th) and embarked *Mauretania*. Sailed 5.45 p.m. Arrived Lemnos (16th). Remained in Mudros Harbour. Landed (20th) and to bivouacs on a small plateau half mile from pier. Battalion had no tents and suffered greatly from severe heat.

AUGUST

Sailed for Gallipoli (5th). Landed Anzac Cove 9 p.m. and to reserve dug outs at Bridges Road on south side of Shrapnel Gully. Bryan Cooper in his history of the 10th (Irish) Division records that men of the battalion had stencilled a large black "L" on the side of their helmets for unit identification. Moved north towards Russell's Top (7th) and attached to 1st Australian Division. "B" Company to Courtney's Trench, "C" Company to Quinn's Post. Retired to Shrapnel Gully (8th). Attached to New Zealand Brigade and moved northwards towards Rhododendron Ridge (9th). Came under heavy shell fire – 12 killed, 35 wounded. Arrived foot of ridge 3 p.m. "A" and "D" Companies moved forward and relieved New Zealanders in line at nightfall. Remainder took up position behind crest in support. Enemy attacked day-break (10th). "A" and "D" Companies held line then reenforced by "B" and "C". Eye-witnesses record that the support companies were warned of the attack by a New Zealander who came running down the hill crying "fix you bayonets boys, they're coming!" The Leinsters, led by their commanding officer – Lieutenant-Colonel J. Craske, D.S.O., then charged up the hill without waiting to put on their putties or jackets. Turks driven back after hand to hand fighting. Lieutenant-Colonel J. Craske wounded. International tennis player – Captain J.C. Parke also among casualties. No. 9 Platoon under Lieutenant J. Barnwell sent out to clear enemy snipers after dark. Overran by large numbers loosing half its strength killed or wounded. Positions held against repeated attacks during night. Enemy driven back by close range fire and bayonet charges. Lieutenant-Colonel F.E. Whittons in his history of the Leinster Regiment records final enemy attack of the night being met by counter-charge – "With a ringing yell the line of bayonets surged forward against the foe . . . the Turks faltered as the charge swept against them, and the Leinsters were at last able to take revenge for the losses of the night." Captain C.W. D'Arcy-Irvine and 2nd Lieutenant J.V.Y. Willington noted as leading "D" Company – "they were cut off and have never been heard of again." Enemy driven back. Rest of day (11th) recorded as quiet. Relieved and withdrew to beach. Carried fatigue duties unloading lighters between tours in trenches at Russell's Top.

SEPTEMBER
Sailed for Mudros (29th).

THE ROYAL MUNSTER FUSILIERS

"Helles" "Landing at Helles" "Krithia" "Suvla" "Landing at Suvla"

"Scimitar Hill" "Gallipoli, 1915-16"

1ST BATTALION

MARCH

Coventry, Warwickshire. Part of 86th Brigade, 29th Division. Left in 3 trains for Avonmouth (15th). Headquarters, "A", "B", "C" Companies embarked *Anson*, "D" Company *Alaunia*, Transport *Haverford*. Sailed (16th). Called Malta (24th). Arrived Alexandria (29th) and to Mex Camp. Strength – Officers: Lieutenant-Colonel H.E. Tizard (Commanding); Majors R.H. Monck-Mason, W.A. Hutchinson, C.H.B. Jarrett; Captains G.W. Geddes, E.L.H. Henderson, H.S. Wilson (Adjutant), C.R. Williams, E.C. Dorman, R. Lane, T.S. Tomlinson, R.T. Baxter (Quartermaster); Lieutenants G.E.G. Pollard, G.W. Nightingale, F.X. Russell, F.J.F. Lee, Attlee (R.A.M.C., Medical Officer); Second-Lieutenants G.R. Prendergast, T. Sullivan, F.S. Waldegrave, E.J. Perkins, H.A. Brown, N. Dewhurst, W. Cooch, S. Watts, J. Watts, G.J. Griffin. Rev. Fr. Harkins (Chaplain); Other Ranks: 1,002.

APRIL

Sailed *Caledonia* (8th). Arrived Mudros (10th). Sailed *Caledonia* (23rd). Arrived Tenedos early (24th) and embarked *River Clyde*. Sailed for Cape Helles (25th). Run aground at "V" Beach 6.25 a.m. Captain S. McCance in his history of the Royal Munster Fusiliers (Vol. II) records that boats being towed by the *River Clyde* were swept by fire, the men (1st Royal Dublin Fusiliers) being "wiped out." Very few managed to reach the shore – "the sight was ghastly, the water all along the shore and especially round the boats was red with blood." Sir Ian Hamilton reports the landing of the Battalion in his Despatch of 29th May . . . "a company of Munster Fusiliers led the way, but, short as was the distance, few of the men ever reached the farther side of the beach through the hail of bullets which poured down upon them from both flanks and the front. As the second company followed, the extemporised pier of lighters gave way in the current. The end nearest to the shore drifted into deep water, and many men who had escaped being shot were drowned by the weight of their equipment in trying to swim from the lighter to the beach. . . . the third company of Munster Fusiliers rushed ashore, suffering heavy loss this time from shrapnel as well as from rifle, pom-pom, and machine gun fire." Survivors advanced (26th) and cleared enemy from Sedd el Bahr village on right and fort to the left. Corporal W. Cosgrove awarded Victoria Cross. Hill 141 attacked and also occupied. In his introduction to Sir Ian Hamilton's Despatches, Field-Marshal Sir Evelyn Wood, V.C. notes – "It is perhaps only soldiers who can fully appreciate the enduring courage of the Munster Fusiliers, who, after losing half their numbers by drowning, and by fire of shrapnel and bullets, with their Brigadier-General, his Brigade Major, and most of their regimental officers down, could re-form into remnants of companies, and after a night without food, follow a staff officer, Lieutenant-Colonel Doughty-Wylie, from the beach up to the Old Castle, and assault successfully Hill No. 141. These men are, indeed, worthy descendants of their predecessors who carried the walls of Delhi in 1857." Relieved by French troops early morning (27th) and returned to "V" Beach. Casualties – Major C.H.B. Jarrett, Captain E.C. Dorman, Lieutenant G.E.G. Pollard, Second-Lieutenant T. Sulivan killed; Captain E.L.H. Henderson mortally wounded; 12 officers wounded; approximately 600 other ranks killed or wounded. Moved to Hill 138 later in day. Advanced towards Krithia (28th) and at night held line. Due to high casualties, formed composite battalion "The Dubsters" with 1st Royal Dublin Fusiliers – "W and "X" Companies from Munsters, "Y" and "Z" from Dublins.

MAY

Enemy attacked from rear (1st) but beaten of after hand to hand fighting by part of "W" Company. Further attacks during night. Reinforced by 1st Essex dawn (2nd) and charge forced enemy to return to their own lines. Captain E.C. Dorman killed, Lieutenant T. Sullivan mortally wounded. It was noted by one witness that many of the dead had been killed while sleeping and their trench ankle-deep in blood. Relieved by 4th Worcestershire and 1/5th Royal Scots then to reserve positions across Krithia Road. To front line (4th). Advanced line 200 yards (7th) – 7 killed, 41 wounded. Moved to left of line at "Y" Beach (8th). Attacked 1 a.m. (9th) and advanced 500 yards. Heavy cross-fire forced withdrawal during afternoon. Moved back to Gully Beach (10th). Strength (11th) – 7 officers, 372 other ranks. Separated from 1st Royal Dublin Fusiliers (19th).

JUNE

Took turns in firing line, reserve at Eski Line. Drafts arrived. Strength (17th) – 23 officers, 588 other ranks. Moved forward to Bruce's Ravine (28th) then advance for attack on trenches J12 and J13. Objectives gained and consolidated. Enemy counter attacked with bombs, but line held. Relieved (29th). Captain McCance records the relief – "The men were then in a very bad state from exhaustion, want of water and food; many collapsed and were unable to get out of the trenches without assistance." Withdrew first to Gurkha Ravine then to Eski Line. Casualties – 20 killed, 8 officers, 112 other ranks wounded, 19 missing.

JULY
To firing line – Worcester Flat. Enemy attacked (5th) – letter written by Captain Geddes notes that the Turks lost heavily and that the reserve companies ran forward keen to take part, the men "started squabbling with each other to get a shot in." He also records that the attack ended by 6 a.m. and was "a hopeless failure." Relieved and to "Y" Beach (15th). Embarked Savage for Mudros (16th). Embarked *Basilisk* for Cape Helles (21st). Landed "V" Beach 4 a.m. (22nd) and moved to Gully Beach. Captain McCance records that only Major G.W. Geddes, D.S.O.,Captains C.R. Williams and G.W. Nightingale remained out of the officers that had landed on 25th April. Of the other ranks, there were 314 originals, some 155 of the wounded having returned for duty.

AUGUST
Moved forward to reserve position, then front line (6th). Relieved by 4th Worcestershire (13th) and to Gully Ravine. Sailed *Osmanieh* for Suvla (20th). Landed and to Chocolate Hill. Took part in unsuccessful attack on Hill 112 (21st). Casualties – 3 officers, 13 other ranks killed; 5 officers, 149 other ranks wounded; 143 missing. Many of the wounded and missing burn alive in brush fires. Relieved and to Lala Baba.

SEPTEMBER
Relieved 1st Royal Dublin Fusiliers in firing line (1st). Embarked for Imbros (8th). To Suvla Bay (21st) and to reserve at Karakol Dagh. Moved forward to trenches below Jephson's Post (22nd).

OCTOBER
Came under gas attack (9th).

NOVEMBER
Heavy casualties during the storm (26th). Men drowned in trenches and dug-outs. Major Geddes records that the Battalion's position bore the full force of the blizzard that followed (28th) – "men lay dead from exposure."

Withdrew to shelter. Casualties – 12 officers, 20 killed, 268 sick or died from exposure.

DECEMBER
Evacuated to Mudros (14th). Strength – 10 officers, 164 other ranks. Moved straight to Cape Helles, landing "V" Beach early (15th) then to reserve at "X" Beach.

JANUARY, 1916
To "V" Beach (2nd) and embarked *Princess Alberta* for Mudros.

6TH (SERVICE) BATTALION

JULY
Basingstoke, Hampshire. Part of 30th Brigade, 10th (Irish) Division. Entrained for Liverpool and sailed *Mauretania* (9th). Arrived Lemnos (16th) disembarking Mudros (19th).

AUGUST
Embarked *Hazel* (6th) – strength, 25 officers, 749 other ranks. Arrived Suvla Bay about noon (7th) and landed east of Ghazi Baba. War Diary records many lighters running aground and officers and men required to enter the water waist deep and wade ashore. Some casualties from land mines on beach. Advanced up western end of Kiretch Tepe Sirt Ridge about 2.30 p.m.- 6th Munsters on left, 7th on right. Large numbers of fly-infested corpses noted from previous action fought by 11th Manchester. Manchester's line – some 800 yards west of Turkish strong-point on summit of ridge reached. Attacked and advanced to within 100 yards of enemy by nightfall. Renewed attack (8th) – "A" Company and part of "B" led by Major J.N. Jephson gained top of mound. Position consolidated and later called "Jephson's Post." Casualties included Major E.P. Conway and Lieutenant J.B. Lee killed. The area between Jephson's Post and the Turkish line was lit at night by a search light provided by a destroyer. This service prohibited any enemy attacks during darkness hours and the ship was soon christened "Munster's Guardian Angel." Carried out successful attack on enemy advanced post (12th). Second-Lieutenant L.A. Gaffney mortally wounded. Drafts of 3 officers and 174 other ranks arrived (14th and 15th). Attack along crest of Kiretch Tepe Sirt Ridge (15th). Some ground gained, Major Jephson mortally wounded. Two companies attacked (with 6th Dublins) along north slope of ridge. Turkish line charged – whole of northern slope cleared. Almost one mile of ground gained by nightfall.

Enemy counter attack at 10 p.m. repulsed. Captain J.B.T. Grant and Lieutenant G.W. Burrowes killed. Further advance recorded as impossible. Positions held under heavy bombing attacks.Relieved and withdrew to original line after dark (17th). To bivouacs at Lala Baba (20th). Moved forward under heavy shrapnel fire and relieved 1/1st Nottinghamshire Yeomanry in captured enemy trenches during night (21st).

SEPTEMBER
Relieved (5th). Later carried out further tours of duty in trenches facing Scimitar Hill.

OCTOBER
Relieved by 8th Cheshire in trenches B58 and B59 (1st) and sailed for Mudros.

7TH (SERVICE) BATTALION

JULY
Basingstoke, Hampshire. Part of 30th Brigade, 10th (Irish) Division. Entrained for Liverpool (8th) and sailed *Mauretania* (9th). Strength – 29 officers, 984 other ranks. Arrived Mudros (12th), disembarked (19th).

AUGUST
Sailed (*Rowan*) for Gallipoli (6th). Strength – 28 officers, 750 other ranks. Transferred to lighters and landed Suvla Bay about 1 p.m. (7th). Moved of from beach about 2.30 p.m. Major Bryan Cooper in his history of the 10th (Irish) Division records that Battalion went into action wearing green shamrocks on each arm for unit identification. Advanced along eastern side of Kiretch Tepe Sirt Ridge. Came under heavy enemy fire and withdrawal forced. Casualties – Captain R.H. Cullinan and 2nd Lieutenant F.E. Bennett and 9 other ranks killed; 2 officers and 58 other ranks wounded; 5 other ranks missing. Attacked 9.30 a.m. (8th) – "A" and "B" Companies in front, "C" and "D" in support. "A" Company reached position facing Kidney Hill, "D" with remains of "B" forced to halt some 400 yards from enemy's line on Beacon Hill. Three companies ordered to withdraw 3.30 p.m., "C" remaining forward throughout night. Casualties – Lieutenants E.M. Harper, S.R.V. Travers and 32 other ranks killed; 6 officers, 77 other ranks wounded; 10 men missing. Records show that the action was fought in intense heat, the men having no water. The enemy were seen to fire on the wounded lying out in the open, and on stretcher-bearers. One wounded man who was not brought in for two days reported seeing a number of

Turks, possible snipers, that were painted green. Draft of 150 arrived from Mudros (14th). Advanced about 4.30 p.m. (15th) reaching a line running from The Pimple to the Gulf of Saros. Received orders to retire to original line and relieved by 7th Royal Dublin Fusiliers 8.30 p.m. Casualties – Captain J.V. Dunn, Lieutenant K.E. O'Duffy and 10 other ranks killed; 3 officers and 42 other ranks wounded; 7 men missing. Returned to previous day's line (16th). Position heavily bombed and shelled and orders received to withdraw to line behind Jephson's Post 7.30 p.m. – Sergeant Mason and 25 men remaining at their posts throughout night repulsing a number of enemy attacks. Casualties – Lieutenant W.H. Good and 18 other ranks killed; 63 other ranks wounded; 12 missing. Moved to Lala Baba (20th) and forward towards Hetman Chair 4.20 p.m. (21st). Enemy's first line crossed, met by heavy shell fire at second. Another advance of 500 yards made but consolidation difficult. Casualties – 47 killed and wounded. Joined 6th Royal Munster Fusiliers in trenches (22nd). Carried out duties deepening and strengthening line.

SEPTEMBER
Relieved by 1/1st Hertfordshire Yeomanry (4th). Took over trenches from 6th Battalion under Scimitar Hill (13th).

OCTOBER
Moved to South Pier (1st) and embarked for Mudros. Strength – 8 officers, 315 other ranks.

The Royal Dublin Fusiliers

"Helles" "Landing at Helles" "Krithia" "Suvla" "Sari Bair" "Landing at Suvla" "Scimitar Hill" "Gallipoli,1915-16"

1st Battalion

MARCH
Nuneaton, Warwickshire. Part of 86th Brigade, 29th Division. To Kenilworth (12th). Entrained for Avonmouth (15th) and embarked *Ausonia*. Sailed (16th). Officers – Lieutenant-Colonel R.A. Rooth (Commanding); Major E. Fetherstonhaugh; Captains E.A. Molesworth, W.F. Higginson (Adjutant), C.T.W. Grimshaw, D.S.O., A.M. Johnson, H.C. Crozier, D. French, A.W. Molony, J.M. Mood, D.V.F. Anderson, J.R.W. Grove; Lieutenants H.M. Floyd, C.G. Carruthers, L.C. Boustead, F.S. Lanigan-O'keeffe, R. Bernard, G.M. Dunlop, C.W. Maffett, H.D. O'Hara, R.V.C. Corbet, R. de Lusignan, J. Hosford, J.P. Walters, W. Andrews, M.J. Kennedy (Quartermaster), H.S. de Boer (R.A.M.C., Medical Officer); Reverend Father W.J. Finn (Chaplain). Other ranks – 988. Called at Gibraltar (20th), arrived Malta (24th). Sailed (26th), arrived Alexandria (29th). Disembarked (30th) and to Mex Camp.

APRIL
Embarked *Ausonia* (7th) and sailed for Lemnos (8th). Arrived Mudros (10th). To Tenedos (23rd). Sailed for Cape Helles (25th) – 3 companies *Clacton*, "W" Company *River Clyde*. Landed "V" Beach under heavy fire. Many men shot while still in landing boats, other while wading ashore. Many wounded drowned, some burned alive when boats caught fire. Early casualties included Colonel Rooth, shot as he came ashore, Major Fetherstonhaugh, mortally wounded in boat and Father Finn, killed while tending the wounded. Survivors record beech being covered in dead and dying and almost impossible to move from what little cover these was due to enemy maintaining fire throughout day. After dark Turks came down to beach where there was much hand to hand fighting throughout the night. Advanced on Sedd el Bahr (26th) – enemy driven back. Moved inland (27th) for attack on Krithia. In action throughout (28th-30th). Command passed to Lieutenant H.D. O'Hara – the only surviving officer. He recalled digging in on the night of (28th) and holding his position for 2 nights. On the 3rd night the enemy came on 20,000 strong at 10.30 p.m. and there

followed a battle which lasted until 5 a.m. next morning. At one point the enemy entered the Dublin's line but were soon driven out by the bayonet – the fighting, he notes, was of a ".nost desperate kind" – very little quarter being given by either side. The Turks were driven on to their own barbed wire by German officers and "shot down in large numbers." The survivors of 1st Royal Dublin Fusiliers amounted to 1 officer and 374 other ranks, none having slept for 3 nights or had food for 36 hours. Battalion temporarily amalgamated (29th) with 1st Royal Munster Fusiliers ("W" and "X" Companies from Munsters, "Y" and "Z" Companies from Dublins) and known as the "Dubsters."

MAY
Relieved (1st) and to reserve. Returned to firing line (4th) and in action (7th). Line advanced 200 yards. Attacked 1 a.m. (9th) – advance of 500 yards made, but heavy cross-fire forced withdrawal during afternoon. Lieutenant O'Hara records "appalling" casualties and the Dubster's strength as 400. Relieved and to Gully Beach (10th). Reinforcement of 10 officers and 46 other ranks arrived and Battalion became separate unit (19th). Returned to front line.

JUNE
Strength – 19 officers, 830 other ranks. Relieved by 2nd South Wales Borderers in trenches near Geoghegan's Bluff (4th) and to Gully Beach. To front line – Turkey Trench (12th). Two attacks by enemy (16th) – 12 killed, 31 wounded, 4 missing. Took part in successful operations (28th-29th) – 9 officers, 45 other ranks killed, 1 officer, 138 other ranks wounded, 1 officer, 42 other ranks missing. Relieved and to Gully Ravine (29th). Strength – 8 officers, 595 other ranks. To Geogheghan's Bluff in reserve to 87th Brigade (30th).

JULY
To "V" Beach (15th), Gully Beach (19th). Embarked for Mudros. Embarked for Cape Helles (21st), landing "V" Beach and to Gully Ravine in Corps Reserve.

AUGUST
To firing line right of Gully Ravine (7th). In action at Southern Barricade (8th) – 25 other ranks killed, 3 officers, 150 other ranks wounded, 30 missing. Relieved and to "Y" Ravine (16th). To "W" Beach and embarked *Prince Abbas* for Suvla Bay (18th). Landed early morning (19th) and to firing line – Chocolate Hill. In reserve at Green Hill during 86th Brigade's attack

on Hill 112 and Scimitar Hill (21st). Relieved by 5th Royal Irish Fusiliers during night and to forward trenches – Kuchuk Anafarta Ova.

SEPTEMBER
Relieved in firing line by 1st Royal Munster Fusiliers (1st). Embarked for Imbros (8th). Arrived (9th) and to Kephalos Camp. Embarked for Suvla Bay (21st). Landed 11 p.m. and to Reserve Nullah. Relieved 1st King's Own Scottish Borderers in firing line between Chocolate Hill and Scimitar Hill (22nd). War Diary notes high sickness rate. Strength at end of month – 15 officers, 608 other ranks. Drafts of over 300 had been received throughout August and September.

OCTOBER
Continued tours in trenches.

NOVEMBER
Tours in trenches. Battalion suffered from storm and subsequent severe weather conditions during last week of month. War Diary records . . . "impossible to estimate number of sick." Strength at end of month – 12 officers, 332 other ranks.

DECEMBER
Draft of 3 officers and 168 other ranks arrived. Received orders to evacuate (13th). Left Reserve Nullah (14th) and embarked *Hazel*. Arrived Mudros during morning (15th). Remained on board then sailed 7.30 p.m. for Helles. Landed midnight and to bivouacs. Later moved to lines above "X" Beach then into firing line – Gully Ravine. Enemy attacked "Z" Company's line (23rd) and gained some ground. Later driven out by bombing party led by Lieutenant H.L. Ridley. Casualties – 12 killed, 18 wounded.

JANUARY, 1916
To "V" Beach (1st) and embarked *Ausonia* at midnight. Arrived Lemnos (2nd). and to camp at East Mudros.

6TH (SERVICE) BATTALION

JULY
Basingstoke, Hampshire. Part of 30th Brigade, 10th (Irish) Division. Entrained for Devonport (9th) and embarked *Alaunia*. Called Gibraltar (14th), Malta (17th). Arrived Alexandria (20th). Sailed for Lemnos (22nd). Arrived Mudros Bay (24th). Sailed for Mitylene (25th).

August
Inspected by General Sir Ian Hamilton (2nd). Headquarters, "C" and "D" Companies transhipped to *Fauvette*, "A" and "B" Companies to *Sania* (6th) and sailed for Gallipoli. Landed "C" Beach, Suvla (7th). Moved to reserve positions and attached to 31st Brigade. Placed on water and ammunition fatigues. Attached to 33rd Brigade (9th). Moved forward to positions near Chocolate Hill in support of Brigade attack. Major J.G. Jennings (66th Punjabis attached), Lieutenant J.J. Doyle, Second-Lieutenants W.F.C. McGarry, R. Stanton killed; 6 other officers wounded; 1 missing; 259 other ranks killed, wounded or missing. Took over part of firing line in captured trenches. Relieved (12th) and to rest camp at "A" Beach. Rejoined 30th Brigade on Kiretch Tepe Sirt (13th). War Diary records fighting strength (14th) as 15 officers, 463 other ranks. Took part in attack along ridge (15th). Two companies in support of 7th Royal Munster Fusiliers on right. Turkish strong point taken along with number of prisoners. Captains A.J.D. Preston killed; 2 other officers wounded; 45 other ranks killed, wounded or missing. Took over positions at Spion Kop (16th). Second-Lieutenant W.C. Nesbitt killed, 2 other officers wounded; 17 other ranks killed, wounded or missing during enemy counter attacks. First reinforcements arrived – 3 officers, 157 other ranks. Relieved and to "A" Beach (17th). To rest camp near Hill 145 (18th). To Lala Baba (20th). Moved forward in reserve for attack on Hetman Chair – Kazlar Chair line (21st). Casualties – 41 other ranks. Fighting strength now 4 officers, 429 other ranks. Moved into firing line near Susak Kuyu (22nd) – fighting strength – 4 officers, 364 other ranks. War Diary notes (29th) – Brigadier-General P.A. Kenna, V.C., D.S.O. mortally wounded close to right of Battalion's line.

SEPTEMBER
Relieved by 1/1st Buckinghamshire Yeomanry (4th) and to reserve trenches near Ali Bey Chesme. To front line – Chocolate Hill – Sulajik line (5th). Relieved by 7th Royal Dublin Fusiliers (13th) and to rest trenches at Ali Bey Chesme. To firing line (21st). Fighting strength – 9 officers, 357 other ranks. War Diary notes (27th) naming of trenches started. Sanction given to "Dublin Road" and "Sackville Street." Also recorded heavy firing and shell fire on Battalion's front. All reserves brought up to firing line. Casualties – 1 officer wounded, 1 other rank killed, 13 wounded. Relieved and to "C" Beach (30th). Embarked and sailed for Mudros.

7TH (SERVICE) BATTALION

JULY

Basingstoke, Hampshire. Part of 30th Brigade, 10th(Irish) Division. Entrained for Devonport (9th). Embarked *Alaunia* (10th). Called Gibraltar (14th), Malta (17th). Arrived Alexandria (20th). To Lemnos (22nd) Strength – 29 officers, 915 other ranks. Arrived Mudros Bay (24th). To Mitylene (25th). Three officers, 165 other ranks transhipped to *Osmanieh* (29th) and to Lemnos.

AUGUST

Inspected by General Sir Ian Hamilton (2nd). Transhipped to *Fauvette* and sailed for Gallipoli (6th). Landed "C" Beach, Suvla (7th). War Diary records heavy and accurate shrapnel fire during landing – Second-Lieutenant C.D. Harvey seriously wounded, 1 man killed, 14 wounded. Attached to 31st Brigade. Moved forward to south-east corner of Lala Baba and stored packs. Continued march and joined attack on Chocolate Hill. War Diary records . . . "hill captured by parts of "A" and "D" Companies and details of other regiments." Casualties – 3 officers, 109 other ranks. Major C.H. Tippet killed. Gains held and consolidated at Fort Waller. Relieved by 9th West Yorkshire during night (12th) and to rest area at "C" Beach. To Kiretch Tepe Sirt (13th). Rejoined 30th Brigade. In reserve during successful attack on Green Knoll (15th). Moved forward during night and relieved 6th Royal Dublin Fusiliers in captured positions. Enemy attacked about 3.30 a.m. (16th). War Diary records "Battalion made two counter attacks but their success was only temporary, the Turks being in great force. Major R.S.M. Harrison (51st Sikhs attached), Captains P.H. Hickman, R.P. Tobin; Lieutenants A.J. Russell, M.J. Fitzgibbon; Second-Lieutenant E.T. Weatherill killed. Relieved about 10 a.m. and withdrew to Brigade Headquarters. War Diary records strength on going into action – 21 officers, 532 other ranks. On coming out of action – 10 officers, 375 other ranks. First reinforcement arrived – 2 officers, 150 other ranks. Moved forward 9 p.m. to positions east side of ridge. Relieved from trenches (17th) and to rest camp at "A" Beach. To bivouacs on western slope of Hill 145 (18th). Commanding Officer – Major M.P.E. Lonsdale sent to hospital and battalion reorganised – Captain C.B. Hoey (Commanding), Lieutenant R.G. Kelly (Acting Adjutant and Signals Officer), Lieutenant R.G. Douglas (Machine Gun Officer); "A" Company – Captain L.S.N. Palmer, Second-Lieutenant T.G. Hicks; "B" Company – Captain J.A. Lucie-Smith, Lieutenant G.N. Wilkinson, Second-Lieutenant F.H. Doran; "C" Company – Captain A.W. Macdermott; "D" Company

– Second-Lieutenant E.J. Hamilton. To Lala Baba (20th). Captain Palmer, Second-Lieutenants Doran and Hamilton to hospital (20th). Moved forward 4.45 p.m. (21st). In general reserve during attack on Turkish Line – Hetman Chair to Kazlar Chair. Came under heavy shell fire. Captain Macdermott, Second-Lieutenant Hicks and 36 other ranks wounded. Moved forward from support trenches to front line 11 p.m.. War Diary records fighting strength – 5 officers, 424 other ranks.

SEPTEMBER
Relieved by 1/1st Worcestershire Yeomanry and to Chocolate Hill (4th). Casualties (1st-4th) – 2 killed, 7 wounded. Lieutenant Kelly sick. Withdrew to Lala Baba (9th). Came under heavy shell fire (13th) – Medical Officer wounded, 5 other ranks killed, 20 wounded. Later relieved 6th Royal Dublin Fusiliers in front line – Chocolate Hill – Sulajik. Lieutenant Douglas sick and to hospital (16th). Received draft of 1 officer, 58 other ranks (20th). Relieved by 6th Royal Dublin Fusiliers (21st) and withdrew to reserve dug outs. Relieved by 6th South Lancashire (29th) and to "C" Beach. Embarked *Abassieh* and sailed for Mudros (30th).

The London Regiment (Territorial Force)

"Suvla" "Landing at Suvla" "Scimitar Hill" "Gallipoli,1915" "Gallipoli,1915-16"

2/1st (City of London) Battalion (Royal Fusiliers)

FEBRUARY
Sailed for Malta. Arrived (11th).

AUGUST
To Egypt (27th). Arrived (30th) and to Abbassia Camp, Cairo.

SEPTEMBER
Sailed for Gallipoli. Landed "W" Beach, Suvla Bay about midnight (24th) and to bivouacs. Attached to 88th Brigade, 29th Division. Re-armed with short Lee Enfield rifles at Ordnance Stores, West Beach (26th) then moved forward to Brigade Reserve area. Work party provided for sapping in front line (28th) – 3 killed, 6 wounded. War Diary records movement in and around camp as nearly always attracting shrapnel fire. Work parties left for front line in groups of not more than 6, and at intervals of 100 yards.

OCTOBER
Machine gun section to Gun Hill (1st). Detachments attached to 1st Essex for instruction in firing line – Kiretch Tepe Sirt sector (2nd). To Borderers Gully (5th). Continued suppling working parties to front line. "A" Company in firing line (6th/7th), "B" Company (8th), "C" Company (9th), "D" Company (10th). Battalion relieved 1st Essex in firing line (12th). Relieved by Newfoundland Regiment (19th) and to Essex Ravine. Relieved Newfoundland Regiment in firing line (26th).

NOVEMBER
Relieved by Newfoundland Regiment (2nd) and to Essex Ravine. To front line (10th), Essex Ravine (16th). War Diary records (21st) total casualties to date – 17 killed or died of wounds, 1 died of disease, 51 wounded, 448 to hospital sick. Many cases of jaundice noted and frost bite after severe weather. Casualties at end of November – 22 killed or died of wounds, 57 wounded, 445 sick.

DECEMBER

Sickness from frost bite continued. All available men working on communication trench to beach. Took over positions from 2nd Hampshire behind 2nd-line trenches (7th). "Y" Company to Essex Ravine (14th). Evacuated (18th). Moved out 7.30 p.m., Embarked (19th) for Mudros. The following extracts are from a Battalion Order issued regarding the evacuation :

3, (a) Unconsumed food is to be dealt with as follows:-
Part issued to the men to carry and the remainder to be buried.

(b) Odd blankets over and above one blanket per man are to be buried.

4, When leaving the dug-outs all fires and light usually shown at 1900 are to be left burning.

5, The lines vacated by the Battalion this evening will be occupied later in the night by other troops. The lines should be therefore left reasonable clean and latrines empty.

15, (b) The Signallers will disconnect the Telephone wire at 1900 and will wind in the wire for a distance of 200 yards.

16, (b) Magazines will be charged, cut-offs closed and rifles kept at safety.

21, (b) As little noise as possible will be made in assembling the troops calling the roll, and throughout the operations. Silence must be preserved, there must be no smoking, and the utmost care must be taken to see that the dixies and picks and shovels do not rattle against the equipment.

23, The answer to challenges will be "London Regt, 88th Brigade", to be given in a low voice.

Embarked *Princess Alberta* for Cape Helles (26th). Could not land due to rough seas and to Imbros 6 a.m. (27th). Sailed 5 p.m. Landed via *River Clyde* at "V" Beach during night and to bivouacs 88th Brigade Reserve area. Provided fatigue parties – Gully Beach and Eski Line.

JANUARY, 1916

Evacuated (7th/8th). Extracts from Battalion Orders regarding evacuation issued (6th):-

1, (a) Unconsumed food – part issued to the men to carry and the remainder to be buried.

(b) Odd blankets over and above 2 per man are to be buried. Both food and blankets before being buried should be so damaged as to make them unfit for use. For instance bully beef tins should have a hole pierced i them, and blankets should be cut into strips with a knife.

2/2ND (CITY OF LONDON) BATTALION (ROYAL FUSILIERS)

JANUARY
Valletta Harbour, Malta having arrived from England on *Neuralia* (31st December, 1914). Disembarked (2nd) and to St. Andrew's Barracks.

AUGUST
Sailed *Ivernia* for Egypt (26th). Officers – Lieutenant-Colonel A.G. Houlder (Commanding), Major W. Whitaker Thompson (Second-in-Command), Captain S. Jones (Adjutant), Lieutenant W.R. Rawle (Transport Officer), Lieutenant H.S. Elton (Machine Gun Officer), Lieutenant G.J. Bradley (Quartermaster), Lieutenant E.P. Carey (Medical Officer), Captain O. Shimwell (Commanding "A" Company), Captain H.M. Thin (Commanding "B" Company), Captain G.N. Hunter (Commanding "C" Company), Captain D. Dutfield (Commanding "D" Company). Disembarked Alexandria 2.45 am. (31st) and entrained for Cairo. Billeted at Abbassia Camp. Bandleader Billy Cotton served with the battalion as a bugler and recalls in his book *I Did It My Way* – route-marches in the desert clothed in khaki service dress instead of the drill uniforms worn in Malta, and 112-pound packs.

OCTOBER
To Alexandria (5th) and sailed *Simla* for Lemnos. Arrived (8th) and remained on board in Mudros Harbour. Transhipped to the *Sarnia* (13th) landing "W" Beach, Helles 9 p.m. Attached to 2nd Brigade (1st and 2nd Battalions Royal Marine Light Infantry, Anson and Howe Battalions), Royal Naval Division. Billeted behind Divisional Headquarters. Party of officers and N.C.Os began instruction under 2nd R.M.L.I. in forward trenches – Northern and Southern Barricade sector; Howe Battalion – Worcester Sap and 1st R.M.L.I. – right sector (15th). Two companies to reserve positions – the Eski Line and 2 to front line under instruction from units of 2nd Brigade (17th). Relieved by 2/4th London and to rest camp (20th). War Diary records first casualty during move. Began work on new winter quarters. Returned to reserve and front lines (27th).

NOVEMBER
Relieved by 2/4th London and to rest camp (3rd). Draft of officers – 2nd Lieutenants A.J. Whittle, H.F. James and G.H. Ticehurst arrived from England (5th). To reserve and front lines (10th) – 3 men killed, 2 wounded ("A" Company) during shelling at Northern Barricade. Billy Cotton recalls Lord Kitchener's visit to Gallipoli (14th) and his walking over "W" Beach

and inland for some half mile. Assisted during 156th Brigade's (52nd Division) attack on right (15th). Provided rifle fire and bombing with machine guns operating from Munster Terrace and Fusilier Street. Heavy casualties, including Captain Dutfield wounded from shell-fire. Relieved and to rest camp (17th. Relieved Drake and Nelson Battalions in line – right sub-sector (24th). Two companies in part of front line from Sap "D" to right of Sap 26 – Rue de Paris, one company in support – Worcester Flat, one company in reserve – Munster Terrace. Violent storm (26th). Historian of the 2nd London Regiment, W.E. Major Grey, notes torrential rain rapidly flooding trenches "converting them into foaming water-courses . . . the men in danger of being swept away." Letter from Private T.J. Unerwood (origi- nally published in the Drapers' Record describes how he was sleeping on a ledge in the support trenches when it began to rain . . . "within a minute I was swept off the ledge and lay in a foot of water . . . I began to think that the Turks were letting a dam loose, as the water was steadily rising." Severe frost recorded (27th) – water freezing around men's feet, oil solidifying in rifles and machine guns. At one time only 30 rifles were operational and a machine gun belonging to 2/2nd London the only one working on entire brigade front. Captain Bateman noted intense cold – "The men's joints were so stiff from the cold that they had to be lifted on to the fire step and lifted off again when their turn of duty was over."

DECEMBER

Relieved by Drake Battalion and 2/4th London (1st). War Diary notes (2nd) that Captain Thin went to Malta to give evidence in an espionage case. While stationed there a patrol from the battalion had caught two natives signaling out to sea. "A" and "B" Companies moved into new bivouacs (6th). Draft of officers – 2nd Lieutenants A.S. Gillespie, C.A. Stubbs, W.F. Strange and A.M. Manson arrived from England (8th). Enemy shell-fire recorded as "much more heavy altogether." Returned to line (11th) relieving Senegalese troops behind French front in part of Tranchée d' Amade – a continuation of Eski line. War Diary records that this was the last occasion on which troops were moved by day. The Senegalese could take the cold no longer and according to Billy Cotton, had lost heart. Their black faces were now plum-coloured and the men had been bribing the Turks not to fire on them by throwing tins of jam over into their lines. He also recalls an inci- dent where one of the Royal Naval Division units opened fire on 2/2nd London thinking that these new white faces were Turks. Half battalion to Brown House (15th). Draft from 2/1st London joined from Suvla Bay (16th). Relieved 2nd Royal Marine Light Infantry in Horseshoe sector of front line (18th) – positions astride the Achi Baba Nullah, from Small Nullah on west of it to Eglinton Tunnel to the east. In support of 52nd Division attack (19th). Relieved by 1/1st Lanark Yeomanry and 1/1st Ayrshire Yeomanry (21st). Moved to right and took over from Nelson Battalion – Esplanade sector. Here, War Diary records, the Turks had become "more daring – possibly they were used to being opposed by Senegalese troops only. Several losses occurred in establishing superiority." War Diary notes first "silent period" carried out 5 p.m. – 9 p.m. (25th). Relived by 2nd Royal Marine Light Infantry and to Ceasar's Camp (26th). A letter written by Captain Bateman notes relief as "a pitiable sight." Majority of battalion suffering from trench foot and frost-bite. The three-mile journey taking several hours. Heavy Turkish shelling records night and day (27th-31st).

JANUARY, 1916
Headquarters and 313 men evacuated to Mudros during night (1st). A second party left (3rd). Two parties among last British troops to leave Gallipoli (9th) – one attached to Royal Engineers for work on "W" Beach, another employed in connecting up mines. Second-Lieutenant Strange one of last to leave via *Grasshopper.* Strength at Mudros (11th) – 20 officers, 549 other ranks. Major Grey records that no record of casualties was kept during battalion's service in Gallipoli. He estimates, however, that some fifty officers, and men were either killed or wounded. In addition, a number died of exposure or disease.

2/3RD (CITY OF LONDON) BATTALION (ROYAL FUSILIERS)

JANUARY
Malta.

AUGUST
Sailed for Egypt (27th). Arrived Alexandria and from there moved to Port Said. Later served in The Sudan.

SEPTEMBER
Returned to Alexandria and sailed for Lemnos. Arrived Mudros (18th). Landed Suvla (23rd) and attached to 86th Brigade, 29th Division – "C" Section, Dublin Castle sector. War Diary of 2nd Royal Fusiliers records (26th) that "A" Company of 2/3rd London were attached.

NOVEMBER
The Regimental Magazine notes that the Battalion was in the line (24th) with a strength of 429 all ranks. Losses since landing had been over 400

killed, wounded and sick. During the great thunder storm (26th), the Magazine records, the men were at first amused to seen No Man's Land turned into a lake. The water, however, quickly rose and flooded the trenches . . . "standing on the firestep the men were up to their waists in water." Many suffered as a result of the blizzard that followed – 50 drowned or died of exposure, over 300 evacuated with frost bite. An effective strength of 6 officers, 50 other ranks remained.

DECEMBER
Evacuated to Mudros (12th). To Helles (16th). Located Gully Beach area.

JANUARY, 1916
Evacuated (2nd).

2/4TH (CITY OF LONDON) BATTALION (ROYAL FUSILIERS)

JANUARY
Malta.

AUGUST
Sailed *Southland* for Egypt (21st). Strength – 30 officers, 750 other ranks. Lieutenant-Colonel V. Dunfee (Commanding). Arrived Alexandria (25th). Disembarked and moved to camp on seashore near Sporting Club.

SEPTEMBER
Service dress issued (18th) and drill uniforms returned to stores.

OCTOBER
Camp handed over to 2/8th Middlesex and embarked *Karroo* (8th). Sailed 7.30 a.m. (9th). Arrived Mudros Harbour (12th). Damaged *Southland* noted in harbour, the vessel having been hit by a torpedo just after disembarking battalion at Alexandria. Transferred to *Sarnia* during morning (15th) and left for Gallipoli 3 p.m. Arrived Cape Helles around midnight. Disembarked "W" Beach and attached to 1st Brigade (Drake, Nelson, Hawke, Hood Battalions), Royal Naval Division. Parties of officers visited forward area (17th-18th). Relieved 2/2nd London in reserve positions – Eski Line (20th), Captain H. Morris and two men wounded on march. Began instruction in front line (23rd). Records note telescopic rifle issued (24th) – Sergeant Raymond making "good practice on Turks at 1000 yards." Relieved by 2/2nd London (27th) and to rest camp. War Diary records

(29th) heavy bombardment from guns in Asia Minor ("Asiatic Annie") the shells dropping "far too close to our camp to be pleasant."

NOVEMBER

Moved forward (3rd) – "A" and "B" Companies Eski Line, "C" attached to Hawke Battalion, "D" attached to Drake, Nelson, Hood and Hawke Battalions in front line. First man killed in battalion (7th) – Private F.C. Pfeiffer shot in head. Battalion records note how off duty men often went down to the pier at Gully Beach. There bread would be thrown into the sea which attracted large numbers of fish. A Mills' grenade tossed into the water at the right moment "would usually provide a good haul". Relieved and to rest camp (10th). Lance Corporal S. Gardiner and Private H. Waller accidentally killed during bombing practice (14th). To Eski Line (17th) – "B" Company attached to Hawke Battalion, "A" Company attached to Hood Battalion in front line for three days. Private R.E. Gate killed by sniper (20th). Strong enemy attack noted on right of Brigade sector (21st). Working party came under shrapnel fire (22nd) – Private A. Chick killed. Relieved (24th). Severe weather conditions noted in battalion records – "drenched greatcoats grew so stiff that they would stand up by themselves" men were kept from freezing to death "by being made to work hard all day with pick and shovel."

DECEMBER

Took over front line trenches (1st) – "A" Company from sap "B" to sap "H", "C" Company sap "H" to sap "N", "D" Company in support at Worcester Flat, "B" in support Munster Terrace. Privates A. Loneragan and G. Cracknell killed by heavy fire from Achi Baba (3rd). "D" and "B" Companies relieved "A" and "C" (4th). Colonel Vickers Dunfee returned to England (5th), Major V.H. Seyd taking over command. "A" and "C" Companies relieved "D" and "B" (7th). Privates W. Cope and W.J. Jefferies killed (7th). Private W.L. Gilbert killed by shell (8th). Battalion records note that he was sitting on a fire-step writing home to his mother when hit. Inter-company relief (9th). Private H.C. Pearse killed. Second-Lieutenants J.W. Price and S. Davis arrived with draft of 49 other ranks. "A", "B" and "C" Companies relieved (10th). "D" Company remained in line (with four machine guns) attached to Drake Battalion until following day. Battalion Orders (12th) noted the bravery of Private F. Hedger who threw back a live grenade which had fallen into the trench. To trenches (14th) – two Companies front line, two in reserve at Tranch,e d' Amade. Private T. Mallindine and Drummer G. Blake killed (20th). "A" and "B" Companies relieved and to Caesar's Camp (22nd). Second-Lieutenant C.S.G . Blows arrived from England. Shell hit dug-out at rest camp (23rd) – Private S.R. Griffin killed, six men wounded. "B" and part of "A" Company joined "C" and "D" in Tranch,e d' Amade (25th). Machine guns to front line. Private L.L. Thompson killed (31st). Lieutenant S.N. Davies and 113 other ranks evacuated to Mudros.

JANUARY, 1916
Relieved (1st). Captain R.N. Keen, 2nd Lieutenants W.A. Stark, H.W. Vernon, D. Giannacopulo, H.G. Hicklenton, J.W. Price evacuated with 147 other ranks. Captain R.N. Arthur, Captain H.G. Stanham, 2nd Lieutenants F.R.C. Bradford and .C.S.G. Blows evacuated with 118 other ranks (6th). Remainder of battalion left Gallipoli (7th).

Officers that seved on Gallipoli – Lieutenant-Colonel Dunfee; Major V.H. Seyd; Captains R.N. Arthur, L.C. Coats, H. Morris, H.G. Stanham, W.N. Towse, F.C.J. Read; Lieutenants W.R. Botterill, D.N. Giannacopulo, G.D. Haigh, R.C. Dickins, L.A. Dickins, R. Keen, J.E.W. Lambley, J.R. Webster; 2nd Lieutenants V.S. Bowater, S.Davis, C.P. Darrington, S.N. Davies, C.F. Dyne, H.G. Hicklenton, F.R.C. Bradford, N.L. Thomas, C.S.C. Blows, E.G. Lovell, J.W.P. Price, W.A.Stark, W.H.S. Stevens, H.W. Vernon, N.W. Williams, B.F.L. Yeoman.

1/10TH (COUNTY OF LONDON) BATTALION (HACKNEY)

JULY
St. Albans, Hertfordshire. Part of 162nd Brigade, 54th (East Anglian) Division. Sailed end of month for Lemnos.

AUGUST
Arrived Mudros Harbour during first week and then via Imbros to Suvla. Moved forward and present during action at Kiretch Tepe Ridge (15th). Took turns in forward area – Lone Tree Gully, Kidney Hill. To Lala Baba (26th) and later reserve positions – Aghyl Dere area. Relieved 9th Royal Warwickshire in trenches left of Farm Gully (30th).

SEPTEMBER
Major M.B. Buxton (1/5th Norfolk) records that his battalion manned the forward area stretching along the brow of a ridge rising above Aghyl Dere alternatively with 1/10th London Regiment. Tours in front line normally about a week. Rest area was on other side of ridge, just 200 yards from front line.

OCTOBER
Relieved (13th) and to Brigade Reserve. War Diary records (16th) – men's
health better and "flies still troublesome." To front line (20th), Brigade
Reserve (27th). Strength at end of month – 13 officers, 268 other ranks.

NOVEMBER
Tours in trenches throughout month. War Diary of 1/11th London records
1/10th as holding forward position at Bedford Ridge. Strength at end of
month – 13 officers, 261 other ranks.

DECEMBER
Sailed for Mudros (3rd).

1/11TH (COUNTY OF LONDON) BATTALION (FINSBURY RIFLES)

JULY
St. Albans, Hertfordshire. Part of 162nd Brigade, 54th (East Anglian)
Division. To Liverpool and embarked *Aquitania* (29th). Sailed (30th).

AUGUST
Arrived Mudros Bay, Lemnos (6th) and remained in harbour. Transferred
to *Charron* (9th) and sailed for Imbros. Left for Suvla Bay (11th). Landed,
then with 163rd Brigade moved to reserve positions 2 miles due north.
Moved position 1 mile east (11th). Moved forward (12th) Took part in
action at Kiretch Tepe Ridge (15th). Withdrew at night to positions about
Lone Tree Gully. Major G.F. Davis killed. Position heavily shelled
throughout (16th). Total casualties (15th-16th) – 9 officers and approximately 350 other ranks. Relieved by 1/4th Northamptonshire (19th) and to
rest area. Relieved 1/5th Bedfordshire in firing line at Kidney Hill (20th).
Relieved by 1/5th Royal Scots (22nd) and to rest camp. To Lala Baba
midnight (26th), reserve positions, Aghyl Dere (28th).

SEPTEMBER
Relieved 1/5th Bedfordshire in fire trenches facing Sandbag Ridge (4th).
Relieved by 1/5th Bedfordshire (11th) and to Finsbury Vale. To front line
(17th). War Diary records (22nd) enemy aeroplane over trenches about 11
a.m. and heavy bombardment between 4.30 – 5.30 p.m. Relieved by 1/5th
Bedfordshire during night (22nd) and to bivouacs in Divisional Reserve. To
front line (29th). War Diary records Sandbag Ridge bombarded by British
howitzers with little effect. Big fire noted at The Apex (30th).

OCTOBER
Patrol sent out after dark (1st) to fix flags with "proclamations" in Turkish attached as near to enemy's lines as possible. Patrol brought in white flag left by enemy during night (6th). Relieved by 1/5th Bedfordshire (7th) and to reserve at Finsbury Vale. Moved to Hay Valley (8th). To front line (13th). "B" Squadron, 1/1st Suffolk Yeomanry attached for instruction. Relieved by 1/5th Bedfordshire (19th). Took over forward trenches – Aghyl Dere area (21st). Relieved by 1/1st Suffolk Yeomanry (26th) and to rest camp. To front line (31st).

NOVEMBER
War Diary records (1st) few shells falling short during bombardment of Franklin's Post. Relieved by 1/1st Suffolk Yeomanry and 1/5th Norfolk (5th) and to rest camp. War Diary records camp now known as "Penton Hill." Relieved 1/1st Suffolk Yeomanry in trenches left of Hill 60 (10th). War Diary records 2 Turks giving themselves up near The Barricade (11th), enemy occupying trench on summit of Bulgar Bluff (12th). Fired on enemy during attack on 1/10th London position at Bedford Ridge (14th). Relieved by 1/1st Suffolk Yeomanry dawn (15th) and to rest camp. To front line (20th). War Diary notes that patrol found Bulgar Bluff unoccupied by the enemy and considerable drainage work done in Stafford Gully. Relieved and to rest camp (25th). Moved to 1st Australian Hospital pending embarkation (28th).

DECEMBER
Sailed *El Kahirah* for Mudros (3rd). Arrived 10 a.m. (4th) and to Portianos Camp.

HEREFORDSHIRE REGIMENT
(TERRITORIAL FORCE)

"Suvla" "Landing at Suvla" "Scimitar Hill"
"Gallipoli,1915"

1/1ST BATTALION

JULY
Irchester, Northamptonshire. Part of 158th Brigade, 53rd (Welsh) Division. Entrained for Devonport (15th). Embarked and sailed *Euripides* (16th). Called Gibraltar (20th), Malta (24th). Arrived Alexandria, Egypt (27th). Sailed for Port Said (30th). War Diary notes (31st) that the distinguishing mark of the Battalion consisted of a strip of cloth 1 inch wide on each shoulder strap; half green, half black.

AUGUST
Captain G. Barker, Second-Lieutenant W.H. Lloyd and 193 other ranks put ashore (4th) and went by train to Alexandria. Remainder – 25 officers, 750 other ranks sailed for Lemnos. Arrived Mudros Harbour 6 a.m. (7th). *Euripides* went to ground on edge of a reef. Men transferred to *Snaefell* and sailed for Imbros (8th). Arrived 11 p.m. and sailed immediately for Suvla. Landed "C" Beach 8.30 a.m. (9th) and moved forward to Lala Baba. War Diary records Quartermaster Stores set up on "C" Beach, the men having bully beef, biscuit and lime juice about 1 p.m. Enemy shelled position with 75mm gun. No casualties among the Battalion, shells all failed to explode. Ordered forward to assist 9th Sherwood Foresters (33rd Brigade) in firing line Azmak Dere. War Diary notes that instructions were received verbally from G.O.C. 53rd Division, and notes the wording as being more or less "place yourself in communication with him (Colonel L.A. Bosanquet, 9th Sherwood Foresters). I do not think you will have much to do or will get a dusting. Get away as quickly as possible." Moved forward about 4.30 p.m.- "B" and "C" Companies leading under Major W.T. Carless. Came under heavy shrapnel fire after about 1 mile. Later made contact with right flank of Sherwood Foresters but leading companies lost touch with 2nd line. Second line led by Commanding Officer Lieutenant-Colonel G. Drage. He recalls . . . "It became increasingly difficult, owing to the dust raised by the enemy's shrapnel, and the nature of the terrain, to see anything to the flank as we approached the Azmak Dere. We pushed on and eventually reached

a low hill covered with scrub, to our immediate front . . . The position of the two second line companies was now at the foot of Damakjelik Bair . . . The Company Commanders, Rogers and Capel, came to me for orders. I was in a quandary and confess I did not know what to do. I had lost touch with my two leading companies." Lieutenant-Colonel Drage and 4 other officers wounded by shell. Second line companies then withdrew to Azmak Dere. Message received from G.O.C. 53rd Division to the effect that all previous orders had been cancelled and to return to Lala Baba. "B" and "C" companies joined Battalion in trenches at Lala Baba early morning (10th). Moved forward to firing line – Azmak Dere about 6 a.m. Some casualties from shrapnel fire during advance – Captain Sir Herbert Archer Croft, Bart reported as missing (killed). Three companies withdrew to western slopes of Lala Baba (11th). "C" Company remained in line, rejoining Battalion (12th). Later moved under heavy shrapnel fire to reserve positions Sulajik sector. Major W.T. Carless killed. Relieved 1/7th Royal Welsh Fusiliers in firing line (13th). War Diary records position as poor and with very little cover. Relieved by 2/4th Queen's same night and withdrew to positions around Salt Lake. Moved west side of Hill 10 to positions in Azmak Dere (14th). War Diary notes (16th) . . . "This was a very trying day for the men, being for many hours under fire without being able to reply." Moved forward during night. Withdrew to Brigade Headquarters (21st). War Diary records . . . "quiet night on our front, but big battle in front of Chocolate Hill." War Diary records (22nd) "Two men accidentally shot themselves." Moved during night to Hill 10. Relieved 1/5th Welsh and 1/4th Cheshire in firing line – Sulajik sector (27th).

SEPTEMBER
Relieved during night (4th) and to Rest Camp "B" near "A" Beach. War Diary records that camp was very dusty and full of flies – "The Battalion would rather be in the trenches." Relieved 1/4th Cheshire in firing line – Sulajik sector during night (7th). War Diary notes (8th) that 10 platoons were kept in firing line while 26 held support. Fire trench line comprised 567 yards. Orders received to the effect that there should be 1 man to every 1« yards of fire trench. Relieved by 2/4th Queen's (16th) and to Rest Camp "B". Moved to new camp (21st). To reserve camp – Karakol Dagh (25th). War Diary records (30th) – 1 man killed, 1 man wound by blasting operations of 6th East Yorkshire (Pioneers).

OCTOBER
To reserve trenches "A" Section (31st).

NOVEMBER

Took over part of firing line – Azmak Dere sector from 1/2nd Lovat's Scouts and 1/1st Fife and Forfar Yeomanry (2nd). Began wiring front south of Fort Conan (3rd). Began work on new fire trench from Fort Conan to White House (7th). Also new communication trench from head of Beaufort Sap to White House. War Dairy records enemy's use of "Broomstick" bombs. which contained a heavy charge of high explosive and quantities if old rivet punches. Some 50% failed to explode. Also (16th) a sniper using "exploding" bullets. These explode on impact, 1 man having his head shattered. Heavy thunderstorm (26th). Enemy's Highland and Calgary Barricades swept away, water level in Azmak Dere rose to 7-8 feet, trenches flooded to depth of 3-4 feet in a matter of minuets. Relieved by 1/1st Fife and Forfar Yeomanry (27th). Blizzard began during march to Lala Baba. War Diary notes that about 10.30 p.m. it was found impossible to reach bivouacs and Battalion spent night in sand dunes south west of Salt Lake. Many men taken to hospital (2/1st Welsh Field Ambulance) suffering from exposure and frost bite. To Lala Baba (29th).

DECEMBER

War Diary records (2nd) strength about 130. Began work digging trenches. Evacuated (12th) sailing *El Kahira* for Lemnos (13th).

Yeomanry Regiments
(Territorial Force)

(All Regiments Served Dismounted)

1/1st Ayrshire Yeomanry (Earl of Carrick's Own)

"Gallipoli, 1915"

SEPTEMBER
Annsmuir, Fifeshire. Part of Lowland Mounted Brigade. Entrained Ladybank (26th). Arrived Devonport (27th) and sailed *Arcadian.*

OCTOBER
Arrived Malta (5th). Sailed for Lemnos (7th). Arrived Mudros (9th). Transferred to *Partridge* (11th) and sailed for Cape Helles. Landed during evening and to rest camp. Attached to 52nd (Lowland) Division. To firing line on right of The Vineyard – Main Street, Argyle Street (24th) and attached to 1/4th Royal Scots Fusiliers for instruction. Relieved and to Eski Line (31st).

NOVEMBER
To firing line – Hope Street (6th). Took part in successful attack on trenches G11 and G11A (15th). Gains held and consolidated. Part of captured line named Carrick Street. Relieved (16th) – "A" and "B" Squadrons to No.1 Australian Line, "C" to No.2 Australian Line. To rest camp (17th). Relieved 1/5th King's Own Scottish Borderers in forward area – Main Street, Argyle Street, Redoubt Line (28th). Headquarters in Wigan Road.

DECEMBER
Relieved and to rest camp (12th). To Eski Line (20th). Relieved 2/2nd London in front line – Eglinton, Horseshoe sector (21st). Relieved by 1/1st Lanarkshire Yeomanry and to support line (25th). "B" and "C" Squadrons to firing line to reinforce 1/1st Lanarkshire during heavy bombardment (27th). Casualties – 3 killed, 3 wounded, 1 missing. Relieved and to Eski Line (29th) then to rest camp. To "V" Beach (30th) and embarked *Princess Alberta* for Mudros.

1/1st Berkshire Yeomanry (Hungerford)

"Suvla" "Scimitar Hill" "Gallipoli, 1915"

APRIL
Fakenham, Norfolk. Part of 2nd South Midland Mounted Brigade, 2nd Mounted Division. To Avonmouth and sailed for Egypt (5th).

MAY
Brigade redesignated as 2nd Mounted Brigade (2nd South Midland).

AUGUST
Sailed *Lake Michigan* from Alexandria (14th). Landed "A" Beach, Suvla Bay (18th) and to bivouacs west side of Lala Baba (20th). Moved forward and took part in attack on Scimitar Hill (21st). Advanced 5.15 p.m. Enemy's first line taken 6.15 p.m. Gains held under heavy counter attacks then forced to retire. Commanding Officer, Major E.S. Gooch mortally wounded, Lieutenant W.E.G. Niven, Second-Lieutenant T.E. Ainger killed. Strength on going into action – 9 officers, 314 other ranks. Private F.W.O. Potts awarded Victoria Cross . . . "Although himself severely wounded in the thigh in the attack on Hill 70 on the 21st August, 1915, he remained out over forty-eight hours under the Turkish trenches with a private of his regiment who was severely wounded and unable to move, although he could himself have returned to safety. Finally he fixed a shovel to the equipment of his wounded comrade and using this as a sledge, he dragged him back over six hundred yards to our lines, though fired at by the Turks on the way. He reached our trenches at about 9.30 p.m. on the 23rd Aug" (*London Gazette*). Regiment remained in Chocolate Hill area.

SEPTEMBER
Due to heavy casualties – strength upon coming out of action on 21st August – 4 officers, 150 other ranks, regiment (with 1/1st Buckinghamshire and 1/1st Dorsetshire Yeomanries) became 2nd South Midland Regiment, 1st Composite Mounted Brigade (4th).

OCTOBER
Left Suvla for Mudros during night (31st).

1/1ST BUCKINGHAMSHIRE YEOMANRY (ROYAL BUCKS HUSSARS)

"Suvla" "Scimitar Hill" "Gallipoli, 1915"

APRIL
Foulsham, Norfolk. Part of 2nd South Midland Mounted Brigade, 2nd Mounted Division. To Avonmouth (5th) and embarked *Menominee* for Egypt. Arrived Alexandria (19th).

MAY
Brigade redesignated as 2nd Mounted Brigade (2nd South Midland).

AUGUST
Sailed for Gallipoli (13th). Landed "A" Beach, Suvla Bay (18th) and to bivouacs at Lala Baba (20th). Took part in attack on Scimitar Hill (21st). Advanced to Chocolate Hill via Salt Lake and Hetman Chair. Followed Berkshire and Dorset Yeomanries into action 5.15 p.m. Charged and captured enemy's first line 6.15 p.m. Gains held, but forced to retire at dusk, Strength upon going into action – 9 officers, 312 other ranks. Casualties – 6 officers, 134 other ranks. Adjutant – Captain G. Gardner (21st Lancers) killed.

SEPTEMBER
Relieved 6th Royal Dublin Fusiliers in trenches Chocolate Hill area (4th). Due to casualties and sickness reorganised as part of 2nd South Midland Regiment, 1st Composite Mounted Brigade.

OCTOBER
Sailed for Mudros (31st). Strength – 60 all ranks.

1/1st Derbyshire Yeomanry

"Suvla" "Scimitar Hill" "Gallipoli, 1915"

APRIL
Holt area, Norfolk. Part of Notts and Derby Mounted Brigade, 2nd Mounted Division. To Avonmouth (7th) and sailed for Egypt. Arrived Alexandria (24th) and to Cairo.

MAY
Brigade redesignated as 3rd Mounted Brigade (Notts and Derby).

AUGUST
To Alexandria (14th) and sailed for Lemnos. Arrived Mudros (17th), tran-shipped and to Gallipoli. Landing Suvla Bay during night (17th/18th). Moved to Lala Baba (20th), forward position at Chocolate Hill (21st). Took part in fighting for Scimitar Hill (21st). Relieved (22nd) after heavy casual-ties and to Lala Baba. Later began tours in forward area – Chocolate Hill.

SEPTEMBER
Became part of (with 1/1st South Notts Hussars and 1/1st Sherwood Rangers) 3rd Notts and Derby Regiment, 2nd Composite Mounted Brigade (4th). Tours in forward area – Cater's House sector.

NOVEMBER
To Lala Baba (1st) and embarked for Mudros (2nd).

1/1st Royal 1st Devon Yeomanry

"Gallipoli, 1915"

SEPTEMBER
Colchester, Essex. Part of 2nd South Western Mounted Brigade. Entrained for Liverpool and embarked *Olympic* (24th). Sailed (25th).

OCTOBER
Arrived Mudros (1st). Remained in harbour then to Suvla Bay. Landed (9th) and to bivouacs -- Oxford Street, Karakol Dagh attached to 11th Division. Began work digging trenches.

NOVEMBER
Relieved 8th Northumberland Fusiliers in firing line – Jephson's Post (3rd). Relieved and to Oxford Street (11th). Marched via Lala Baba and Salt Lake to support trenches "A" Section. attached to 2nd Mounted Division (15th). To front line – White House sector (18th). Relieved and to Lala Baba (29th). Attached to 53rd Divison.

DECEMBER
Attached to 2nd Mounted Division (9th). Returned to forward area (10th). Evacuated to Imbros during night (19th).

1/1st Royal North Devon Yeomanry

"Gallipoli, 1915"

SEPTEMBER
Colchester, Essex. Part of 2nd South Western Mounted Brigade. Entrained for Liverpool and embarked *Olympic* (24th). Sailed (25th).

OCTOBER
Arrived Mudros (1st) Remained in harbour then to Suvla Bay. Landed (9th) and to bivouacs – Oxford Street, Karakol Dagh. Atached to 11th Division. Began work digging trenches.

NOVEMBER
Relieved 8th Northumberland Fusiliers in firing line – Jephson's Post (3rd). Relieved and to Oxford Street (11th). Marched via Lala Baba and Salt Lake to support trenches "A" Section. Attached to 2nd Mounted Division (15th). To Brigade Support – Willow Tree, Cater's House, Tint's Corner (18th). Relieved 1/1st West Somerset Yeomanry in front line – White House sector (24th). Relieved and to Lala Baba (29th). Attached to 53rd Division.

DECEMBER
Attached to 2nd Mounted Division (9th). Returned to forward area (10th). Evacuated to Imbros during night (19th).

1/1st Dorset Yeomanry (Queen's Own)

"Suvla" "Scimitar Hill" "Gallipoli, 1915"

APRIL
East and West Rudham, Norfolk. Part of 2nd South Midland Mounted Brigade, 2nd Mounted Division. Entrained at Fakenham for Avonmouth (7th). Embarked *Karoa* (8th) – 21 officers, 318 other ranks. Horses with 5 officers and 189 other ranks embarked *Commodore*. Sailed (9th). *Karoa* arrived Alexandria (20th), *Commodore* (21st). Marched to El Zarieh Camp.

MAY
Entrained for Cairo (3rd). Arrived (4th) and to Kasr-el-Nil Barracks. Brigade redesignated as 2nd Mounted Brigade (2nd South Midland).

AUGUST
Entrained for Alexandria (13th). Two squadrons embarked *Lake Michigan*. Officers – Lieutenant-Colonel E.G. Troyte-Bullock (Commanding); Majors J.B.H. Goodden, E.W.F. Casteman, V.C.M. Reeves; Captains R.G.S. Gordon, F.J.B. Wingfield-Digby, A.D. Pass, G.V. Carter; Lieutenants and Second-Lieutenants G.M. Dammers, A.L. Kennaway, Hon. G.S. Dawson-Damer, F.W. Gray, L.F.R. Livingstone-Learmonth, O.C. Bragge, H.C.A. Hoare; Captain N.J.C. Livingstone-Learmonth (15th Hussars, Adjutant), Major W.P. Parsons (Quartermaster). Other ranks – 362. Arrived Lemnos (17th). Transferred to *Sarnia* and sailed for Suvla. Landed "A" Beach during morning (18th) and marched to camp South Side, Karakol Dagh. To Lala Baba (20th) and bivouacked on beach. Advanced south of Salt Lake (21st). Halted at Chocolate Hill. Took part in attack on Scimitar Hill – took and held Turkish forward trenches. Ordered to retire early (22nd). Fell back to dug-outs below Chocolate Hill. Casualties – 7 officers, 182 other ranks. To trenches north side Chocolate Hill (30th).

SEPTEMBER
With 1/1st Berkshire and 1/1st Buckinghamshire Yeomanries formed 2nd South Midland Regiment, 1st Composite Mounted Brigade. Relieved by Royal Dublin Fusiliers (5th) and to Support line east of Chocolate Hill. To front line (13th), reserve trenches (25th).

OCTOBER
To front line (8th). Relieved (20th). Embarked for Mudros (31st). Strength
– 65 all ranks. Arrived and to camp at Portianos.

NOVEMBER
Embarked *Hannibal* for Egypt (27th).

1/1st Fife and Forfar Yeomanry

"Gallipoli, 1915"

SEPTEMBER
Fakenham, Norfolk. Part of 1st Highland Mounted Brigade. To Devonport and sailed (8th). Arrived Alexandria (18th). To Lemnos (20th). Landed Suvla (26th) and joined 2nd Mounted Division – Salt Lake area.

OCTOBER
Began tours in forward area – "A" Section. General Sir Ian Hamilton recalls passing through the Regiment's trench (8th) in his book *Gallipoli Diary*.

NOVEMBER
Relieved by 1/1st Herefordshire in firing line – Azmak Dere sector (2nd). Relieved 1/1st Herefordshire in firing line (27th).

DECEMBER
Evacuated to Imbros during night (20th).

1/1st Gloucestershire Yeomanry (Royal Gloucestershire Hussars)

"Suvla" "Scimitar Hill" "Gallipoli, 1915"

APRIL

King's Lynn, Norfolk. Part of 1st South Midland Mounted Brigade, 2nd Mounted Division. Entrained at Hunstanton for Avonmouth (10th). Embarked *Minneapollis* (11th). Called Malta (21st). Arrived Alexandria (24th) and to camp at Chatby Beach.

MAY

Brigade redesignated as 1st Mounted Brigade (1st South Midland).

AUGUST

Embarked *Haverfield* and *Ascania* (14th). Officers – Lieutenant-Colonel W.H. Playne; Majors H.C. Elwes, A.J. Palmer, R.M. Yorke; Captains J. Godman (Adjutant), M.G. Lloyd-Baker, T.J. Longworth, C.E. Turner; Lieutenants Viscount Quenington, A.H.S. Howard; Second-Lieutenants A.G. Wykeham-Musgrave, A.W. Strickland, H.B. Gething, the Hon. E.J.B. Herbert, E.T. Cripps. Other ranks – 346. Arrived Mudros (17th) and transferred to *Queen Victoria*. Proceeded to Suvla Bay, landing "A" Beach during night. Moved to Lala Baba in reserve during night (20th). Advanced to Chocolate Hill under heavy fire (21st). Took part in attack on Hill 112. Advanced behind 1/1st Worcestershire Yeomanry 5 p.m. Withdrew to Chocolate Hill during night. Casualties – Second-Lieutenant Gething and 11 other ranks killed; 4 officers, 44 other ranks wounded; 1 man missing.

SEPTEMBER

Due to casualties and sickness reorganised (with 1/1st Warwickshire and 1/1st Worcestershire Yeomanries) as 1st South Midland Regiment, 1st Composite Mounted Brigade (4th). To forward area – Cater's House sector (7th). Carried out tours in firing and support lines, exchanging with 1/1st Warwickshire Yeomanry. Relieved by 1/1st South Notts Hussars and to reserve at Salt Lake Line (25th). Strength (29th) – 169 all ranks.

OCTOBER

Relieved 1/3rd London Yeomanry in "A" Section front line (8th). Four killed during trench mortar attack (10th). Strength (17th) – 95 all ranks. Relieved and to Salt Lake Line (20th). Embarked for Mudros (31st), strength – 81 all ranks.

1/1st Hertfordshire Yeomanry

"Suvla" "Scimitar Hill" "Gallipoli, 1915"

JANUARY
Abbassia, Egypt. Became part of Yeomanry Mounted Brigade (19th).

FEBRUARY
To Ismailia (3rd). Served on Suez Canal Defences. To Abbassia (24th).

AUGUST
To Alexandria (13th). Embarked *Knight Templar* for Lemnos (14th). Arrived Mudros (17th). Transferred to *Queen Victoria* and to Suvla Bay during night. Landed (18th) and to rest camp. Yeomanry Mounted Brigade redesignated 5th Mounted Brigade and attached to 2nd Mounted Division. Left "A" Beach for Lala Baba 7.30 p.m. (20th). Advanced to Chocolate Hill. In reserve during attacks on Scimitar Hill and Hill 112 (21st). Commanding Officer – Lieutenant-Colonel Samuel Gurney Sheppard and 11 other ranks killed. About 30 others wounded. Relieved and to Lala Baba (22nd). Returned to front line on Chocolate Hill during night.

SEPTEMBER
Regiment (with 1/2nd County of London Yeomanry) became 5th Yeomanry Regiment, 1st Composite Mounted Brigade (4th). Releived by 1/1st County of London Yeomanry at Tint's Corner (25th).

OCTOBER
Relieved 1/1st South Notts Hussars in front line – Cater's House sector (8th). Relieved and to rest camp (20th). Evacuated to Mudros during night (31st).

1/1st Royal East Kent Yeomanry (The Duke of Connaught's Own) (Mounted Rifles)

"Gallipoli, 1915"

SEPTEMBER
Canterbury, Kent. Part of South Eastern Mounted Brigade. Entrained for Liverpool and embarked *Olympic* (24th). Sailed (25th).

OCTOBER
Arrived Lemnos (1st). Remained in Mudros Harbour then to Helles. Landed (8th). Moved forward up Gully Ravine and to bivouacs near Gully Farm. Attached to 42nd (East Lancashire) Division. General Sir Ian Hamilton recalls in his book *Gallipoli Diary* meeting the Regiment in Gully Ravine (10th). He noted that "they made a brave showing" and was informed that many of the men had caught enteritis. Relieved by 1/10th Manchester at Fusilier Bluff (12th).

NOVEMBER
Tours of duty in forward area – Border Barricade, Fusilier Bluff.

DECEMBER
Evacuated to Mudros from "V" Beach during night (30th).

1/1st West Kent Yeomanry (Queen's Own)

"Gallipoli, 1915"

SEPTEMBER
Canterbury, Kent. Part of South Eastern Mounted Brigade. To Liverpool and embarked *Olympic* (24th). Sailed (25th).

OCTOBER
Arrived Lemnos (1st). Remained in Mudros Harbour then to Helles. Landed (8th). Moved forward up Gully Ravine and to bivouacs near Gully Farm. Attached to 42nd (East Lancashire) Division. General Sir Ian Hamilton recalls in his book *Gallipoli Diary* meeting the Regiment in Gully Ravine (10th). He noted that "they made a brave showing" and was informed that many of the men had caught enteritis. Relieved by 1/10th Manchester at Fusilier Bluff (12th). To front line (26th).

NOVEMBER
Tours in forward area – Border Barricade, Fusilier Bluff.

DECEMBER
Relieved 1/5th East Lancashire in firing line (24th). Relieved by 9th Royal Warwickshire in trenches – Essex Ravine (30th) and evacuated during night to Mudros.

1/1st Lanarkshire Yeomanry

"Gallipoli, 1915"

Cupar, Fifeshire. Part of Lowland Mounted Brigade. To Devonport (26th). Embarked *Arcadian* (27th).

OCTOBER

Arrived Malta (5th). Sailed (7th). Arrived Mudros (9th). Transferred to *Partridge* (11th) and to Cape Helles. Landed "W" Beach and to bivouacs. Attached to 52nd (Lowland) Division. Began instruction in firing line (19th). Attached to units of 156th Brigade on right of The Vineyard – Main Street, Argyle Street.

NOVEMBER

Moved forward to Eski Line (7th), Redoubt Line (15th). Relieved 1/1st Ayrshire Yeomanry in captured line – Carrick Street (15th). Relieved and to rest camp (21st). To Eski Line (27th). Later to firing line, reserve in Plymouth Avenue.

DECEMBER

Relieved and to rest camp (12th). To Eski Line (19th). Relieved 1/1st Ayrshire Yeomanry in firing line – Horseshoe sector (25th). Heavy bombardment (27th) – 15 killed, 11 wounded. Reinforced by 1/1st Ayrshire Yeomanry. Relieved and to rest camp (29th). Embarked for Mudros (30th).

1/1ST CITY OF LONDON YEOMANRY (ROUGH RIDERS)

"Suvla" "Scimitar Hill" "Gallipoli, 1915"

APRIL
Happisburgh, Norfolk. Part of London Mounted Brigade, 2nd Mounted Division. Entrained Mundesley for Avonmouth (10th). Embarked *Scotia* (11th). Sailed (15th). Arrived Malta (22nd). Sailed (23rd). Arrived Lemnos (25th). Sailed for Gallipoli (28th). Moored of mouth of Gully Ravine, Cape Helles. In his history of the Regiment, A.S. Hamilton, M.M. records the Regiment standing by to land. Warships were firing, their shells bursting on the crest of Achi Baba. Krithia was burning and shrapnel bursts marked the front lines and main advances.

MAY
Sailed for Tenedos (1st), Alexandria (3rd). Arrived (6th) and by trams to camp at Sidi Bishr. To Suez Defences (11th). Brigade redesignated as 4th Mounted Brigade (London).

AUGUST
Entrained for Alexandria (13th). Embarked *Caledonia* (14th) and sailed for Lemnos. Strength – 17 officers, 315 other ranks. Arrived Mudros (16th). Transferred to *Doris* (17th) and sailed for Suvla. Landed during morning (18th) and to reserve at Karakol Dagh. To "C" Beach, Lala Baba (20th). Advanced to Chocolate Hill (21st) then moved towards Hill 112. Held up by wounded returning from 86th Brigade. Reached Green Hill and occupied trenches. A.S. Hamilton notes that these were "chock-full of dead and dying." Ordered to retire (22nd). Arrived Lala Baba 4.30 a.m. Casualties – Second-Lieutenant A.H. Ridsdale and 7 other ranks killed; 5 mortally wounded, 22 wounded. To firing line – Chocolate Hill after dark. Major F.R.A.N. Knollys received fatal wounds from shelling (23rd). Movement during day noted as restricted. Work carried out after dark on new trench in front of Scimitar Hill. Also carried rations forward to units holding line south of Green Hill.

SEPTEMBER
Due to casualties and sickness reorganised (with 1/1st and 1/3rd County of London Yeomanries) as 4th London Regiment, 2nd Composite Mounted Brigade. Relieved after dark (4th) and to support trenches. Relieved 1/3rd

County of London Yeomanry in firing line (9th). Strength – 200. Relieved by Scottish Horse during night (17th/18th) and to reserve trenches. Took over positions near Tint's Corner (28th).

OCTOBER
Began work on right of line (3rd) extending positions towards Black and White House. Detachment held position in No Man's Land – Owls Barn. Relieved (8th). Strength in 3rd week of month recorded as less that 100. 40 men to firing line near Worcester Sap (18th).

NOVEMBER
Relieved and to Lala Baba (1st). Strength – 5 officers, 46 other ranks. Sailed *Ermine* for Mudros (2nd).

1/1st County of London Yeomanry (Middlesex, Duke of Cambridge's Hussars)

"Suvla" "Scimitar Hill" "Gallipoli, 1915"

APRIL
Mundesley, Norfolk. Part of London Mounted Brigade, 2nd Mounted Division. Entrained for Avonmouth (11th). Embarked *Nile* (14th) and sailed for Egypt. Horses and transport sailed *Crispin* and S.F. Hatton in his book *The Yarn of a Yeoman* recalls the cramped and unsanitary conditions in the stalls. Some 32 horses died during the voyage. Arrived Alexandria (27th). Disembarked (28th) and to camp at Sidi Bishr.

MAY
To Moascar, Suez Canal Defences (10th). Brigade redesignated as 4th (London) Mounted Brigade.

AUGUST
Entrained for Alexandria (13th). Sailed *Caledonia* for Lemnos (14th). Strength – 16 officers, 320 other ranks. Arrived Mudros (16th). Transferred to *Doris* (17th) and to Suvla. Landed (18th) and to Karakol Dagh. To "C" Beach, Lala Baba (20th). Advanced towards Chocolate Hill under heavy fire (21st) and halted. In their history of the Regiment, C. Stoneham and B. Freeman note how the men watched other units of 2nd Mounted Division advancing through the shell fire. After the war, they record, a Turkish artillery officer commented that "the Division presented a target such as artilleryman thought impossible outside the world of dreams." During its 2-mile advance across open ground the 2nd Mounted Division sustained more than 1,200 casualties. S.F. Hatton recalls the march being in perfect order, mouth-organs were being played and officers led their men carrying walking-sticks. He was told not to take any notice of the Turkish shells "as most of them were duds." Continued advance on right flank of Chocolate Hill. Halted at Green Hill then continued forward to trenches on west slope of Hill W. Ordered to withdraw (22nd) and moved back to Lala Baba. Casualties- 10 killed or died of wounds, 46 wounded. Moved forward to trenches at Chocolate Hill after dark. To reserve line (28th). Began tours in forward area – Beggar's Bush sector (30th).

SEPTEMBER
Due to casualties and sickness reorganised (with 1/1st City and 1/3rd County of London Yeomanries) as 4th London Regiment, 2nd Composite Mounted Brigade (4th). Relieved by Scottish Horse (17th) and to Salt Lake Line. S.F. Hatton recalls the relief being late. At one point a look-out reported that the enemy had broken into the line – he could hear them talking. It was the Scottish Horse, many of whom spoke Gaelic. Relieved 1/1st Hertfordshire Yeomanry in firing line – Tint's Corner (25th). Position faced Dead Man's Gully where S.F. Hatton noted unburied and rotting bodies lay at least one every yard and in places pilled into heaps.

OCTOBER
Relieved by 1/1st Worcestershire Yeomanry and to Salt Lake Line (8th). Strength – 8 officers, 119 other ranks. Parties reinforced Scottish Horse in firing line (22nd) and (28th).

NOVEMBER
To Lala Baba (1st). Strength recorded as being less that 50. Embarked *Ermine* for Mudros (2nd). Arrived and to camp at Portianos.

1/2ND COUNTY OF LONDON YEOMANRY (WESTMINSTER DRAGOONS)

"Suvla" "Scimitar Hill" "Gallipoli, 1915"

JANUARY
Egypt. Became part of Yeomanry Mounted Brigade (19th).

AUGUST
Became part of 2nd Mounted Division (13th). Sailed from Alexandria (14th), arriving Mudros (17th). Sailed for Gallipoli, landing Suvla (18th). Brigade now designated as 5th Mounted Brigade, 2nd Mounted Division. Moved from "A" Beach to Lala Baba (20th) then forward to Chocolate Hill. Took part in attacks on Scimitar Hill and Hill 112 (21st). Relieved and to Lala Baba (22nd). Carried out further tours in forward area – Chocolate Hill.

SEPTEMBER
Regiment (with 1/1st Hertfordshire Yeomanry) became 5th Yeomanry Regiment, 1st Composite Mounted Brigade (4th).

OCTOBER
Tours in forward area – Cater's House sector. Sailed for Mudros (31st).

1/3RD COUNTY OF LONDON YEOMANRY (SHARPSHOOTERS)

"Suvla" "Scimitar Hill" "Gallipoli, 1915"

APRIL
North Walsham area, Norfolk. Part of London Mounted Brigade, 2nd Mounted Division. To Avonmouth (11th). Embarked (12th) and sailed for Egypt (14th). Arrived Alexandria (27th).

MAY
Brigade redesignated as 4th (London) Mounted Brigade.

AUGUST
Sailed from Alexandria (14th). Arrived Mudros (16th) then to Gallipoli (18th). Landed Suvla Bay and to reserve positions at Karakol Dagh. To "C" Beach, Lala Baba (20th). Advanced towards Chocolate Hill under heavy fire (21st) and halted. Took part in operations at Scimitar Hill and "W" Hills. Withdrew to Lala Baba (22nd). Later Took turns in forward area – Chocolate Hill.

SEPTEMBER
Due to casualties and sickness reorganised (with 1/1st City and 1/1st County of London Yeomanries) as 4th London Regiment, 2nd Composite Mounted Brigade (4th). Located in reserve at Salt Lake Line, forward area – Tint's Corner area.

OCTOBER
Began work on right of line (3rd) extending positions towards Black and White House. Detachment held position in No Man's Land – Owls Barn.

NOVEMBER
To Lala Baba (1st) and sailed for Mudros (2nd).

1/1ST LOVAT'S SCOUTS YEOMANRY

"Gallipoli, 1915"

SEPTEMBER
Hunstanton, Norfolk. Part of 1st Highland Mounted Brigade. To Devonport and sailed *Andania* for Egypt (8th). Arrived Alexandria (18th). To Lemnos (20th), Suvla Bay (26th). Landed during night and to Salt Lake Line attached to 2nd Mounted Division.

OCTOBER
Began tours in front line – "A" Section.

NOVEMBER
Relieved by 1/5th Royal Welsh Fusiliers (1st) and to Salt Lake Line. To front line (27th).

DECEMBER
Began evacuation. Last party left firing line (20th) and to Imbros.

1/2ND LOVAT'S SCOUTS YEOMANRY

"Gallipoli, 1915"

SEPTEMBER
Hunstanton, Norfolk. Part of Highland Mounted Brigade. To Devonport and sailed *Andania* for Egypt (8th). Arrived Alexandria (18th). To Lemnos (20th), Suvla Bay (26th). Landed during night and to Salt Lake Line attached to 2nd Mounted Division.

OCTOBER
Began tours in front line – "A" Section. General Sir Ian Hamilton recalls visiting the trenches held by both 1st and 2nd Lovat's Scouts (8th). Just after leaving those of the latter, the General, accompanies by "Birdie" (General Sir W.R. Birdwood) became lost and found themselves standing just 200 yards from the enemy's line – about half way between 2nd Lovat's Scouts and the Turks. Noticing this both officers turned . . . "and ran for it – for our lives, I mean." Lieutenant I. Forsyth-Grant died of wounds (19th) received during patrol prior to attack on enemy strong point at Azmak Dere Barricade (17th). Operation successful and position named "The Highland Barricade."

NOVEMBER
Relieved by 1/1st Herefordshire (2nd) and to Salt Lake Line. Relieved 1/7th Royal Welsh Fusiliers in front line (27th).

DECEMBER
Began evacuation. Last party left firing line (20th) and to Imbros.

1/1ST NORFOLK YEOMANRY
(THE KING'S OWN ROYAL REGIMENT)

"Gallipoli, 1915"

SEPTEMBER
Norfolk Coast. Part of Eastern Mounted Brigade, 1st Mounted Division. With Brigade left Division and to Liverpool (23rd). Embarked *Olympic* (24th) and sailed (25th) for Lemnos. Officers – Lieutenant-Colonel A.F. Morse (Commanding); Majors A.R. Buxton, J.F. Barclay, M.E. Barclay; Captains H.A. Birkbeck, E.C. Ruggles-Brise, J.D. Paul, N.A.C. Flower; Lieutenants Sir J.F. Ramsden, Bt., T.F. Preston, G. Fenwick-Owen, L.S. Hill, Second-Lieutenants J.G. Frere, F.G.L. Worster, M.C. Bonsor, J. Harbord, A.C. Cannan, A.T. Gimson, J.H. Michell, C.P. Wyatt, T.R. Swift, J.S. Goslett. Captain J.T. McMurrough Kavanagh (7th Hussars, Adjutant), J.A. Sayer (Quartermaster), B.N. Ash (R.A.M.C., Medical Officer). Other ranks – 504.

OCTOBER
Arrived Mudros (1st). Remained on board. Sailed *Abassieh* for Anzac (8th). Unable to land due to weather conditions and put back to Imbros. Landed Walker's Pier (10th) then to bivouacs – Dixon's Gully. Attached to 54th (East Anglian) Division. Joined 1/8th Hampshire and 1/4th Essex for instruction in trenches – Hill 60 area (14th). Relieved 1/6th Essex in Norfolk Street (21st). Relieved by 1/4th Norfolk and to rest camp – New Bedford Road. (26th).

NOVEMBER
Returned to front line. Took turns in trenches on right of Hill 60. Second-Lieutenant J.S. Goslett killed (11th). Many casualties from sickness. Strength (27th) – 14 officers, 301 other ranks.

DECEMBER
First party evacuated to Mudros (14th). Remainder followed during night (19th).

1/1st Nottinghamshire Yeomanry (Sherwood Rangers)

"Suvla" "Scimitar Hill" "Gallipoli, 1915"

APRIL
Holt area, Norfolk. Part of Notts and Derby Mounted Brigade, 2nd Mounted Division. To Avonmouth (7th) and sailed for Egypt. Arrived Alexandria (24th) and to Cairo.

MAY
Brigade redesignated as 3rd Mounted Brigade (Notts and Derby).

AUGUST
To Alexandria (14th) and sailed for Lemnos. Arrived Mudros (17th), transhipped and to Gallipoli. Landing Suvla Bay during night (17th/18th). Moved to Lala Baba (20th), forward position at Chocolate Hill (21st). Took part in fighting for Scimitar Hill (21st). Relieved (22nd) after heavy casualties and to Lala Baba. Later began tours in forward area – Chocolate Hill.

SEPTEMBER
Became part of (with 1/1st Derbyshire Yeomanry and 1/1st South Notts Hussars) 3rd Notts and Derby Regiment, 2nd Composite Mounted Brigade (4th). Tours in forward area – Cater's House sector.

NOVEMBER
To Lala Baba (1st) and embarked for Mudros (2nd).

1/1st NOTTINGHAMSHIRE YEOMANRY (SOUTH NOTTINGHAMSHIRE HUSSARS)

"Suvla" "Scimitar Hill" "Gallipoli, 1915"

APRIL
Blakeney, Norfolk. Part of Notts and Derby Mounted Brigade, 2nd Mounted Division. Entrained at Melton Constable for Avonmouth (7th). Embarked *Saturnia* and sailed for Egypt (9th). Arrived Alexandria (24th) and to Abbassia Barracks, Cairo.

MAY
Brigade resesignated as 3rd Mounted Brigade (Notts and Derby).

JULY
To Kasr-el-Nil (20th).

AUGUST
"B" and "D" Squadrons to Alexandria (14th) and sailed for Lemnos. Strength – 360 all ranks. Officers – Colonel E.H. Cole (Commanding); Major T.P. Barber; Captain E. Sopper (Adjutant); Lieutenant H.T. Roach (Quartermaster); Lieutenant W.G.. Heymann (Machine Gun Officer); Captain W.T. Rowe (Medical Officer); "B" Squadron: Captain P.H. Warwick; Lieutenants L.C. Coventry, S. Hanson, L.C. Hodges, C.F.A. Ley, C.T. Repton; "D" Squadron: Major H.L. Birkin; Lieutenants G.G. Milwood, T.R.C. Birkin, F.W. Piggin. Arrived Mudros (17th) and after dark trans-shipped and sailed for Suvla. Landed during night and to bivouacs. To Lala Baba (20th). Moved forward towards Chocolate Hill 4 p.m. (21st). Shelled during march. In his history of the Regiment, B. Freeman notes many dead and wounded from leading regiments passed on march. Shelling caused shrub to catch fire and work of Medical Officer – Captain W.T. Rowe in rescuing wounded noted. Arrived at Chocolate Hill and after short halt led Brigade attack on right flank of Hill 112. B. Freeman records – "It was then so dark that the officer commanding could not tell if the troops in front were British or the enemy. Desperate fighting took place before the enemy's trenches were gained." Covered retreat of Brigade then fell back to trenches about 300 yards to the rear. Relieved by 6th Royal Munster Fusiliers (22nd) and to Lala Baba. Moved forward to Chocolate Hill (23rd). Took over position – River Bed Trench in support of 1/1st

Sherwood Rangers (25th). Began work digging new communication trench (26th). Took over front line from Sherwood Rangers (31st).

SEPTEMBER

Became part of (with 1/1st Derbyshire Yeomanry and 1/1st Sherwood Rangers) 3rd Notts and Derby Regiment, 2nd Composite Mounted Brigade (4th). Relieved by 1/1st Derbyshire Yeomanry (7th) and to reserve trenches. Relieved 1/1st Sherwood Rangers in firing line (11th). Lovat's Scouts and Scottish Horse attached for instruction (12th). Relieved by Scottish Horse (6th). Relieved 1/1st Gloucestershire Hussars in firing line Cater's House sector (25th).

OCTOBER

Began work on new communication trench – Pope's Seat (2nd). Large numbers of unburied dead lay in the area and casualties from sickness were high – "In the day time men lay exhausted on the fire steps, their faces covered with swarms of flies which they had not the energy to brush away" (B.Freeman). Relieved by 1/1st Hertfordshire Yeomanry (8th) and to reserve trenches.

NOVEMBER

To Lala Baba and bivouacked on beach (1st). Embarked *Ermine* during night and to Mudros.

1/1st, 1/2nd, 1/3rd Scottish Horse

"Gallipoli, 1915"

AUGUST
The 3 regiments comprised 1st Scottish Horse Brigade. Embarked
Transylvania (17th) at Devonport.

SEPTEMBER
Landed Suvla (2nd) and joined 2nd Mounted Division. Relieved 6th Loyal
North Lancashire in support trenches at Kazlar Chair (3rd). General Sir Ian
Hamilton recalls in his book *Gallipoli Diary* that the Scottish Horse were
bivouacked on Lala Baba Beach (3rd). They had just landed and there had
been a number of casualties among the officers from shell fire. He later
visited the Regiment in its trenches on left of the Indian Brigade (25th).
Some of the men had been issued with rifles fitted with telescopic sights and,
the General notes, "are as keen as schoolboys out for their first shoot."

NOVEMBER
In a letter dated 4th November, 1915, Lieutenant-Colonel A.D. Borton,
DSO, VC recalled an incident regarding the Scottish Horse in which their
C.O. and a look-out were speaking Gaelic. They were arrested by a patrol
from the Lancashire Fusiliers as Turkish spies wearing British uniform.

DECEMBER
Evacuated to Imbros during night (19th/20th).

1/1st West Somerset Yeomanry

"Gallipoli, 1915"

SEPTEMBER
Thorpe-le-Soken, Essex. Part of 2nd South Western Mounted Brigade. Entrained for Liverpool (23rd). Embarked *Olympic* (24th). Sailed (25th).

OCTOBER
Arived Mudros (1st). Transferred to *Osmanieh* and sailed for Suvla Bay. Strength – 25 officers, 477 other ranks. Landed (9th) and to bivouacks at Oxford Street, Karakol Dagh. Attached to 11th Division. Began work digging trenches. Two men fatally wounded.

NOVEMBER
Releieved 9th Lancashire Fusiliers in forward trenches – Lone Tree Gully sector (3rd). Relieved by 9th Sherwood Foresters (11th) and to Oxford Street. Marched via Lala Baba and Salt Lake to support trenches – "A" Section. Attached to 2nd Mounted Division (15th). Took over forward trenches – White House sector (18th). Headquarters – Pope's Seat. Relieved by 1/1st Royal North Devon Yeomanry (24th) and to support line – Willow Tree, Cater's House, Tint's Corner. "B" Squadron reinforcved North Devons in firing line (27th). "C" Squadron reinforced 1/1st Royal 1st Devon Yeomanry in firing line (28th). Attached to 53rd Division. Willow Tree positions hevilly shelled (29th). Releieved and to Lala Baba. Casualties (27th-29th) – 3 officers, 78 other ranks.

DECEMBER
Strength (2nd) – 294. Many men to hospital sick. Strength (4th) – 111. Attached to 2nd Mounted Division (9th). To Willow Tree sector (10th). Evacuated to Imbros during night (19th).

1/1st Suffolk Yeomanry (The Duke of York's Own Loyal Suffolk Hussars)

"Gallipoli, 1915"

SEPTEMBER
Leiston, Suffolk. Part of Eastern Mounted Brigade, 1st Mounted Division. With Brigade left Division and to Liverpool (23rd). Embarked *Olympic* and sailed (25th) for Lemnos. Officers – Lieutenant-Colonel F.W. Jarvis (Commanding); Majors Hon. W.E. Guinness, J.W.R. Tomkin, F. Goldsmith, C.E. Pym; Captains Viscount Duncannon (Adjutant), E.A. Greene, T. de la G. Grissell, Hon. E.C.G. Cadogan, Lieutenants G.P. Barker, R.O.W. Pemberton, H. Musker, E.C.M. Flint, J.F. Crisp, G.R. Arbuthnot-Leslie; Second-Lieutenants C.B.A. Jackson, R.E. Eversden, A.C. McKelvie, D.E. Ginn, G.B. Horne, A.L. Martin-Linnington, R.P. Woodhouse, E.W. Tuttle (Quartermaster). Rev. J.W. Blencowe (Chaplain); Captain Taylor (R.A.M.C., Medical Officer).

OCTOBER
Arrived Mudros (1st) and remained on board. Sailed *Abassieh* for Anzac (8th). Unable to land due to weather conditions and put back to Imbros. Landed Walker's Pier (10th) then to dug-outs at New Bedford Road. Attached to 54th (East Anglian) Division and began tours of duty in front line – Sandbag Ridge area. To New Bedford Road (21st). Relieved 1/5th Bedfordshire and 1/11th London in front line – Aghyle Dere area (26th). Relieved by 1/5th Norfolk and 1/11th London (31st) and to New Bedford Road.

NOVEMBER
To trenches left of Hill 60 crossing Kaiajik Dere (5th). Major Hon W.E. Guinness records (6th) how Captain Hon. E.C.G. Cadogan had received slight injuries to his face when a Turkish sniper hit the officer's periscope. He also notes the use of a new catapult that had been manufactured by Harrods (see *Staff Officer – The Diaries of Lord Moyne 1914-1918*). High casualties from sickness recorded. Relieved by 1/11th London and to rest camp (10th). Returned to front line (15th). Major Guinness records Turkish deserters coming in from their unit on Sandbag Ridge. They reported that one of the bombs fired from the catapult had hit one man on the head and that the Turks were looking forward to "annihilating" the British when guns and shells promised by the Germans arrived. Enemy noted improving their

positions and putting out wire at rear of Smythe's Spur. Major Guinness records the chance death of Private H.W. Day (16th), the case of a shell fired at an aeroplane coming through the roof of a dug out, hitting him between the shoulder blades and killing him instantly. "A" Squadron dug out in Aghyl Dere flooded (18th) – water knee-deep. Relieved (20th). To front line (25th).

DECEMBER
First party evacuated to Mudros (14th). Remainder followed during night (19th).

1/1st Sussex Yeomanry

"Gallipoli, 1915"

SEPTEMBER
Canterbury, Kent. Part of South Eastern Mounted Brigade. Entrained for Liverpool and embarked *Olympic* (24th). Sailed (25th).

OCTOBER
Arrived Lemnos (1st). Remained in Mudros Harbour then on *Sania* to Cape Helles (7th). Moved forward up Gully Ravine and to bivouacs near Gully Farm. Attached to 42nd (East Lancashire) Division. General Sir Ian Hamilton recalls in his book *Gallipoli Diary* meeting the Regiment in Gully Ravine (10th). He noted that "they made a brave showing" and was informed that many of the men had caught enteritis. Began instruction in front line – Border Barricade, Cawley's Crater, Fusilier Bluff.

NOVEMBER
Took over line – Border Barricade (5th). Relieved (7th) and to Brigade Reserve. Began digging fatigues at Fusilier Bluff. To bivouacs (14th), front line – Fusilier Bluff (26th).

DECEMBER
Relieved and to bivouacs (10th). Moved forward to the Zig Zag (19th). In his history of the Regiment, Lieutenant-Colonel H.P. Powell-Edwards, D.S.O. recalls the move as being under heavy shell fire. One shell that had landed on the cliff above caused the air to be filled with flying legs, all of them black. It was later discovered that a dump containing a supply of waders had been hit. Bombers under Captain H. Sayer assisted with consolidation of positions in front line near Cawley's Crater. To Geogheghan's Bluff in reserve then "Y" Ravine (24th). Relieved (30th) and to Gully Beach. Later moved to "V" Beach and during night embarked *Princess Alberta* for Mudros.

1/1ST WARWICKSHIRE YEOMANRY

"Suvla" "Scimitar Hill" "Gallipoli, 1915"

APRIL
Norwich, Norfolk area. Part of 1st South Midland Mounted Brigade, 2nd Mounted Division. To Avonmouth and sailed (11th). *Wayfarer* carrying 763 horses torpedoed 60 miles north west of Scilies and later towed to Queenstown. Four men lost at sea. Regiment arrived Alexandria, Egypt (24th).

MAY
Brigade redesignated as 1st Mounted Brigade (1st South Midland).

AUGUST
Sailed *Ascania* (14th). Arrived Mudros (17th). Transhipped to *Doris* and sailed for Gallipoli (18th). Landed "A" Beach, Suvla and moved to Lala Baba in reserve during night (20th). Regimental historian – the Hon. H.A. Adderley, records that the journey to Lala Baba was at night. The men carried no packs, cloaks or blankets and had been issued with 200 rounds of ammunition and 2 days rations. . Advanced to Chocolate Hill under heavy fire (21st) and took part in attack on Hill 112. The Hon. H.A. Adderley records the advance as being over 2½ miles of flat country, the Regiment in the centre of the Brigade coming under heavy shrapnel fire half-way across. He notes that shells were bursting about 30 foot overhead "with deadly effect." Withdrew to Lala Baba (22nd). Casualties – 6 other ranks killed, 2 officers, 65 other ranks wounded. Moved back to Chocolate Hill during night and dug in.

SEPTEMBER
Due to casualties and sickness reorganised (with 1/1st Gloucestershire and 1/1st Worcestershire Yeomanries) as 1st South Midland Regiment, 1st Composite Mounted Brigade (4th). To forward area – Cater's House sector. Carried out tours in firing and support lines, exchanging with 1/1st Gloucestershire Yeomanry. The Hon. H.A. Adderley records a heavy reduction on strength due to sickness. Of the 308 men that landed in August, just 41 of these remained fit for duty. Relieved and to reserve at Salt Lake Line (25th).

OCTOBER
To front line – "A" Section (10th). Positions running south from Green Hill

– Munster Sap and Dorset Alley. The Hon. H.A. Adderley notes trenches as being full of mud and filth. There were also many dead from the August fighting still unburied. Relieved and to Salt Lake Line (20th). Embarked for Mudros (31st). Total casualties for Gallipoli – 15 other ranks killed; 2 officers, 92 other ranks wounded.

1/1st Welsh Horse Yeomanry

"Gallipoli, 1915"

SEPTEMBER
Woodbridge, Suffolk. Part of Eastern Mounted Brigade, 1st Mounted Division. With Brigade left Division and to Liverpool (23rd). Embarked *Olympic* and sailed (25th) for Lemnos.

OCTOBER
Arrived Mudros (1st). Remained on board. Transferred to *Partridge* (8th) and to Anzac Cove. Landed Walker's Pier and to rest camp at Burnt Gully. Moved foreword to Hill 60 (10th) and attached to 163rd Brigade, 54th (East Anglian) Division began work mining and sapping.

NOVEMBER
Five mines exploded (15th). Brigade War Diary records "mine craters were not occupied and the line not advanced. Result of explosion disappointing." Enemy exploded mine (20th) – Lieutenant W.L. Renwick and 8 men buried. War Diary records Lieutenant Renwick dug out, but "The 8 men all perished, as they could not be got out."

DECEMBER
First party evacuated to Mudros (15th). Enemy mine exploded near Ivy Lane (19th) – 5 wounded. Later same night, provided rearguard of 4 officers and 39 other ranks in line at Hill 60. Withdrew 4 a.m. (20th) and to Mudros.

1/1st Worcestershire Yeomanry (The Queen's Own Worcestershire Hussars)

"Suvla" "Scimitar Hill" "Gallipoli, 1915"

APRIL
King's Lynn, Norfolk. Part of 1st South Midland Mounted Brigade, 2nd Mounted Division. Entrained for Avonmouth and sailed *Saturnia* Egypt (8th). Arrived Alexandria (24th) and to camp at Chatby Beach.

MAY
Brigade redesignated as 1st Mounted Brigade, (1st South Midland).

AUGUST
Sailed *Ascania* (14th). Arrived Mudros (17th) and transferred to *Doris*. Proceeded to Suvla Bay, landing "A" Beach during night. Moved forward to reserve positions at Lala Baba during night (20th). Advanced to Chocolate Hill (21st). Took part in attack on Hill 112 (21st) – 43 casualties.

SEPTEMBER
Due to casualties and sickness reorganised (with 1/1st Gloucestershire and 1/1st Warwickshire Yeomanries) as 1st South Midland Regiment, 1st Composite Mounted Brigade (4th). Carried out tours in firing and support lines – "A" Section and reserve at Salt Lake Line.

OCTOBER
Relieved 1/1st County of London Yeomanry in firing line – Tint's Corner (8th). Embarked for Mudros (31st).

Regimental Index